Google+™
Marketing
FOR
DUMMIES®

Google+™ Marketing FOR DUMMIES®

by Jesse Stay

WILEY

John Wiley & Sons, Inc.

Google+™ Marketing For Dummies®

Published by
John Wiley & Sons, Inc.
111 River Street
Hoboken, NJ 07030-5774

www.wiley.com

WILEY

About the Author

Jesse Stay began his career as a software developer, where in an era of social media he quickly became immersed in the world of marketing technologies. An entrepreneur at heart, he has consulted with industry players both large and small to create some of the most social technologies on the web. Jesse's approach is not a one-size-fits-all approach of just Google+ and Facebook Pages or Twitter accounts, but rather looking at the overall business objectives of each business he consults with to build the most effective strategy available. Author of three other books on social media, Jesse has also helped write documentation for blogs such as AllFacebook.com, has contributed to InsideFacebook.com and TechCrunch.com, and has even helped document, as clients, some of the major social networks themselves. Jesse was named by both *Mashable* and *Entrepreneur* magazine as one of 20 developers to follow on Twitter and by *Mashable* as one of 10 entrepreneurs to follow on Twitter. This inside knowledge of the industry has enabled Jesse to understand the ins and outs of how social networks work and set the stage for documenting an emerging network like Google+. It has enabled him to provide a unique view into marketing that all can understand.

Jesse is currently employed as a social strategist for The Church of Jesus Christ of Latter-day Saints. In his spare time he runs his current entrepreneurial endeavor, `socialtoo.com`, and continues to document the social networks he uses in his marketing approaches on the educational site, Pluralsight.com. Jesse also consults for businesses large and small as he gets time. He is a professional speaker and loves to share his techniques with all that want to learn.

You can follow Jesse on his blog at `http://staynalive.com/` and you can always circle him at `http://google.com/+jessestay`.

Dedication

To Rebecca, Elizabeth, Thomas, Joseph, JJ, Alex and baby-on-the-way.

Author's Acknowledgments

Thanks to my beautiful wife for putting up with me while spending late nights working on this. I'm grateful for all of her hard work — without her, I couldn't do this. She deserves all the credit for this book.

Others who have influenced me in my writings include my good friend and mentor Guy Kawasaki — your friendship and willingness to listen and provide advice is something I will never forget. Also, thanks to my good friend Jeremiah Owyang — an all-around smart guy who truly puts research before anything. Lastly, thanks to my former employers, CWDKids.com and Backcountry.com, who allowed me to build the software that lead me to a true interest and experience in marketing.

Publisher's Acknowledgments

We're proud of this book; please send us your comments at http://dummies.custhelp.com. For other comments, please contact our Customer Care Department within the U.S. at 877-762-2974, outside the U.S. at 317-572-3993, or fax 317-572-4002.

Some of the people who helped bring this book to market include the following:

Acquisitions and Editorial

Project Editor: Pat O'Brien

Acquisitions Editor: Amy Fandrei

Senior Copy Editor: Barry Childs-Helton

Copy Editor: Tonya Cupp

Technical Editor: James H. Russell

Editorial Manager: Kevin Kirschner

Editorial Assistant: Leslie Saxman

Sr. Editorial Assistant: Cherie Case

Cover Photo: © iStockphoto.com / Cary Westfall

Cartoons: Rich Tennant (www.the5thwave.com)

Composition Services

Project Coordinator: Patrick Redmond

Layout and Graphics: Joyce Haughey, Corrie Niehaus, Christin Swinford

Proofreader: Kathy Simpson

Indexer: Potomac Indexing, LLC

Publishing and Editorial for Technology Dummies

> **Richard Swadley,** Vice President and Executive Group Publisher
>
> **Andy Cummings,** Vice President and Publisher
>
> **Mary Bednarek,** Executive Acquisitions Director
>
> **Mary C. Corder,** Editorial Director

Publishing for Consumer Dummies

> **Kathleen Nebenhaus,** Vice President and Executive Publisher

Composition Services

> **Debbie Stailey,** Director of Composition Services

Contents at a Glance

Table of Contents

Introduction

As a prolific user of Google's early attempts at socializing their services — such as Google Buzz or even Wave — I've been through the wringer when it comes to Google and social media. I've been burned, time and time again, so I entered Google+ with skepticism. Google was going to have to prove to me that this was *the* social network.

I was pleasantly surprised at first use of the service — Google had finally created a social application that had a future! The more I used it, the more I realized that this venture into social networking wasn't going away. It had, and has, a real audience and real users, and I was seeing its growth — practically in real time — on my individual Google+ profile. It was an online social experience like no other.

The success of this new Google product spelled opportunity for me. Here I was, on a social network owned by a huge company like Google, one of the first users trying out the service. I'd used social networking before, but here was a fresh range of new opportunities:

- I could grow my audience and meet new people in the process.
- I could introduce the brands I work with to new people.
- I could participate in an active online community — very friendly to brands — whose members were all anxious to see the community grow.

As I got to know the Google+ team, I realized that this project was top priority for Google. The Google+ team was working late hours, full speed ahead, hoping to catch up with other equivalent social networks on the market. The effort was impressive.

Even as new as it was, Google+ had one secret weapon that its competitors didn't — Google itself. That's because Google+ is essentially a social layer on top of all Google products and services. It's not really a standalone social network at all, but a second — socially networked — version of Google. This "Google 2.0," if you will, was a network with vast capabilities already in place, beyond those of Facebook or Twitter or similar social networks.

Here's how it works: Google+ serves as the lifeblood of Google by connecting all the other Google properties together. If you're currently using Google+ — especially if your brand has established a presence on the service — you're poised to have a more prominent place in the rankings that show up in all of Google's properties. That's right — search, YouTube, hosted images, Gmail, Google Contacts, and Google Voice are all now integrated with Google+.

A word to the wise: The more your brand is integrated with Google+, the more your brand will appear in the results that Google shows to your fans on each of the Google properties.

Google+ is legit, thriving, and a serious contender for your brand's attention in this era of social networking.

I wrote this book to help you get a handle on where to start with Google+, why it is a valuable tool for your brand, and how you can get the most out of the service. My hope is that you can grab that handle and make the most of the fast-growing value of Google as a marketing tool that can also create a whole new bond between your brand and your followers, fans, and customers.

About This Book

Whether you're an experienced online marketer, a marketer just now getting your feet wet with social media, or a newcomer to marketing in general, this book will be comfortable for you. I wrote this book to help marketers, small businesses, and even enterprise-level business owners and executives understand the value of Google+ and how it can help your brand's presence on the web through the power of Google itself.

This book covers a range of approaches to revving up your market presence — from search engine optimization to building an audience, to using Google+ as a CRM (Customer Relationship Management) tool for tracking the people you interact with across Google properties. And that's just for openers. I also cover strategies for making the most of your ads and analytics to increase your brand's online voice using Google+.

Feel free to pick and choose your favorite topics and chapters as you read this book; you can get something from any part you read, in whatever order you read. You don't have to read it right through from front to back — although if you do read it that way, you'll see it from the perspective of how I wrote it. Whichever way you read it, you'll grow your understanding of Google+.

That said, keep in mind that Google+ changes — frequently — as does any social network. Some of the features I describe may have changed by the time you read this book. That's okay; I've set up a Google+ Group where you can ask questions at `http://stay.am/gplusmarketinggroup`. Feel free to join and ask questions as you read, or share a success story or two with the rest of the readers of this book!

Conventions Used in This Book

If you've read a *For Dummies* book before, you're probably familiar with the convention I use in this book. It's pretty simple. For code snippets, HTML, and URLs, I use a monospace font like this:

```
www.staynalive.com/dummiesbook
```

Foolish Assumptions

Just so you know, I don't claim to be an SEO (Search Engine Optimization) expert, and this book's focus isn't on SEO per se. Because Google+ is so engrained in Google.com search, I offer a close-up view of how a social product like Google+ can affect the process of online search. Always consult an SEO consultant as you take my advice on using Google+ as a marketing tool — and before you do, consider doing some supplemental reading on SEO. There are entire books on that subject, including Peter Kent's *Search Engine Optimization For Dummies* (John Wiley & Sons, Inc.)

This book gives you a thorough understanding of "thinking social" as you work out your online marketing strategy. You take into account why people share, how to get people sharing, and how to bring more eyes to your content on Google+. I give you a crash course in customizing and tailoring your content, and in shaping your web presence or mobile app into a more social and engaging experience. You'll get the goods on building community and getting more people interacting with every piece of content you post.

This book assumes that you've used a Google product or two before, although even that isn't 100 percent necessary. To get the most out of this book, just give it a good read, watch online for examples of what it presents, and follow the directions I include.

Oh, and keep in mind that the *most* up-to-date information probably hasn't made it into print yet! This book will give you a firm foundation for using Google+, but treat it as a starting point. The service is also a living, evolving platform; it changes frequently. Always verify that the data you read here is still applicable, and when you have questions, ask in this book's Google Group at `http://stay.am/gplusmarketinggroup`. If there are updates, you'll also find them at `dummies.com/go/googleplusmarketingfor dummiesupdates`.

How This Book Is Organized

This book is organized to help you understand why Google+ is a valuable social network. I start there and then take you on a journey through the elements of Google+ that will help your brand or company grow. If you read through the entire book, you'll have a thorough understanding of what you can get from Google+ and how you can integrate your brand into a Google+ presence.

Part I: Seeing How Google+ Benefits Marketers

In this part, I show you why Google+ is important. I talk about how Google+ is about people and how it's more than just a social network. I also talk about ways you can use it to get benefits and cover the basics of what Google+ is.

Part II: Fishing Where the Fish Are

In this part, I talk about finding your market — a concept that marketers call "fishing where the fish are." I show you how to bring your brand presence and messaging to the places where your customers hang out online — focusing on the elements of Google+ you can embrace right away and use as places to insert your messaging. You'll learn about Facebook Pages and messaging, how to build your audience on the network there as well, and how to link the two venues.

Part III: Going from Fisher to Fish-Farmer

Here's where I show you how to expand your Google+ presence beyond the `plus.google.com` website and onto your own website. I show you how to use Google+ to grow your audience on your website, bring more referrals, keep customers on the site longer, and improve your website's search presence — all by using Google+.

Part IV: Taking Google+ Further

Here's where I get to have some fun and show you a few advanced tips and tricks for improving your Google+ presence. I zoom in on how to use Google+ APIs to improve your website, as well as other advanced topics to hone your edge as a marketer.

Part V: The Part of Tens

For some folks, this is the best part! Here, I give you three chapters with ten tips each, showing you how to improve your presence on Google+. I cite some prime examples of successful Google+ use and offer some practical Google+ tips for the small-business owner.

Icons Used in This Book

Where necessary, you'll see little icons that call attention to information you can respond to in various ways — some you ignore, some you pay attention to so as to nail down the subject matter, and some you (ahem) just heed, okay? Hey, at least you get some cute little pictures to look at instead of just writing.

Wherever you see this cute little Dummies head, I'll leave a tip that will sharpen your savvy about the subject matter. These are the places you'll probably find yourself saying, "Hmm, I didn't realize that!"

I promise not to bore you by becoming too repetitive, but if I get a sudden urge to remind you to duct-tape something to your memory, this is where I put it. If it's here, there's a good chance you should pay attention. These are the things I want so stuck in your head that you'll be able to recite them by memory when you're done with the book. (Just kidding. There won't be an exam. Honest.)

Anywhere you see this, you should probably pay attention. It means there's something you should watch out for — and I don't want you to run afoul of it.

If you're a dyed-in-the-wool marketer, you can probably ignore these tidbits, but if you really want to understand the tech that makes this process tick, you'll want to read 'em. They're where I get back to my techie roots for a minute.

Where to Go From Here

Well, the first step is to start reading! Go ahead — pick any chapter. Some like to read from the beginning and go to the end (that's how I wrote it). But you can drop into the book anywhere and go from there if you like. Pick a chapter that looks useful to you and get going!

You might want to start by following this book's Google+ Page, as well as my personal account and this book's Google Group. You can find those here:

- *Google+ Marketing For Dummies* Google+ Page: `http://stay.am/gplusmarketing`

- Jesse's personal Google+ profile (This is my personal profile, so you'll get some personal things here! Follow at your own risk, but all are welcome!): `http://profiles.google.com/jessestay`

- *Google+ Marketing For Dummies* Google Group (Ask questions here, and share your success stories!): `http://stay.am/gplusmarketinggroup`

I hope you'll come by and say, "Hi — I'm your biggest fan!" (or just "Hi!") at any of the channels listed here. Above all, get out there and create a Google+ account. Then create a Google+ Page for your brand, and start following people online who are interested in your brand. Soon, you'll see the value of Google+ that I saw when I first joined.

Part I

Seeing How Google+ Benefits Marketers

The 5th Wave By Rich Tennant

"Has the old media been delivered yet?"

In this part . . .

I've heard it over and over again: "I get on Google+, and no one ever talks to me over there, so I go back to Facebook." Or perhaps you've seen others find success on Google+ — and you want to learn how you can do it too.

Whatever the reason, Google+ is a tool all marketers should consider as an option to increase the presence of the brands they represent. In this part of the book, I show you why you can, and how you can see the success that many others have seen through the use of Google+. You'll learn what Google+ is, and why it's a valuable tool for anyone trying to build a network, an audience, or even more clicks that lead new customers toward their brand or website.

Chapter 1

A Marketer's Overview

*T*he future of Google+ is Google.

If there's one phrase I want you to remember, it's that one. The fact is, as a marketer you're not going to get the same results on Google+ (said *Google Plus)* as you do on Facebook or Twitter or any other social network.

Google+ is a social layer on top of the entire Google experience. The destination site centralizes it all: `plus.google.com`. The cool part is that you don't even have to visit `plus.google.com` to use Google+. The team working on Google+ frequently calls it "the Google+ Project," and for a reason — it's a layer (maybe even a glue?) that gives the entire Google infrastructure a comon social bond.

In this chapter, I give you a look at what Google+ is and help you get acclimated to the environment. You'll quickly find it isn't the same as Facebook or Twitter. It has its own personality, strengths, and quirks. This chapter gets you going quickly so you can hit the ground running and not the wall.

This book doesn't explain how to set up a Google+ account or how to circle people. For that information, I recommend my other book, *Google+ For Dummies,* Portable Edition (John Wiley & Sons, Inc.). However, I do show you the different pieces of Google+ so you're familiar with the tools at your disposal.

Appreciating the Typical Google+ Audience

As with any social network — or marketing strategy — understanding your audience is your number-one priority. The minute you set up your Google+ profile, or a Google+ page after that, you'll notice that your audience just isn't the same as the one you're seeing on Facebook or Twitter. Maybe you're seeing no audience at all. That's okay, because on Google+, you have opportunities to grow new audiences while bringing existing audiences to your Google+ presence through Google search.

Besides remembering that the future of Google+ *is* Google, keep in mind that Google+ is about people. The more you focus on people and building real relationships, the more success you're going to see on Google+.

The following points can help you:

✔ Google+ is a powerful way to bring together like-minded interests. This point is most important for effective marketing.

✔ If you focus on just your brand, and not the people within your brand, you probably won't survive on Google+.

✔ Audiences on Google+ are typically a little more analytical than usual.

✔ Typically, at least at the start, you won't find close friends and family of individuals on Google+.

Because Google+ caters to a more analytical audience, it's easy to find people who like the same things you do — or people who like the same things your customers like — and start conversations with them. Photographers are a good example: They can see their photos right in line with the stream. In addition, I can search for *photography* and find a whole list of people with the same interest.

As a marketer or business owner, you can take advantage of how easy it is to find people this way. Say your customers are moms. Search for *mom* and you'll find a whole bunch of moms on Google+. (See Figure 1-1.) Add your favorites to your circles and have a few conversations with them; you'll be building community and relationships with other moms all around the world. That's when you start to create a platform for your brand.

Figure 1-1:
Searching
for *moms*
on Google+
reveals
a list of
people who
are moth-
ers (or are
interested in
moms).

Becoming a Member of the Google+ Community

As I mentioned, Google+ is about people. This means you have to focus on people to see results. Building community and relationships within your community is an important aspect of your Google+ strategy. Think about who your audience is, and how you can build community with those folks from the very start.

Reading books and influencing people

Consider reading *How to Win Friends and Influence People* by Dale Carnegie or *Enchantment* by Guy Kawasaki for some great tips on how to build genuine relationships with people and build your network the way Google+ intended.

Because you can bring people with like interests together so easily with Google+, seek out people who have interests like yours. As a marketer or business owner, you may also consider seeking out people whose interests match those of your customers. If your customers like toothbrushes, find people who like toothbrushes and participate in the conversation with them. Use your own personal profile and employee profiles to do so.

Consider these tips when you're trying to make yourself or your brand a member of the Google+ community:

- ✔ **Treat people with respect.** Remember that others do have different ideas and interests — and that you represent more than just yourself; you represent your brand. Users are always notified when you comment on their posts or mention them. If you say something negative, you can get blocked — possibly resulting in a loss of respect for you and your brand.

- ✔ **Comment, comment, comment.** Of course, commenting on every single post a person makes can make you come across as annoying, but showing interest in an individual — and in what he or she says — has a personal effect. Commenting on someone's posts leaves an impression on that individual, and the more you participate in his or her conversations —especially when you build up and contribute to what that person has to say — the more he or she remembers you. That person is more likely to follow you in return and participate in your conversations.

- ✔ **The power of the +1.** A +1 button is next to every post (and now on many websites). If you like the post, click the +1 button. (To see what the +1 button looks like, look at Figure 1-2.) When you "+1" a post (click the +1 button), its author sees that you've done so. People notice +1s especially well among the people they're following — and they take note. The attention you generate by +1'ing posts helps you build further relationships.

- ✔ **Participate in Hangouts.** I have a tough time doing this myself. Believe it or not, I'm actually a shy person and would much prefer to write out my thoughts than to engage someone in person. Participating in Google+ Hangouts, which allow up to ten people at a time to chat through video, can be a painless way to build relationships. Start your own Hangouts or join others. The more potential customers see your face and hear your voice, the more "real" the Google+ experience becomes for them; in turn, they recognize and pay attention to you. In addition, you can broadcast your Hangouts to the world through Google's On Air feature, giving even greater opportunities to meet new people. You can read more about Hangouts in Chapter 9.

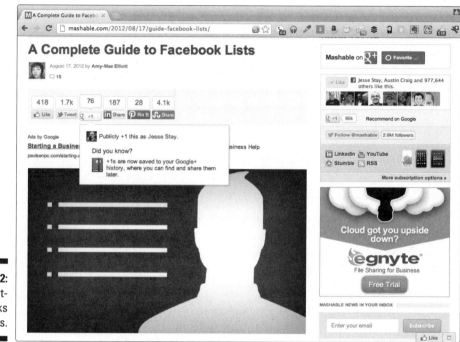

Figure 1-2:
The +1 button looks like this.

✔ **Focus on relationships.** Find ways to help and build up relationships with the people you're following.

The word *hate* should not be in your vocabulary. Avoid harsh criticism. Instea, seek to grow — and to show you're on the same team as those you're following. The words your mom always told you ring true: If you can't say anything nice, don't say anything at all. This is especially true on Google+.

Discovering Google+ Tools

The following sections explain the most important components, which are the basic building blocks for your marketing strategy on Google+.

User profiles

Your user profile is the foundation of Google+; look at Figure 1-3 to see my profile. Every post on Google+ is by an actual person. Even brands, through Google+ Pages, have to be linked to an actual person's Google+ profile in order for that person to post on behalf of the brand. (In Chapter 12, I talk later about linking content from your website to the Google+ profiles of people who create that content.)

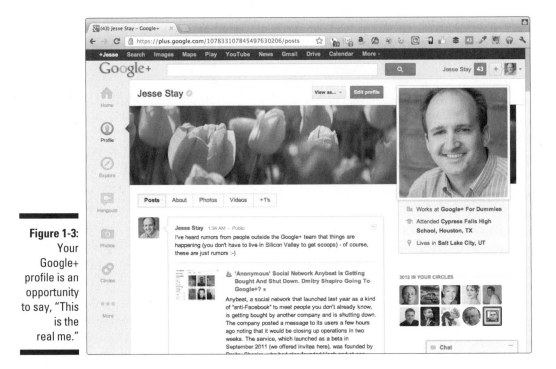

Figure 1-3: Your Google+ profile is an opportunity to say, "This is the real me."

When, as a marketer, you're thinking about Google+ profiles, think about *who* in your company is behind the brand. Your Google+ presence should be less about the brand itself than it is about the people who make the brand what it is. For example, your employees or notable execs can share content from your Google+ page or participate in Hangouts representing your brand. Or your Google+ page can share experiences of actual people who have Google+ profiles and use your product. These people and their user profiles are critical in your marketing strategy on Google+.

Circles

On Google+, instead of following, friending, or subscribing to someone, you add a person to one of your circles The Google+ Circles feature gives you a way to gather individuals into a group by clicking the Circle button.

By using Circles,

- ✔ You can connect individual user profiles.
- ✔ Users can organize the content they share on the web.
- ✔ You can separate your friends and associates into groups.

Separating people into groups, from the very start of your marketing campaign, allows for some unique opportunities:

- ✔ You can target content to audiences who will be interested in that content.
- ✔ Staying on top of the activities of people with similar interests becomes easier because you can separate your news feed into content only from specific circles you select.
- ✔ You can send an e-mail notification to an entire circle, notifying as many as 100 people of your post.

You must choose which circles to share with when you post content. Google+ leaves the Add Names, Circles, or Email Addresses field blank by default. If you select Public, your posts default to Public until you change the setting (see Figure 1-4). That's important to you as a marketer because you may not see every post that your customers (or folks in other relationships with you) share. Consider it one more reason to focus on relationships among those you work with: You want to get into as many circles as possible so you can see what your contacts are sharing.

You can benefit your marketing strategy in many ways with Google+ Circles. I share several several such techniques throughout the book.

In addition to circles, you can target posts to individual people or e-mail addresses. You can have fun with this. For instance, you can use a special e-mail address Evernote gives you to archive certain posts from Google+. Or you can decide which posts you want to send to your blog.

Publish to Public

Figure 1-4:
Publishing
to Public
puts my
posts
available to
anyone by
default.

Google+ Pages

Google+ Pages are your brand's presence on Google+. When this book went to press the pages were sparse, but expect them to become more a part of the core Google experience when they represent businesses on Google itself.

The pages created in Google+ Pages are timeless, and specific to your brand. Google+ Pages can add people to circles, but only people who have added *them* first. People with Google+ profiles can add brands to their circles just as they can add people. Make sure, however, that your employees, owners, and executives are interacting on your brand's Google+ pages in a responsible manner.

To help prevent spam, Google+ holds a No Touch policy for Google+ Pages. Bottom line: Your Google+ page can't *touch* (circle, interact with, or notify, among other things) anyone's Google+ user profile unless that person has already added your Google+ page to his or her circle. Thus the following restrictions apply until each user profile you want to touch has first circled your Google+ page:

✔ You can't add other user profiles to your brand's circles.

✔ You can't mention user profiles.

✔ You can't comment on a user's posts until they've added you.

Google+ Events

Google+ Events (see Figure 1-5) are a great way to get the people in your audience coordinated around a specific event related to your brand. When you create an event, it's added to your Google calendar as well. Then the event is added to the Google calendars of everyone who RSVPs your event. The cross-integration between Google+ Events and Google Calendar is a powerful combination.

Figure 1-5:
A simple
Google+
event.

Google+ Events allow you to schedule real-life events and virtual events through Google+ Hangouts (described in the next section). You get to invite guests in the same manner as you add posts to your news feed — select the person, people, or circles you want to invite, and they're added to the guest list with an invite to RSVP.

You can also opt to make the event "on air," and all interaction between the people you invite to the event are made public for the world to watch. This strategy becomes especially interesting when guests turn on party mode. In this mode, all photos that guests take during the event are shown on their phones (that have the Google+ app installed). The event then provides a slideshow of everyone's photos taken during the event. This option can provide a fun way of sharing with your friends what happened at the party.

You can use Google+ Events in a few ways. You can

- **Schedule appointments.** Keeping your event private and visible to only those you invite can be a great way to collaborate among the members of a small group of people — sharing photos, screen shots, and other material with those who were in the meeting. The feature also sends an invitation to each attendee through Google Calendar.

- **Schedule Hangouts.** You can make an event entirely virtual. Just select the Google+ Hangout check box under the Advanced Options for the event; doing so attaches a link to a Google+ Hangout where the event is happening — right when it's time for the event to start. Then all those who were invited can join the Hangout, comment, and post photos, screen shots, and other relevant content inside the event.

- **Remember events.** A Google+ event allows you to capture a snapshot in time for those who attended the event. As users turn on party mode for the event, sharing photos *while they're at the event* is easy as pie. Then the photos are captured in time so everyone can go back and remember — which is hard to beat as a way to get close family and friends using Google+. Everybody can look back and reflect on the good time they had.

Google+ Hangouts

Google+ Hangouts allow up to ten people to chat via a video webcam session. A feature called On Air lets you also broadcast your Hangout to the rest of the world. See Chapter 9 to learn more about Google+ Hangouts.

Invite specific people in particular circles, or invite the entire public, to your Hangout. This means you can invite a group of influencers to join the Hangout, and then broadcast that group of smart and influential people to the world, bringing even more attention to your brand and the people involved with it.

To explore some other highly effective ways to use Hangouts, check out Chapters 9 and 14.

Search

Search is at the heart of Google+; *search engine optimization (SEO)* is just as close to the heart of your marketing campaign. (For a look at farther-reaching implications of SEO outside `plus.google.com`, flip to the "Seeing people as the new SEO" section later in this chapter.)

The search capability on `plus.google.com` itself is very robust compared to what you find on competing platforms. With Google+, images and videos are embedded right in the stream — and the stream is not only real-time but also refreshes automatically as you watch it. However, perhaps the neatest feature is that you can participate in a conversation without ever having to mention the search term itself. For instance, as you watch the Super Bowl, search for *Super Bowl* to see a live view of updates, videos, and images about the game. Now post an update in the same stream, and don't mention *Super Bowl.* Your update appears with the rest of the search results, even though it didn't have that search term in it. You're now a part of the Super Bowl conversation, which is so much more than just a search result on a social network.

Google+ search allows you to search not only content and posts on Google+, but also people. Here are some very marketing-friendly ways you can do so:

- **Use hashtags.** Google+ supports hashtags, one of which you can see in Figure 1-6. When you see a hashtag on Google+, the following word hyperlinks to the search for Google+. Clicking it immediately takes you to a live view of the people talking about that topic. You can also participate in the conversations.

- **Participate in trending terms.** The Trending Terms section at the upper right of your stream (and in the search results) is where you find the most popular topics at any given time. If enough of your customers post about a particular topic, your own products and messages could be reflected in these terms. Even if they aren't (yet, anyway) seek out the trending terms that match your brand's purpose — and make sure you participate in the conversation.

- **Find people with like interests.** Search for *football,* and you'll find people interested in football. Search for *tech,* and you'll find people interested in tech. Also returned in your search results will be circles related to your search that people have shared with their friends. Seek those out as well; you'll find a terrific resource: people's circles in which their friends have identified them as having an interest in the topic of your particular search.

If you're contributing to other people's conversations, don't just broadcast content that reflects only your own interest; that approach smacks of spam. *Join* the conversation — don't pollute it! Finding people with similar interests means you're learning from or associating with other users. The sales and conversions will come naturally from these relationships. Going in and commenting just to comment will never end up well. Focus on real people and relationships.

Figure 1-6:
Hashtags are a great way to organize a conversation about a topic.

Photos (and videos)

Not only can you store photos and video on Google+, you can also upload photos and videos you take on your phone — automatically — through Google+ apps for iOS and Android. Animated images are also supported — what better way to bring attention to your posts or bring home a point? When I add an animated image to a post, my followers are much more likely to see the post because it's moving and drawing their eyes toward my post. (I talk more about content strategy in Chapters 5 and 6.)

Games

Games — at least from a marketing standpoint — are a way to build relationships with people. You may consider building a game that helps integrate your brand in some unique way (see Chapter 14 for that topic). Selected developers can get an API from Google+ for building games; if games are your product, check out *Google+ For Dummies,* Portable Edition (John Wiley & Sons, Inc.), which devotes entire chapter to this API.

Building Social on Top of Google

Because the future of Google+ really *is* Google itself, the `plus.google.com` portion of Google+ will become less significant over time. Google+ allows you to respond, comment, +1, and even start Google+ Hangouts directly inside your Gmail inbox. I don't even have to go to `plus.google.com` anymore to participate in conversations I've started. That's the true power of Google+: It's everywhere in the Google universe because it's simply a social layer on top of everything Google.

Seeing people as the new SEO

Your `www.google.com` search results now include people. If your content has an identified author, it will likely rank higher than content that doesn't have an author listed. For example, because my blog lists my Google+ profile as the author of my content, my content is likely to rank higher than similar content from another website of the same ranking that has no link to Google+. (You can find the details of this topic in Chapter 12.)

Even before Google+, Facebook included websites in its own search rankings through its Open Graph Protocol. These days your content's rank in the search results has a direct connection to how many people click the +1 button to show that they've seen it and have responded positively to it. As people discover more content through their friends, they affect search engine optimization. People are quickly becoming the new SEO.

Making Google+ a path, not a destination

Think about how Google+ integrates with Google Contacts. As you talk with people on Google+, those new contacts get archived in `google.com/contacts`. When you open Gmail, you see the people who have Gmail accounts; you can also see and do much more:

- ✔ You can see which people have their Google+ profile data integrated on the sidebar of Gmail next to their messages.

- ✔ You can see recent conversations you had with those individuals.

- ✔ You can add people to your circles from right inside Gmail.

- ✔ You can search inside `www.google.com` and see content that your friends on Google+ have +1'd or shared.

Knowing when to post on which network

As I write this, Facebook and Twitter are the two biggest social networks — at least they're the ones with which brand managers, marketers, and business owners are most concerned. Google+, as a social network, really carries some of the best elements of each:

- ✔ **Google+ supports threaded comments.** The +1 button is very similar to Facebook's Like button. Google+ has pages similar to Facebook, and its lists format is much more similar to Facebook's than Twitter's.

- ✔ **Google+ has public search, hashtag support, and trending terms.** Although Google+ has no mutual "friend" agreement like the one on Facebook, following people on Google+'s circles is similar to following on Twitter.

Your Twitter strategy may be closer to how you approach Google+:

- ✔ Embracing hashtags

- ✔ Deciding who to follow

- ✔ Posting frequent and real-time content

However, consider that because threaded comments are attached to each post, moderation of comments is also necessary. Also consider how to create engaging posts, much as you might do in your Facebook strategy.

In general, cross-posting the same message to multiple networks won't give you the best results. Your Google+ audience will probably be different from your Facebook and Twitter audiences. Adapt your messaging to fit the audiences and strengths of each network. If you have time and resources, you'll see the best results from this approach.

Getting and Measuring Solid Results

The key to any good social media campaign is to *measure, measure, measure*. This goes for Google+ too. You'll have to do a lot of the measuring on your own. I anticipate at some point Google Analytics will integrate with Google+. Until then, be sure to track your own posts and determine a strategy that works best for you.

I suggest this approach:

1. **Make a spreadsheet.**
2. **Mark the Google+ posts you make.**

   Categorize posts by topic, time, and frequency.
3. **Experiment.**

Look for patterns: Do certain types of content resonate better with your audience? Play with the capabilities of Google+ Circles; does applying different circles to different content produce better results? Experiment with posting at different times or more frequently. Try to duplicate your posting on occasion in order to catch eyes that may have missed your post originally.

Then return and report — look at your results and see what works best for your message. No single formula works the same for every brand or person out there. Come up with a custom formula that works just right for your brand. (I detail some strategies you can try out along these lines in Chapter 13.)

Chapter 2

Getting Started with Google+

In This Chapter

▶ Creating a Google+ account

▶ Understanding circles

▶ Learning the etiquette

*B*efore you can build a marketing strategy, you have to be familiar with the tools. That familiarity starts with creating or enabling your Google+ profile, and increases as you get comfortable using it.

The interface for Google+ changes frequently. Much of this is par for the course in writing about any social network. However, if you're lost because the interface or sounds have changed, wander over to this book's Google+ page at `http://stay.am/gplusmarketingpage`, or ask me via my profile at `http://profiles.google.com/jessestay`. Overall, the concepts in this chapter should remain the same.

Accounting You In

If you haven't already — over 200 million people have, according to Google — create a Google account and set up your Google profile. (I don't add the + next to the word *Google* in the phrase *Google profile*. This profile is on every Google site and refers to it as your *personal profile*.)

The future of Google+ is Google, so your Google+ activity will follow you wherever you go.

Setting up your profile

Your profile is the single most critical point on Google for establishing a presence, seeking engagement, and helping people find you across Google. Marketers who focus on the profile as the source of content see the most success on Google+. Way too often, people don't fill out their profiles — and then complain that they're not seeing anyone engage with their posts.

I'll say it over and over again: Google+ is about people. Google tries hard to ensure that every profile represents a real person. Google prefers that you avoid pseudonyms and other anonymous ways of representing yourself. To keep your profile genuine, follow these tips:

- ✔ **Use your real name.** The more real this is, the more success you'll see. Use circles (which I cover in the next section) if you're concerned about privacy.

- ✔ **Use a profile image with your big, bright, smiling face.** Make people feel like they're talking to a real person. This is how people recognize you on Google+. You'll see much more interaction when your profile is represented by a real representation of yourself.

- ✔ **Fill out your profile's About section.** If someone tells me he's not getting any interaction on Google+, I go to his profile. Usually he hasn't completed the About section. People can learn about you here. Also, the content helps people find you through search.

In my profile tagline, I start with "Google+ For Dummies Author." I did this so that when people search for *Google+* on `plus.google.com`, they find me and my book. Google+ places a fairly heavy weight on your tagline, so be sure to focus on that when you fill out your profile.

Because Google+ has to be turned on if you're an existing Google user, and because you may or may not have set up a Google profile before, the following two sections cover different scenarios. Follow the steps that fit your scenario. If neither fits your situation, pick the closest one.

You don't have a Google account

If you have a Gmail account or use Google Docs, you likely have a Google account.

If you ever log in to any Google-owned product, you have a Google account. If you do, you can skip this section.

If you don't have a Google account, Google makes setting up Google+ easy. In fact, Google now requires all new users to fill out their Google profiles (which link to Google+), automatically giving you a head start on Google+.

Here's how you set up your Google Account and get your Google profile going:

1. **Go to** `plus.google.com`.

   Remember this URL! This is where your main Google+ stream will be. Any time you want to follow people you're following, go here.

2. **Click Create an Account (see Figure 2-1).**

3. **Enter your name, select your username, and enter your information (see Figure 2-2).**

4. **Click Next Step.**

   This is where things might change. Just follow the instructions you see onscreen.

Figure 2-1: Click the Create an Account link to get started.

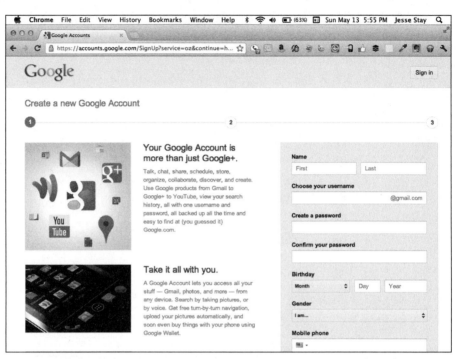

Figure 2-2:
Enter your
name and
information.

Make sure you're using a real name. Google is known to disable accounts that don't represent real people, under their legal, real-world names. Google wants this to be as real an experience as they can get for their users. The more real you can make it, the better an experience you'll have on Google+.

5. Add a profile photo.

While you may feel inclined to remain anonymous, please consider uploading a genuine photo of yourself. You get more out of Google+ if you make your profile as genuine and real as possible. You will see many more comments, +1s, and shares if you have a real profile photo of the real you.

Your profile photo is how people will remember you. Every time you change it, people have to re-recognize you. While you certainly can change the profile image as often as you like, consider selecting a good representation of yourself at the start, and avoid changing it unless there are major changes in your look and appearance.

6. Add friends.

You should have these options:

- Select friends on Google+ from other networks and accounts (such as Yahoo! Mail).

- Select suggestions; see Figure 2-3.

- Click through and select individuals from a list.

Adding too many friends can cause clutter in your stream. When you have too many friends, it can become difficult to sort through your stream and catch everything. At the same time, if you change your mind later, the more friends you have, the harder it becomes to clean up your friends list. For the optimum experience, limit your friends to those you truly have an interest in.

7. **Read the tips that Google+ provides.**

8. **Fill out your employment and work information.**

Completing this information helps fellow alums or former coworkers find you. This information reflects on Google's other products: When someone searches for *Microsoft,* she finds all her friends and others who work (or worked) at Microsoft. The same goes for any educational institution.

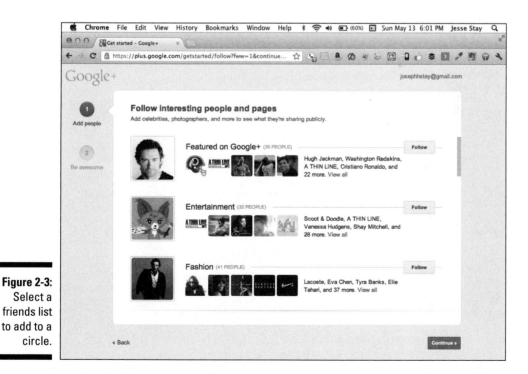

Figure 2-3:
Select a friends list to add to a circle.

9. **Start using Google+.**

   That's it! Proceed to the next section for the details of how to make your first post, utilize circles, and start your first conversation on Google+.

After setting up your Google account, try this:

1. **Go to** www.google.com **and log in.**

2. **Search for the name of a company you've worked for.**

   If you're lucky, a list of other employees at that company will appear on the right side of your Google search results. (See Figure 2-4.)

Figure 2-4: Searching for *Microsoft* returns a list of people who work for Microsoft (shown to the right of www. google. com).

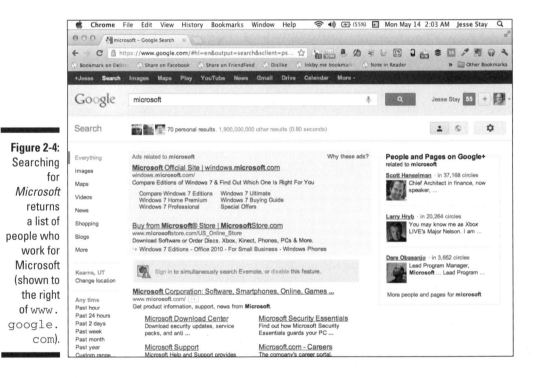

You have a Google account but haven't joined Google+

If you've never joined Google+, but you have a Google account, follow these steps to create a Google+ account:

1. **Go to** `plus.google.com`.

   You have probably been to Gmail or another Google product at this point; `plus.google.com` is where you'll go to get all the news from those you are interested in.

2. **Sign in with your Google account if haven't done so already.**

3. **Fill out the requested information.**

4. **Click Upgrade.**

5. **Follow the directions to add and find friends.**

6. **Enter your work and education info.**

   This step is important. Try following people with the same interests as your customers. The more you interact with these people, the more potential customers you'll accrue and the bigger audience you'll garner.

7. **Start using Google+.**

Going Around in Circles and Privacy

Circles are at the heart of the entire Google+ experience. Google has made an effort to ensure that you have complete control over

- ✔ Who can see the posts you make
- ✔ How you organize your stream

In fact, your very first post on Google+ doesn't appear to anyone. Google+ *asks* you to choose who will see it. From that point until the next post, your privacy settings will be remembered. Everyone you selected to see your first post will continue to see the content you post until you change the audience again.

Google is taking circles through the entire Google experience. You can use the circles you create on Google+ on other Google products as well. Google Contacts, for instance, allows you to organize your contacts by circles. Gmail allows you to add, to your Google+ circles, people who send you e-mail. This linking is a piece of what I consider Google's venture into *social* customer relationship management (CRM); you can use it to easily track the groups you interact with on Google products (and even across the web).

To give you an idea of what can be done with the Google+ Circles feature, consider the following:

- ✔ You can determine who sees the posts you make on Google+.
- ✔ You can organize your news stream by interests or by the groups of people you interact with.

✔ You can control which groups of people see what in your profile.

✔ You can organize your Google contacts.

✔ You can create a Google+ Hangout with a group of friends you choose.

✔ You can share a circle of friends with another group of friends (or with the public).

Google+ circles will be familiar to you if you use Facebook lists; in fact, they're almost identical. However, I feel circles are even more central to the experience in Google+. They're easier to find — and, as I said, Google+ tends to let you decide with whom to want to share; its default is no sharing at all. Facebook, by contrast, defaults to friends and friends of friends. That difference doesn't mean either is better than the other. It's just good to understand how each works so you can use each tool to your best advantage.

Finding people to circle

Google+ isn't the place you're going to interact with your closest personal friends and family. That's what Facebook is for.

First thing to do is find some people with interests like yours and circle them. You can get started finding people to circle a couple of ways. Here are my suggestions:

✔ **Take the suggestions made to you when you signed up.** I cover this briefly in the "Setting up your profile" section of this chapter. See if you can find people with like interests (or of interest to you). If they have stuff you'd like to have appear in your stream, add them to a circle of your choice.

✔ **Go with Google's suggestions from your Google and Gmail contacts.** A You Might Like section is on the right side of the Google+ feed; see Figure 2-5. It lists people from your Google and Gmail contacts who are already on Google+, as well as people your friends are following. Check out their feeds to see if they're interesting.

Here's another way to find people from your existing Google and Gmail contacts, as well as common friends from Google+:

1. *Click the Circles tab on the left.*

2. *Click the Find People tab at the top.*

   The Top Suggestions and Other Suggestions sections will list people who Google+ thinks would be interesting to you.

Feeds you might like

Figure 2-5:
The You
Might Like
section
appears on
the right
side of your
stream.

Users with a little Gmail or mail icon in the upper-right corner of their
profile picture (see Figure 2-6) aren't on Google+, but you can add them
to a circle. When you post to that circle, you can opt to send updates to
those users' e-mail addresses. When they join Google+ with that e-mail
address, they're automatically added to your circle as Google+ users.

WARNING!

Be careful not to spam your friends. If you add an e-mail address to a
circle, you have the option when you post an update to that circle to
also send an e-mail to the people not on Google+. Use this sparingly, as
people who don't use Google+ could consider this spam.

TIP

✔ **Search your other mail contacts.** Try this method:

1. *Look on the Find People tab under Circles on your Google+ stream.*

   Note that you can find people you know from the moment you first
   sign up or fill out your profile on Google+.

2. *Click the drop-down arrow by All Suggestions.*

Mail icons

Figure 2-6:
If it's just an e-mail contact, it has a little mail icon.

3. *Choose a Yahoo! or Hotmail account or upload an address book from a popular e-mail client (see Figure 2-7).*

You'll get instructions to import your contacts from any one of these services into your suggestions to add to circles.

Your Google+ contacts may not be the same as your Facebook contacts. Importing your Facebook contacts into Google+ involves a bit of a hack. See the Lifehacker tutorial at

```
http://lifehacker.com/5817003/import-facebook-friends-
        to-google%252B-by-going-through-yahoo-first
```

✔ **Search by workplace.** Look for any employer in Google+ search to see a list of people who have worked at that workplace. (See why it's important to fill out your work history on Google+?)

✔ **Search by place of education.** In the same way as a workplace, search for your favorite educational institution, whether it's a high school or college; a list of people who attended appears. Add them to your Classmates circle.

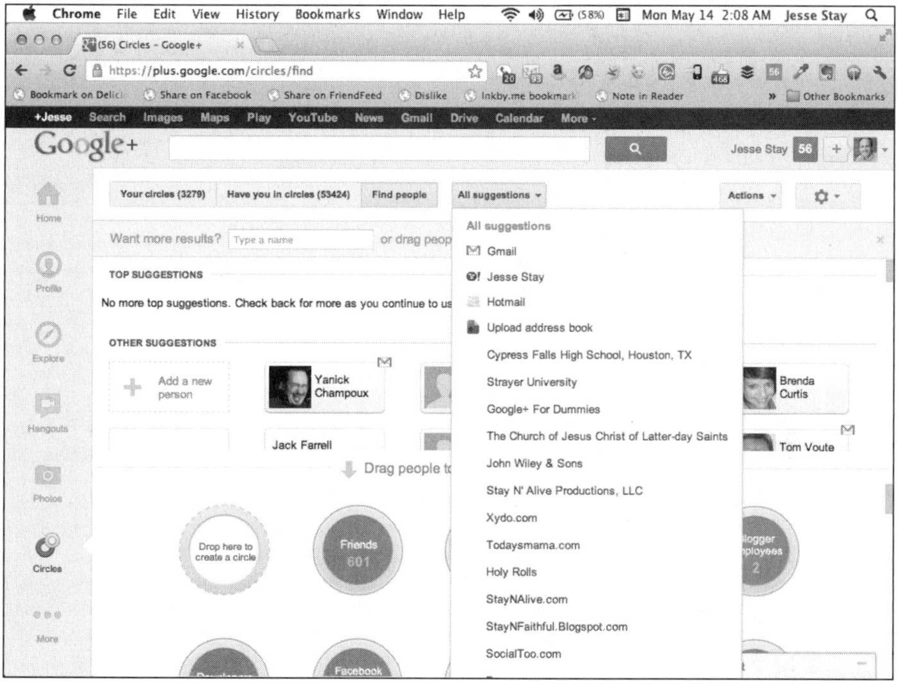

Figure 2-7:
Selecting
the Yahoo!
or Hotmail
options from
the drop-
down menu.

Select the drop-down menu next to Everything in the search results and select People and Pages to see only a list of profiles that match your search criteria.

✔ **Search by name.** There are sure to be people you know and want to add. Just search for their name, and select People and Pages in the drop-down menu next to the search term that's displayed to find individual people that you know.

✔ **Search by interest.** This is one of the best tricks in the book. You'll gain a lot of value trying to find people who have the same interests as you and your customers. Search for *mom* (for example) and you'll find a bunch of moms posting on Google+; see Figure 2-8. Search for *marketing* and you'll find a bunch of marketers on Google+. You get the point. Following people with like interests and participating in their streams will provide some of the most value.

✔ **Look for shared circles.** This is one of my favorite tricks. Search for *"shared a circle"* (with the quotes) followed by any interest. (For example, searching for *"shared a circle" photographers* produces a list of everyone who's sharing their photographer circles with the public; see Figure 2-9. This invaluable list is full of people with specific interests and have already been categorized.

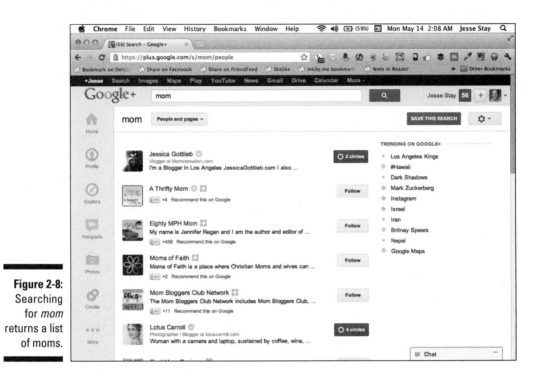

Figure 2-8:
Searching
for *mom*
returns a list
of moms.

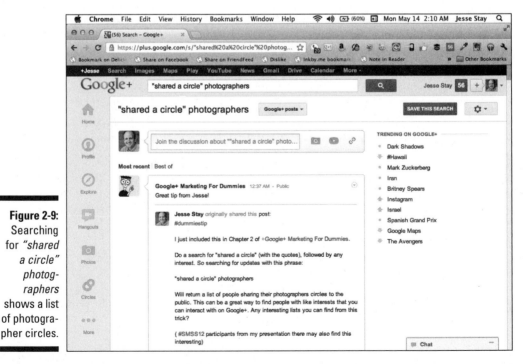

Figure 2-9:
Searching
for *"shared
a circle"*
photog-
raphers
shows a list
of photogra-
pher circles.

✔ **Participate in Hangouts.** You can meet some amazing people in Google+ Hangouts. If you can get out of your shell and talk to people, Hangouts are a great place to "seal the deal" in a relationship. Join a Hangout or two with people who seem interesting to you. That may be just what you need to determine whether they're interesting enough to follow.

If you click the Circles tab on the left side of Google+, you can manage your circles even more. Play around with this page and see the different ways to manage your circles.

Targeting your updates

One of the big advantages of Google+ circles is that you can target your updates to specific audiences. This ensures you always have control over who can see your posts. You choose lists, people, or e-mail addresses.

Want to archive all your updates? If you use the Evernote service, you can. Just store your Evernote e-mail address in a circle named Evernote. When you want to archive an update, add the Evernote circle to the list of circles you're posting to. Now all your posts will save to Evernote. You can take this strategy even further if you want, and use other e-mail addresses. Name the circle Backups, and it will be backed up automatically to every service you choose.

You can target your posts a few different ways:

✔ **To an individual.** If you type in the name of a Google+ user, only that user — or the individual users you specify by name — can see your post. You can send a private message to a friend, for instance. Or maybe you want to send it to a particular circle and just a couple of friends outside that circle.

✔ **To a circle or circles.** Perhaps the most common feature is to specify a single circle or a couple of circles you want to see your post. Maybe the post is just for coworkers. Make sure you specify your coworkers' circles.

The circles you choose are recalled the next time you post. The next time you post, make sure that your post is going to the right people and that your settings are back to where you like them. This particular privacy strength could actually come back to bite you if you're not watching it.

✔ **To an e-mail address.** You can target updates to specific e-mail addresses. Those users get an e-mail message asking them to click through to see the entire update. Users are required to have Google+ accounts to read the messages; each one who comments must have a Google account.

Adding people to circles

Adding people to a circle is quite easy. Google provides a list of default circles from which you can choose. Or you can create your own. When you see a name you'd like to add to a circle, follow these steps:

1. **Mouse over the name.**

2. **Mouse over the Follow or Add button.**

   You'll see the circles available to you. This button may also be the name of another circle to which you have already added this individual.

3. **Look over the circles that are there, and if you see one you like, check the box next to it.**

   You can do this with multiple circles if you like. If you don't see a circle you like, go to Step 4.

4. **Click Create New Circle.**

5. **Type the name of your new circle.**

6. **Click Create.**

✓ **To the public.** I like to post to the public so people can find me more easily. People with like interests will see my posts and want to add me. The more posts they see, the more likely they are to follow me and add me to their circles. Your profile looks blank to people who visit and aren't in your circles. The more often you update publicly, the better the idea you give people about what they can expect from your stream. All public updates are visible in `www.google.com` search. It means friends searching for things related to what you share on Google+ will also see those updates in their `www.google.com` search results. They can +1 them and come back to comment on your original post.

If you mark a post public, *everyone* can see it. Of course, you should never post anything online unless you're okay with the web seeing it, because there is always a risk that friends might share what you post — in spite of your privacy settings.

You can notify your friends by following these steps:

1. **Click any of the circles you're posting to.**

2. **Click Notify About This Post; see Figure 2-10.**

   Each person, up to 150 people, will get a notification about your post. Just be careful not to do this too often, or it may be construed as spam.

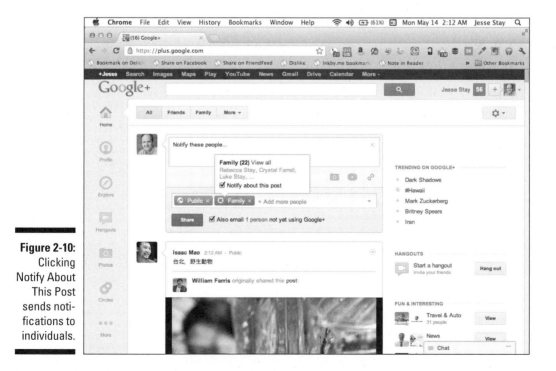

Figure 2-10: Clicking Notify About This Post sends notifications to individuals.

Posting to circles and to individuals

Posting to a specific circle or individual is simple. Below your post, click the box for adding circles, individuals, or e-mail addresses, and then type the name of the circle you want to add.

✔ If you're targeting an individual, type the individual's name.

✔ If it's an e-mail address, type the individual's address.

✔ If you're targeting circles, you're given a list of your circles as you type the circles' names (or you can choose Public). Add as many as you like; your post will be visible only to those people.

Navigating the Interface

As part of your venture into Google+, you should understand the basic elements of the interface you'll be using. There are many features, but I cover the most important here.

Accessing the news feed

The news feed shows *most* of the posts from everyone in your circles; see Figure 2-11. It also updates in real time. This may take some getting used to — especially when you have a lot of people in your circles — but you'll see the beauty of it the more you use it.

Any time you need to access your main news feed, do one of the following:

✔ Click the Home icon.
✔ Click the Google+ logo at the top.

You can also adjust what you see in your news feed. The default shows everything, but your circles are at the top. Click any circle to see the feeds of people in these circles.

Clicking the circles whose feeds you want to see is a handy way to go in and check on groups of people instead of getting the whole feed at once.

Organizing your circles

Google+ has a pretty nifty interface for organizing circles. I don't go into thorough detail here, but clicking the Circles tab at the left takes you to a page where you can fully organize who is in which circle and add new people to circles.

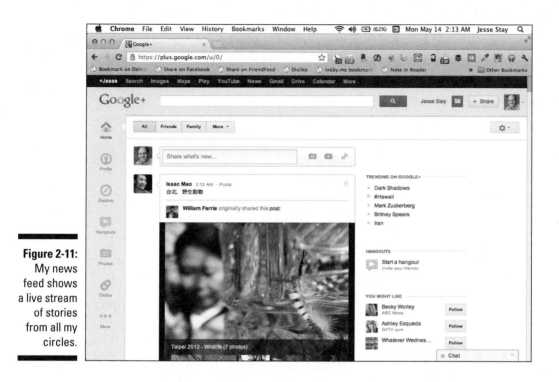

Figure 2-11:
My news feed shows a live stream of stories from all my circles.

Clicking the Circles tab also lets you do the following:

- ✔ **Find new friends.** I show you how to do so earlier in this chapter, in the section "Finding people to circle."

  You also can find other contacts (Google and otherwise).

- ✔ **Add people to existing circles.** Drag a person's card to the circle you want her in. One cool little animation later, she is — poof — added to the circle.

- ✔ **Create new circles.** Drag any name(s) to the Drop Here to Create a New Circle bubble. A form opens. Type a name for — and create — the circle.

- ✔ **Remove people from circles.** To remove someone from a circle, just click any of the circles, and drag the individual outside the circle. The person will then be taken out of the circle.

- ✔ **Delete circles.** Click any circle name. Then click the trash-can icon. The circle spins off the screen, and the circle is deleted.

- ✔ **Share circles.** Click the circle name. Click the icon of a circle with the two arrows pointing up. Type a message and click Share.

  Google+ lets you share only 500 people in a circle at a time.

Adjusting your volume

Your news feed shows *most* updates. In each circle you can adjust the volume of updates you receive from people in that circle. I change all of mine to 100 percent.

To change that throttle, follow these steps:

1. **Click the Home icon to go to your news feed.**

2. **Click a circle name.**

   At the upper right, you'll see a little slider bar. See Figure 2-12.

3. **Slide the bar to adjust the volume.**

   • *Slide it all the way to the right for 100 percent.*

   • *Slide it all the way to the left for no updates.*

Slider

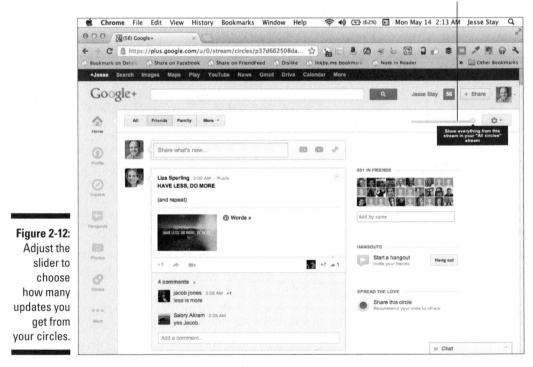

Figure 2-12:
Adjust the slider to choose how many updates you get from your circles.

Adjusting the update volume is a great way to customize what types of updates you see in your default news feed on Google+. The farther to the right you adjust the little volume slider, the more updates Google+ will insert into your feed. If you turn the slider all the way to the right, you'll see not only every update in your news feed, but also an e-mail notification for every update that comes from people and brands in the circle.

Playing Nice: Basic Etiquette

Google+ has its own culture. There is etiquette, perhaps not so different from other networks', that you should adhere to as you use the service.

Seeing how notifications work

When you take certain actions, other users get notifications that you performed those actions. Notifications show up two ways:

✔ **In the dark *sand bar* at the top of Google+:** In the little red bubble at the upper right, you'll see a number — that's how many notifications you have. You may find, after using Google+ for awhile, that the little bubble gets annoying; as the number goes up, you may feel that you always have to check it. Solution: Try setting a standard time for checking notifications, or push notifications to your e-mail so that you don't need to check that box.

✔ **Via e-mail:** In your account settings, you can decide which types of notifications go to your e-mail. It's important to consider that choice; for whatever action you do, you could be filling up someone's inbox. And if that inbox is already full, your actions could be deemed spam. So be sparing in your use of e-mail. As part of the important process of interacting with and building relationships with others, always consider what types of notifications they would want to receive *before* you send the message.

Here are most of the actions that cause notifications to occur on Google+:

- Comment on a post.

- +1 a post.

- Share someone's post.

- Mention someone in a comment or a post (by typing + followed by the person's name).

- Click a circle and select the Notify People About This Post check box. (Again, use this feature sparingly; filling an inbox with unasked-for messages gets annoying fast.)

Avoiding spam

The more you notify people on Google+, the more easily your posts could be deemed spam. It's important to note a couple of rules as you participate on Google+, just to be sure you don't get ignored or blocked.

Here's a good list to keep in mind:

- **Don't comment on every single post an individual makes.** Although commenting helps a person remember your name, doing it too much will likely backfire. He could ignore or block you as a result. Instead, reply sparingly, and focus on building up and helping the individual whose posts you're commenting on.

- **Use the Notify About This Post option sparingly.** The more you force a notification on other users, the more you come across as a spammer. Use this feature only for posts that you think they'll truly find interesting. Look for things they've asked for — and mention in the post why you're sending the notification.

- **Don't reply if your comment isn't related to the original post.** In other words, stay on topic. Keep in mind this general definition of spamming (or, for that matter, trolling): anything that isn't related to the general topic at hand. If you want to start a new topic with an individual, post something new in your own stream, and add that individual to the targeted recipients. Or wait for those folks to post something related to what you want to talk with them about.

- **Never mention individuals only to get their attention about something they never asked for in the first place.** If they didn't ask for it, it's spam — period. Instead, try to find things that help build up and strengthen the individual, and share those. You'll get a much better response that way.

Dealing with trolls

As you post on Google+, you're certain to come across a few *trolls* (people who comment on your posts with irrelevant statements or with content intended to cause angst for you or your followers). It's important that you don't encourage them. Instead, follow these simple tips:

- **Don't feed the trolls.** Whatever you do, don't further the argument. It brings more attention to them, never helps the topic at hand, and usually drives a conversation off topic. Just ignore the post, and follow the next steps in this list as necessary.

✓ **Consider deleting the comment instead of blocking someone.** I generally start by deleting a person's first offensive comment. I only block the person if he or she keeps trolling my posts. Blocking someone's comments at the outset means you might prevent a relationship from growing that could have been there.

✓ **Always take the high road.** Never give in to a troll. It just makes you into another troll. Don't go into the troll's posts and reply. Don't post disparaging remarks. Find ways to build them up where you can while keeping the conversation on topic. Sometimes even trolls can become friends or loyal fans if you try.

✓ **When in doubt, just block the troll.** As a last resort, if a troll continues, just block — then ignore and forget about — him or her. The more you focus on the posts, the more you're tempted to engage the troll further.

Ignore trolls and they'll go away.

Chapter 3

Discovering the "Plus" in Google+

Google+ isn't your average social network. It's much more than that. To understand Google+, you have to take a different approach than you would on any other traditional social network, such as Facebook or Twitter. In this chapter, I show you a few things that are unique to Google+ to give you an advantage as a marketer.

Optimizing Your Profile

Your Google profile is one of the most important parts of Google+ (and Google itself). This is the center of everything about you on Google and where people will identify the content you share. It's important that you get your profile right.

Spend some time on your profile. People who do generally see more engagement in their posts, more likes, more comments. That activity leads to more people liking your brand and brings your content's brand page a better ranking in www.google.com search results.

Your Google profile affects the following:

- ✔ **Your privacy.** You can change your profile so that certain circles can see certain types of information about you. If you have private information you don't want the entire world to know, make it visible only to people you trust.

- ✔ **How other people find you.** Have a particular skill set? Include it in your description or tagline. When people search for that skill set, they'll find your profile.

✔ **How your classmates can find you.** If you fill out your educational history, people (including former classmates) who are searching for your educational institution can find you.

✔ **How your coworkers can find you.** If you fill out your work history, former coworkers can find you when they search for employers, present or previous, that they have in common with you.

✔ **How people see you in their Google Contacts.** As you communicate with people via Gmail, your e-mail address gets associated with their Google+ circles — which associates your Google+ profile with you in their Google contacts. Result: The Google Contact pages they have of you shows much richer detail than just the basic e-mail address and name they would have otherwise. If you include a phone number or address publicly, those are also be visible to your contacts — and they, in turn, now have full contact information for you as they interact with you on other Google services.

✔ **Your** `www.google.com` **search ranking.** The more you interact with Google+, the more you +1, and the more you share on Google+, the more highly your content ranks on Google+. Also, if you associate the content you write on your website with a Google+ profile that identifies the author of that content, your website's content also ranks higher in `www.google.com` search results. (Chapter 12 provides full details of how to make this happen.)

✔ **Your first impression.** Your bright, shining face appears next to your Google interactions. Your profile is the first impression that most Google+ users have of you. Fill out that information. Adjust your privacy settings. Then, if visitors do judge a book by its cover, they know just what you want them to know about you.

Adjusting your profile for search

You can be found more than once. People can find you, follow you, comment to you, shower you with +1s, and share your posts.

Focus on these few elements to optimize your profile for search:

✔ **Your tagline.** If you're looking for people or pages with the main Google+ search, your tagline is one of the most important pieces of your profile to focus on. Start your tagline with the most important keyword. For instance, I want people to find my name when they search for *Google+,* so my tagline is *Google+ For Dummies Author.* If you want people to find you when they search for (say) photographers, include *Photographer* as the first (or only) word here.

✔ **The introduction.** Believe it or not, people look at this field when they're trying to figure out whether you're worth following. The introduction also serves as a source for Google+ search results. The intro doesn't weigh as heavily on search rankings as people and pages do, but it's important to have a few important keywords in here.

✔ **Your employment history.** If you go to your Circles tab (via the circles icon on the left of the stream), under Find People, click the All Suggestions drop-down menu. Your previous workplaces and other options are listed there. Select one to specify a time period. You can see other people who have also worked at those places at those times (see Figure 3-1).

✔ **Your education.** As with your employment history, people you went to school with can find you through Google+ search and the Find People option if you complete your education information.

✔ **The Profile Discovery field.** This field determines whether people can find your profile and *how* they can find it. Make sure Help Others Discover My Profile in Search Results is checked if you want to be discoverable on Google+.

Figure 3-1:
Finding
people
through
your
employment
history.

✔ **Places you've lived.** You can't search specifically for people who live in your former cities. Regardless, filling in where you've lived adds personality to your profile.

✔ **Other profiles and the Contributor To field.** These sections are very important (see Figure 3-2). This is a way to tell Google+ what sites are yours on the web, as well as which sites you contribute to. The more you link here, the more Google knows to look at those sites to find traces of you. (Chapter 12 has all the details.)

Filling out your Other profiles and Contributor fields is even more applicable as you start linking your websites and profiles back to your Google+ profile. (Again, I show you how in Chapter 12.) You can tell Google what sites and contents are yours. On the website, you can tell Google that your Google profile correctly suggests they are yours. This adds a layer of identity and authenticity that will help your www. google.com rankings.

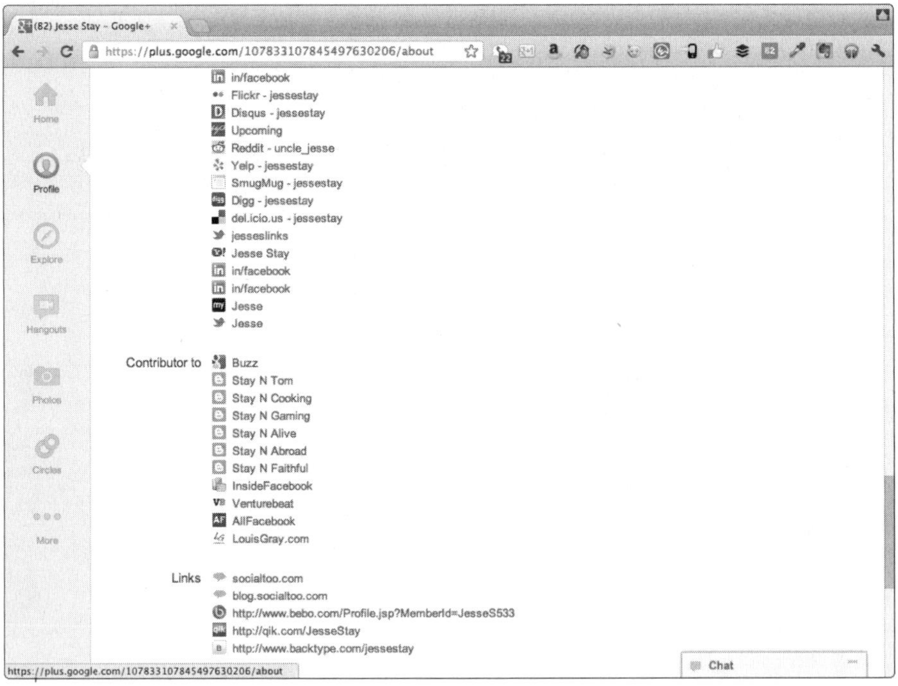

Figure 3-2:
Be sure you fill out your Contributor To section.

To edit your profile, follow these steps:

1. **Click the profile icon to the left of your stream on Google+ (or click your name or image anywhere on a Google sites).**

2. **Click the About tab at the top of the profile.**

3. **Click Edit Profile at the top of the screen.**

4. **Click a section you would like to change.**

5. **Edit or add information to the section.**

   You can also adjust privacy settings, as I show you in the next section.

When you select the appropriate time period, you'll see a list of people you either went to school with or worked with at that place, during that time. Click their names and drag them to a circle of your choice. If you find a lot of these folks, then you have an excellent reason to create a Coworkers or Classmates circle.

Setting your privacy settings

While finding you is certainly important, there may be some elements of your life you want to share — but only with certain groups of people (your phone number, for example). The same goes for your e-mail address. Thus you'll want to know how to adjust your privacy settings on Google+. Stay tuned.

Searching for coworkers and classmates

I got into Facebook itself by searching for old classmates and coworkers and getting in touch with them. Google+ allows this same type of connection. To find an old pal, follow the steps:

1. **Click the Circles icon on the left side of your Google+ stream.**

   Doing so takes you to your Circles page, where you can manage your circles and find new people to follow.

2. **Click Find People at the top of your Circles page.**

   Results for the people you find are based on your profile, Google Contacts, and other

information. This is where you'll find your old classmates or coworkers.

3. **Click the All Suggestions drop-down menu at the top.**

   You see options.

4. **Click a name, click Find Classmates, or click Find Coworkers.**

5. **In either scenario, make sure you fill out the appropriate name for your school or workplace after you click; then select a start and/or end date.**

To change how people see your profile, use the following steps:

1. **Click the profile icon, your name, or your profile image anywhere in Google+.**

   The Google profile page opens.

2. **Click Edit Profile.**

   You're in edit mode, which means you can edit any section on the page.

3. **Click the section whose privacy settings you want to adjust.**

4. **Edit the section.**

5. **Select the circles or individuals (including Public) you want to let see that particular section.**

   The options' appearance varies for each section; in most sections, you can click a drop-down menu like the one in Figure 3-3.

   Typically you see the following options:

   • Extended Circles

   • Public

   • Your Circles

   • Only You

   • Custom

   If you choose Custom, you can select specific circles and individuals.

Audiences love Google+

You have a few basic audiences, on top of your own circles and individuals, to whom you can target updates and profile information. It's important you understand each of these:

✔ **Extended Circles:** Extended circles are the circles of the people you have circled. On Facebook this is called *friends of friends*. This is your second-degree network and a great way to limit your audience (but allow people to discover you through your friends).

✔ **Public:** *Everyone* on the Internet can see any post or profile section, including search engines and non-Google+ users. This isn't necessarily a bad thing if you want to be

discovered. Just don't share those party pictures with a public audience!

✔ **Your Circles:** Only people you have circled (across all your circles) can see your post or profile section.

✔ **Only You:** If you want to keep something to yourself, choose Only You. With this option you can create a personal record. Just don't ever add circles, or what you intended as private could be made public.

✔ **Custom:** Select specific circles and individuals. This is helpful when you need only certain groups of people to see your updates.

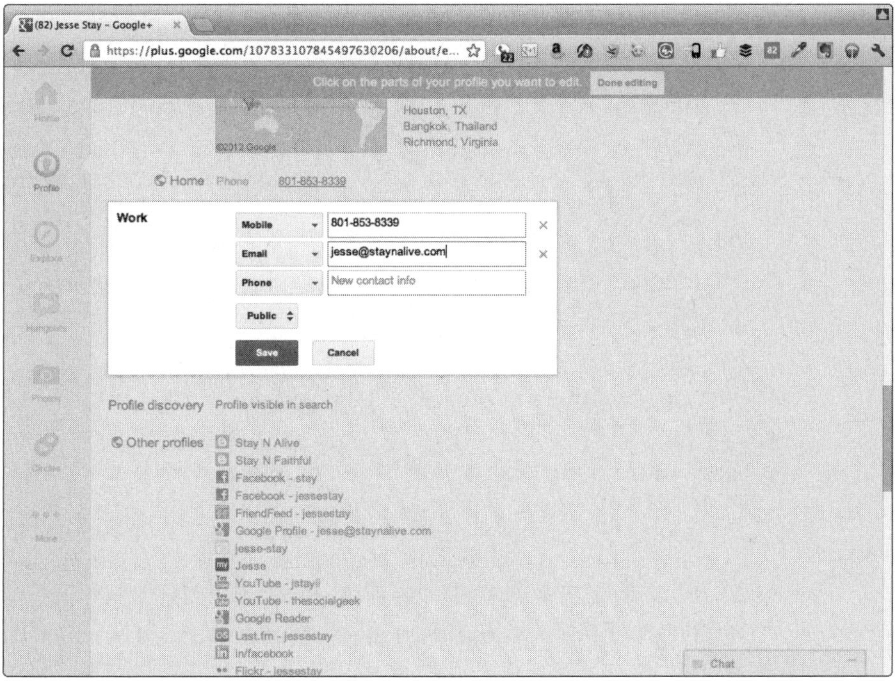

Figure 3-3:
Select the
right privacy
settings for
an e-mail
address.

WARNING!

Don't set everything to Private. Remember, the more you make public, the more people can find you and add you. The more you reveal about yourself on Google+, the more people will find you, and the more your network will grow. That said, use caution and make sure safety and privacy come first.

Building Your Network

How do you find people to follow you? How do you get people commenting on your posts?

Google+ requires an active approach. It has plenty of people to interact with. You just have to find them. As with any other service, you get what you put into Google+. If you spend some time, you'll get a lot of value out of it.

Follow this advice and soon you'll see more activity than ever:

✔ **Seek out people similar to you.** The more you surround yourself with people you want to be like, the more interesting your experience will be. Look for people who have achieved the success you want to achieve. Spend time learning from them. Naturally you'll build friendships — including some friendships with influential people.

Don't get frustrated if someone doesn't follow you or reciprocate when you follow him or her. Getting someone to follow you takes work. People have to get to know you first. Don't ever ask directly, "Why aren't you following me?" It's rude. They'll follow you when you've earned it.

✔ **Find interesting content.** Search for and follow individuals who share interesting content. This fills your stream with interesting things that entice others to comment and participate.

✔ **Build people up, and find ways to help.** This is my biggest secret — and I've met many influential people this way. If you find things that help the people you're trying to connect with (note that I didn't say "suck up"), they remember that. When you help someone, that person wants to reciprocate. Offer to help wherever possible. As my friend Guy Kawasaki likes to say: Whenever someone says thank you, always respond with "I know you would do the same for me." This really works.

✔ **Stop thinking of yourself. Think of others.** Google+ isn't about you. Well, maybe it is, but don't think of it that way. Instead, focus on following rather than being followed. Focus on +1'ing rather than being +1'd. Share, instead of worrying about being shared. When you take this approach, people respond. Don't make self-promotion the main thing.

✔ **Seek out face-to-face interactions.** To me, the final stamp of a relationship is when you meet in person. Google+ makes the online version of this step really easy through Hangouts. Join a Google+ Hangout or two. You may meet a few people in the process. If you meet, bond with, and then follow someone you meet during a Hangout, chances are they'll follow you back. If you get the opportunity to meet them in person, in real life, take it.

✔ **Participate.** I see so many people get on Google+ and just watch the stream go by. They don't comment or post. They just watch. Then they complain that they're not seeing any interaction on Google+. Well, you won't see any interaction on Google+ unless you participate. Make sure you're commenting on others' posts, +1'ing things you like, and engaging in conversations.

Optimizing Your Content Around People

The ultimate way to grow your network on Google+ is to strategize your content on the service.

This same principle applies to any social network. Create content that is engaging and meaningful to your audience, and they will want to comment, +1, and share it.

Here are the most important steps in creating content that engages and entices your audience to comment, +1, or share in your stream:

✔ **Calls to action are key.** Most people really don't know that you want them to comment on your posts, +1 them, or share them:

- If you want someone to +1 a post, ask.

- If you want someone to share a post, ask.

- If you want others to comment, write content that encourages them to comment.

✔ **Ask questions.** A controversial or engaging question (especially one that pulls on your audience's heartstrings) will get them commenting like crazy. Simply posting a link and waiting for comments doesn't create nearly the same level of results.

✔ **Fill in the blank.** Want to see your comments fill up like crazy? Start a fill-in-the-blank post. "I am from _____ (fill in your location)" will fill up with all kinds of people sharing their location. People love to try to guess answers, or come up with their own creative answers for fill-in-the-blanks.

✔ **Share your favorite circles.** There's no greater compliment than sharing a circle of people who have meaning to you; doing so lets your audience know more about you and your circles. Share a circle and ask your audience who else should be added. Lots of people will ask to be added — or will make suggestions. At the same time, people will share it if it's interesting enough for their friends.

✔ **Start a poll.** Create a post with a question in it. Comment with a few optional answers. Tell people to +1 their favorite answers. You can lock the post to force people to +1 their favorite answer without being able to comment. (See Figure 3-4.)

✔ **Start conversations about others' content.** Sharing another person's content can be a great way to get that person's attention in a good way, while still starting a new conversation. If you see something interesting and have something interesting to add to it, share it and encourage your audience to comment.

Figure 3-4:
A simple
poll on
Google+.

Getting into Google+ Pages

Your Google profile represents the real you on Google. Your Google+ Page (also known as Plus Pages) represents your business on Google.

Right now, this feature just exists on Google+, so I include the +. However, I wouldn't put it past Google to remove the + on this as well and use your business profile across all Google products at some point.

If you've haven't already set up your personal profile, now's a good time. Also make sure you read Chapter 1 so you know what you need to about privacy and circles. Finally, you may want to go back to the beginning of this chapter and make sure you've optimized your profile.

Google+ Pages, from the consumer or average-user standpoint, are similar to user profiles in the following ways:

- You can add Pages to your circles.
- You can search for Pages.

✔ You can even comment on posts for Pages, just you can with any profile.

✔ You can mention Pages just as you do profiles.

Chapter 6 covers the brass tacks of setting up your own Google+ Page; in this chapter, I stick to what you can do with Pages as a user and consumer.

Finding Google+ Pages

To find a particular Google+ Page, follow these steps:

1. **Type in your search term into the search bar at the top.**

2. **If it doesn't appear in the drop-down menu, press Enter and select People and Pages in the Everything drop-down menu.**

   You might try a search term such as *Google+* or *For Dummies* and see what appears. (See Figure 3-5.)

3. **Mouse over the Follow button.**

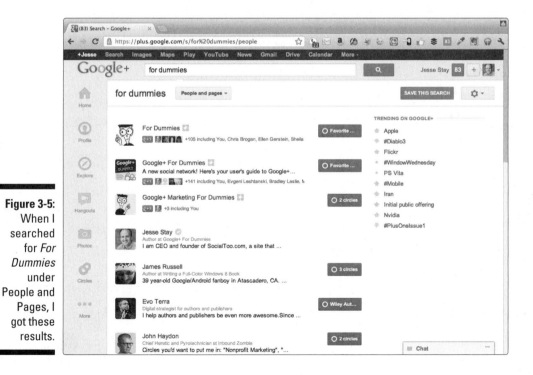

Figure 3-5: When I searched for *For Dummies* under People and Pages, I got these results.

4. **Click the check the box next to the circle you want to add it to.**

   Now that Page will appear in your main news feed every time the Page updates.

Adding Google+ Pages to circles

Adding a Page to a circle is just like adding anyone else on Google:

1. **Mouse over a Page name.**

   A *hovercard* appears, showing the profile image, Page name, and a big Follow button.

2. **In the hovercard that appears, mouse over the Follow button.**

   If you've already added the Page to a circle, then the circles that the Page is already in will take the place of the Follow button. Mouse over the list of circles instead. Then you'll see check boxes next to the names of your circles.

3. **Do one of the following:**

   • *Check the box next to the circles you want to add the Page to.*

   • *Select Create New Circle. (See Figure 3-6.)*

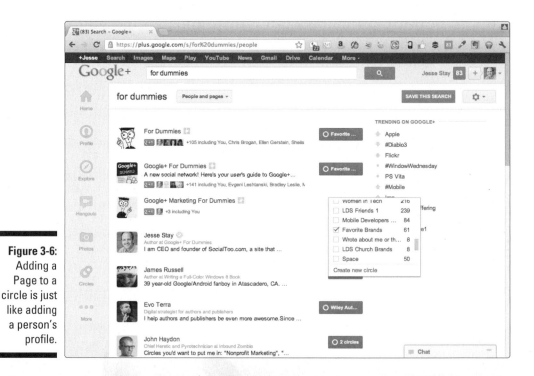

Figure 3-6:
Adding a
Page to a
circle is just
like adding
a person's
profile.

Hanging Out

I've met some wonderful people through Google+ Hangouts. A *Hangout* — a shared video presence online — is a great tool overall for chatting with groups of up to ten people at a time.

Google+ Hangouts let you chat, via your video webcam, with up to ten people at a time (and they're free). Hangouts provide a text chat on the side where those ten people can also text each other. You can mute your audio or mute your video at any time. (Muting your video makes your video go black.) The chat shows the participants in smaller boxes below the main speaker. See Figure 3-7. When a new person speaks, he or she takes over as the main speaking participant.

You boo‎‎‎‎‎ ‎‎‎‎‎‎‎d the capability to share your screen, watch ‎‎‎‎‎‎‎‎‎‎‎‎‎‎‎ other apps.

‎‎‎‎‎‎‎‎n join one, you'll need to find one. ‎‎‎‎‎‎places:

one of your friends start a Hangout your stream with the option to

‎‎‎n: Google+ shows ongoing column next to your main ‎‎ar there. See Figure 3-8.

‎‎‎‎‎‎‎our main stream: Clicking ‎‎‎‎‎n other Google+ users. They ‎‎‎‎‎‎ay include some that you can watch ‎‎ *air*).

✔ ‎‎‎‎‎‎ngouts: Look for a topic you want to discuss. There ‎‎‎‎‎‎‎angout organized around that topic. In the Everything d‎‎‎p-down menu that appears when you search, select Hangouts.

You can join Hangouts on your mobile device. If you see a Hangout in your stream on the Google+ app for iOS or Android devices, just tap Join Hangout.

Figure 3-7:
A Hangout
looks like
this.

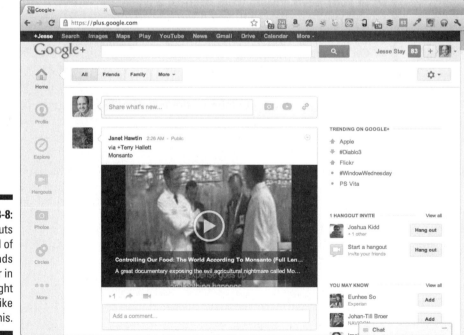

Figure 3-8:
Hangouts
full of
friends
appear in
the right
column like
this.

Starting a Hangout

If no Hangouts are happening, create your own. Discuss a particular issue or talk about your company. If you can fill a Hangout with smart people who provide value, you'll gain the most value.

Here's how you create a Hangout:

1. **Click the Start a Hangout button from the Hangouts page, the right column of your news feed, or anywhere else that you see the option.**

   A window prompts you to fill out a few basic fields. Your webcam will turn on, but don't worry: No one can see you yet.

2. **Select the people or circles you want to invite, just as you would target a status update to a particular audience.**

   If you want the invitees to be notified, click the circle after checking it, and select Notify About This Post. See Figure 3-9.

   Sometimes it's better to limit your Hangouts to just those in your circles. You can always do a Hangout on air (to let people watch) to avoid getting overwhelmed.

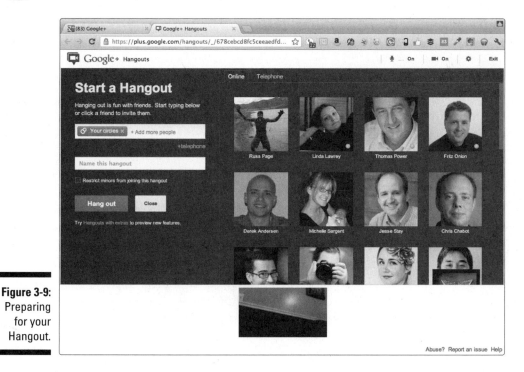

Figure 3-9:
Preparing
for your
Hangout.

3. **Name your Hangout.**

   The name helps people find your Hangout and sets the tone for the conversation.

4. **Check your hair.**

   First impressions mean everything. Make sure you look nice and the lighting is right in the room. Ensure that your background is one that your audience will appreciate. Get rid of anything that might offend others or embarrass you during the Hangout.

5. **Click the Hangout button.**

   You're live! People can start joining your Hangout. If no one joins at first, don't get discouraged. Try, try again as you have the patience to do so. You may also want to notify a few people so they know to join.

Exploring Google+ Search

This chapter has several examples of how to find people and pages using Google+ search. Here's where I show you how Google+ search works — and how you can get involved in it. Google+ search is one of the most powerful pieces of Google+. You'll quickly see why.

Finding people

In the earlier section "Building Your Network," I show you how to find people in various ways to network and grow your audience. Spend some time looking for interesting people and using Google+ search to do so.

To find a person on Google+ search, follow these steps:

1. **Type the person's name in the Google+ search bar.**

   A drop-down menu appears below the search bar as you're typing. Choose the name if you see the person you're looking for. If you don't, go to Step 2.

2. **Press Enter.**

   Another page lists a combination of people who match that name on Google+, as well as content that matches. (See Figure 3-10.) Choose the name if you see the person you're looking for. If you don't, go to Step 3.

Figure 3-10:
Searching
for a name
on Google+
returns a
combined
page of
content and
people.

3. **Click the Everything drop-down menu on the next page.**

4. **Select People and Pages.**

   A list of people and pages that match the search appears.

5. **Choose the person you're looking for.**

Finding content

Finding content on Google+ is as simple as typing in the search bar. You can discover content other ways, as well — and knowing these methods as a consumer will help you determine a good marketing strategy.

Hashtags

Hashtags are simple keywords that start with a # (pound sign), followed by an easily searchable keyword. When you see them in your friends' posts, the hashtags link to a page in Google+ search that shows everyone else on Google+ who has included that hashtag publicly (the effect is the same as if you had inserted the hashtag into the search field yourself).

If you type in a hashtag in your own post, a drop-down menu shows similar hashtags being used on Google+. You can select one of the results or keep typing and use your own. After the post appears, the hashtag is hyperlinked in your own post.

Use hashtags to organize a conversation around a specific event or topic. If you want to get all your friends talking about the same thing at once, use a hashtag. (See Figure 3-11.)

Hashtag

Figure 3-11:
Using a
hashtag in a
post.

Trending terms

Google+ shows the most popular trending keywords at the upper right of your main Google+ stream; see Figure 3-12. Like Twitter, Google+ calls these keywords *trending terms*.

If you want to know what the rest of Google+ is talking about, look at this list. You can click the trending terms to see search results, and you can participate in a live conversation about particular terms with other people who are also mentioning the term on Google+ (by posting an update directly from the search results). You can find friends and grow your audience when a lot of people are looking at the same search results and the same conversation.

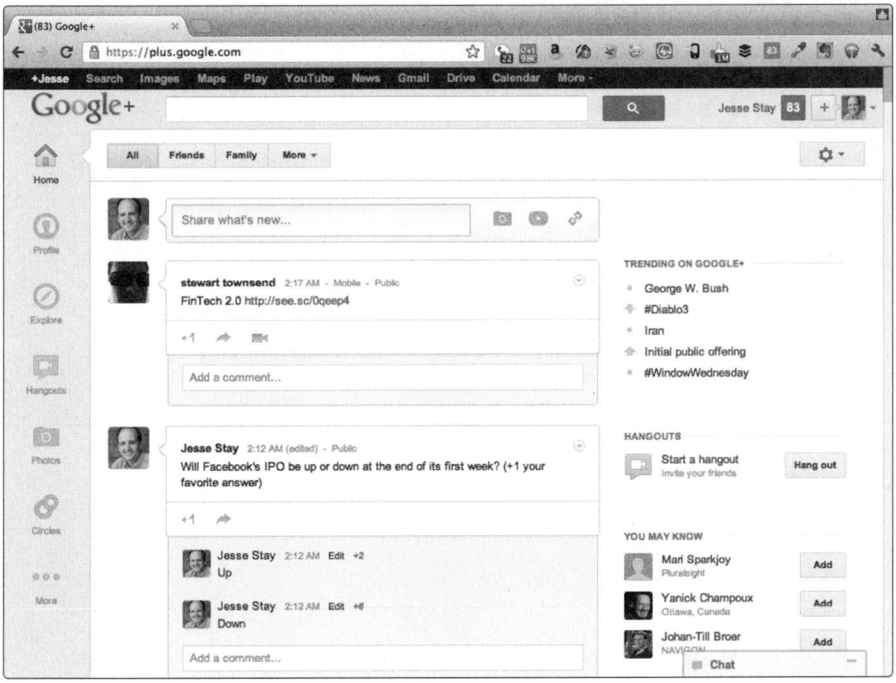

Figure 3-12:
Trending
terms on
Google+.

Because Google+ is young, it is easier to get your own hashtags and keywords to appear as trending terms on Google+ because the audience is smaller. Take advantage of this situation while you can. It won't last long — Google+ is growing pretty fast.

Participating in the conversation

One of the unique advantages of Google+ search over other social network search tools is that you can respond to a conversation directly in the search results.

Search for anything on Google+. Notice how the results pop up in real time, with pictures and videos embedded in the stream. Now type a status update into the Join the Discussion About (your search term) box at the top. It doesn't even need to include the original search word. Notice how your status update from that box goes into the stream as well?

Search is a participatory experience. For example, search for *"Grammys"* during the Grammy Awards show. Then post right from the search results by writing a status update in the Join the Discussion About (*your search term*) box at the top of the search results. Now you're participating in a much larger conversation.

Chapter 4

Embracing the "Google" in Google+

Google lets you create connections and link people together using different Google products, and soon, if the trend of updates to Google+ continues, you'll be able to associate with people you know in every product they own. Google+ isn't just a website. It's an entire platform intended to link together all Google products, and eventually the World Wide Web, in a social manner. In this chapter, I show you how this connection is already happening and where it's headed.

The future of Google+ is just Google.

Exploring the Google Bar

If you ask me, the heart of the Google+ experience is the little bar that follows you from Google site to Google site. I've been told that Googlers (Google employees) call this *the sandbar*. Figure 4-1 shows my Google bar.

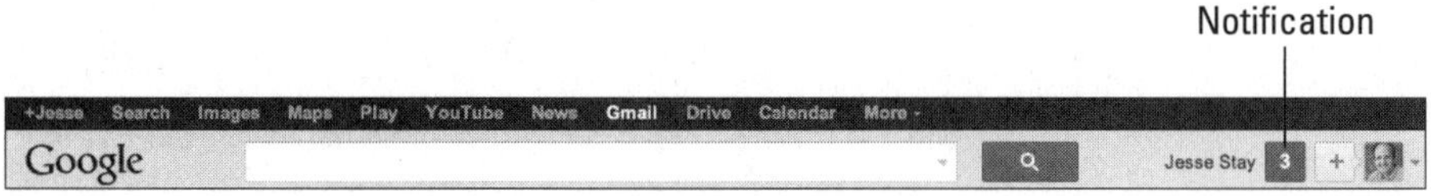

Figure 4-1:
The Google
bar looks
something
like this on
most Google
sites. Gmail
is high-
lighted in
this shot.

Notification

Figure 4-1: The Google bar looks something like this on most Google sites. Gmail is highlighted in this shot.

Whatever you call it, the Google bar links all the Google products together and lets you know when someone comments on your posts or mentions you. The bar also allows you to post right from most of Google's major products. This capability, along with gradual integration of the social Google+ features, will help make it so you never have to visit `plus.google.com` to participate in Google+.

I start by going over the different parts of the Google bar from left to right:

- **+You:** The Google bar is split into two sections on most sites (see Figure 4-1). The top starts with +*your first name,* followed by a list of other Google sites. The bottom part has a bunch of other stuff (mentioned in the next few bullet points). When you click +*your first name,* you're taken to your Google+ news stream.

  Clicking +*your first name* is the fastest way to get to `plus.google.com` from any Google site.

- **Other Google site links:** On my Google bar, I show Search, Images, Maps, Play, YouTube, News, Gmail, Drive, Calendar, and More. These spots link to Google's most popular sites, and they're part of the top bar. The More drop-down menu lists even more Google sites.

- **Search:** Most of the time, the bottom part of the Google bar shows the logo and a search box. This box usually lets you search the site you're currently in.

- **Red notification bubble:** When you get a notification on Google+, the bubble comes up. The number inside it shows how many total notifications you have. When you click it, you see a menu of all your Google+ comments, mentions, and +1s, as well as new people who are following you on Google+. You might need to fight the urge to click the bubble every time you see that number go up.

This little red bubble can get addictive.

From the notification bubble, you can +1, add people to circles, and comment on posts. Between the notification bubble and the Share button, you really don't need to visit `plus.google.com` unless you want to check your news feed.

Make sure you adjust your notification settings. You can do this for both profiles and pages on Google+. You can choose what you get notified for, and how you get notifications. I choose to receive my most important notifications by e-mail; then I can ignore notification bubble in my Google bar (most of the time, anyway) because I know I'll get the important stuff in my Gmail inbox.

✔ **Share button (the + sign in Figure 4-1):** The Share button (the little + sign at the top of most Google products) is useful. If you've got something on your mind and you're using another Google product, just click the Share button, type a message, post an image, or share a link. You'll be sharing to Google+ without having to leave the product you're using. You don't have to open `plus.google.com`.

✔ **Account management drop-down menu (accessed by clicking the profile picture, your name, or the little upside-down triangle):** From here you can visit your Google profile, switch to a Google+ Page that you administer, or switch Google accounts (if, say, you have more than one Google account or your family uses the same computer but has separate accounts).

Posting Outside of plus.google.com

Using the Google bar (in most Google products), you can post directly to Google+ no matter in what Google space you are. For example, in Figure 4-2 I'm in Google Reader and decide to post about how much I like Google Reader.

To post from the Google bar, follow these steps:

1. **Click Share in the Google bar at the top.**

2. **Make your post.**

3. **Choose the circles to share with.**

4. **Click Share.**

That's it! It's pretty simple to share to Google+ from just about any Google website.

Figure 4-2:
Posting to
Google+
from the
Google bar.

You can share to Google+ outside of Google, too. Here are my favorite ways
to share:

- **Click +1 on other websites.** Clicking +1 not only gives rank to that
  website amongst your friends (and Google itself), but it also brings up
  a dialog so you can choose your target audience (through circles) and
  post a comment about that website to Google+.

  More websites are putting the +1 button next to Facebook Like and
  Twitter Tweet This buttons; I show you how to put a +1 button on your
  own website in Chapter 12.

- **Comment inside Gmail.** Whenever you post on Google+, you get an
  e-mail for each comment. Assuming you read them in Gmail, the e-mail
  messages show embedded comments that you can +1 and manage. (For
  other clients, such as Microsoft Outlook, you get a separate e-mail for
  each comment.) Google also lets you comment on a post inside the
  e-mail itself without having to click a link to go to `plus.google.com`.

- **Share from Google Reader.** As a big Google Reader user, I use this
  option a lot. If you click the Share link at the bottom of any post in
  Google Reader (or press the keys Shift+S), a dialog box opens so you can
  share that post. It's a simple way to consume and share your news.

✔ **Use a Chrome extension.** Google+ has many Chrome *extensions* (plug-ins that you can add to the Google Chrome web browser to augment your web browsing experience). Search for *Google+ Chrome Extension* in Google to see what I mean. Two extensions that I particularly like were made by Google itself:

- • A +1 Chrome extension lets you +1 and post links to pages by clicking a +1 button in your browser.

- • A Google+ notification bubble reveals your notifications in your browser for any website you visit. Plus, you can interact in the extension to post on Google+. Figure 4-3 shows what it looks like when you click the Google+ notification bubble.

✔ **Post on your mobile phone.** You can post from most mobile devices. There is a mobile web experience for phones that don't have apps (such as Android and iOS). In fact, on Android devices, for apps that initiate the intents share dialogs, you can share to Google+ within your favorite apps.

Figure 4-3: The Google+ notifications extension.

TIP

Install the Google+ notifications Chrome extension so you can get and respond to notifications even when you're not on Google products. To install it, visit this site and follow the instructions:

```
https://chrome.google.com/webstore/detail/
          boemmnepglcoinjcdlfcpcbmhiecichi
```

Integrating with Google Products

What products is Google+ integrating with? How is it expanding farther? At the time of this writing, the following are already integrated with Google+:

✔ **Gmail:** Gmail puts a profile card next to the e-mails you read that are from other Google+ users. The card gives detailed information about previous interactions you've had with the individual through Google+. See the earlier section "Posting Outside of `plus.google.com`" for more examples. Figure 4-4 shows what this looks like.

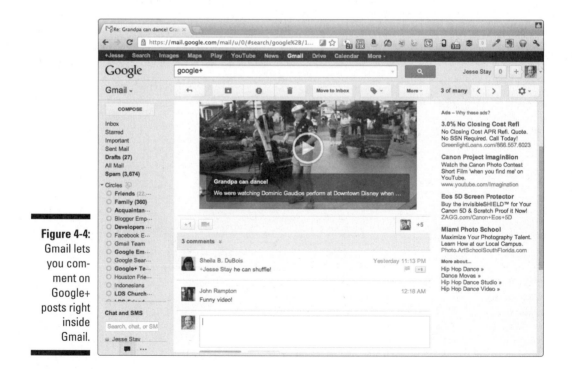

Figure 4-4: Gmail lets you comment on Google+ posts right inside Gmail.

✔ **Google Reader:** Google Reader lets you share articles right to Google+ (through either the Share link or the shortcut key sequence Shift+S). You can also +1 articles you like, improving their rank amongst your friends on Google.com itself.

✔ **YouTube:** YouTube is gradually integrating more and more with Google+. For instance, when you click Like on YouTube, you see a Google+ Share link that lets you +1 and share the video so your friends can comment on it and share it.

I anticipate that YouTube will expand quite a bit in the future, embracing the Google+ social layer. Perhaps eventually the YouTube the Subscribers option will cater just to Google+ followers; then each YouTube channel would become its own Google+ Page. It's hard to tell in what specific ways these changes will hapen, but you can bet YouTube will get more and more integrated in the future.

✔ **Google search:** Google search and Google+ together are referred to as *Google Search Plus Your World.* See Figure 4-5. Google Search Plus Your World starts with the column on the right, which shows people in your circles and recent Google+ content from your friends that matches your search query.

Figure 4-5:
Google's
Search Plus
Your World.

In addition, you can do these things:

- +1 any search result in the main search.

- See the Google+ profiles of authors with properly associated content. (I cover that topic in Chapter 12.)

- In certain cases (defined by an algorithm that only Google knows) you can add authors and websites (through their Google+ pages) to your circles.

✓ **Google Chrome browser:** In Google Chrome, if you want to use an extension to +1, share websites, or see your notifications on any website, you must have the extension (explained earlier in this chapter). There's no telling where Google will take this option in the future, but I wouldn't be surprised if the +1s and notifications you get from Chrome extensions end up directly integrated into Chrome. Only time will tell.

✓ **Google Play:** Google Play is Google's marketplace for media and apps. When you mouse over media, a Share button appears. Clicking the Share button allows you to share things like music to Google+. (When you share music, Google+ formats it so your friends can preview the music on Google+.) In addition, Play lets you +1 albums and shows you which of your friends have +1'd each album on the site.

✓ **Picasa Web:** Google has been integrating its photo-sharing service, Picasa Web, into Google+ photo sharing and storage. Every photo you post to Picasa Web is added as a private photo in your Google+ photos. You can then change the permissions of the album for that photo to a privacy setting in Google+ you are comfortable with.

✓ **Blogger.com:** As an avid Blogger.com user, I love seeing Google+ get more integrated with this service. Blogger.com can prompt you to share each post you make on the service. Google also provides Google+ Badges and +1 buttons for people who host their blogs on the service.

Exploring Google+'s relationship with search

As Google-savvy users may already know, search is perhaps the greatest value of Google+.

After launching Google+, the company integrated many Google+ features into www.google.com itself. In fact, even before plus.google.com launched and people had heard of Google+, www.google.com added +1 buttons to all its search results. That addition let people vote on their *favorite* search results; clearly, Google was trying to socialize search. Google solidified this effort when they launched Search Plus Your World (see Figure 4-6). The service aimed to provide a much more social experience to users who were logged in to their Google accounts when visiting www.google.com.

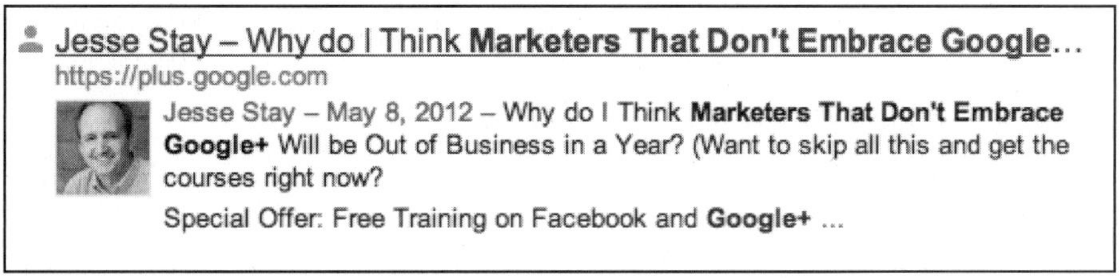

Figure 4-6:
Google's
Search Plus
Your World
within
www.
google.
com search
results.

Figure 4-6:
Google's
Search Plus
Your World
within
`www.google.com` search
results.

These are my favorite features that come with Google search as a result of their integration with Google+:

✔ Friends' Google+ listings that are posting about the keywords you're searching for

✔ Pictures of Google+ users next to their posts, signifying that they authored the posts

✔ The capability to see which friends have +1d a post in your search results

✔ The capability to add people and pages to your circles from search results

✔ The capability to +1 posts within search results on `www.google.com`

Building relationships via Contacts and Gmail

In addition to search, Google+ has a very deep relationship with Contacts. That shows especially in services, such as Gmail, that use contacts heavily. In many ways, Google+ is quickly becoming a *customer relationship management (CRM)* tool. You can manage your contacts and track your communication with people you associate with inside Google products (and possibly, eventually, elsewhere).

Check out this list of some areas that pull together Google+ and Gmail/Contacts:

✔ **Gmail shows profile information for contacts you communicate with as you read their e-mail.** When you open an e-mail from a Google+ user, that person's information from Google+ appears in the upper-right column of Google+. As in Figure 4-7, you can see name and profile photo. If you click More, you can see your most recent communication with that individual. If you haven't added the person to any circles, you can add him or her to a circle from inside the Gmail Web interface.

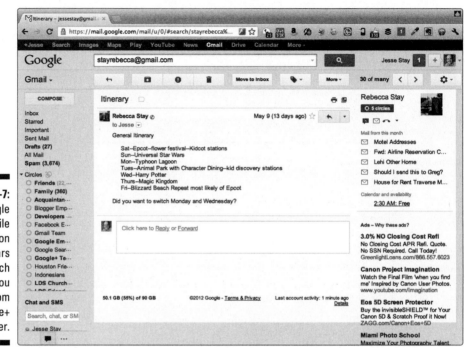

✔ **Gmail search lets you look for e-mail from people in your Google+ circles.** Search right inside Gmail and include *circles:family* or *circles:friends,* followed by your search criteria. For example, to search for *kittens* in your family circle, type *circles:family kittens*. In return you get all the e-mail you received from those circles, with your search criteria.

✔ **Gmail lets you click circles to access e-mail from Contacts in those circles.** Click to expand the Circles link in the left column. Then click the name of any of your circles.

✔ **People you add to circles on Google+ are also added to your contacts.** Now, when you visit `google.com/contacts`, you'll see the circles that each contact is in. The circle appears next to the contact's name, as in Figure 4-8. In addition, if that person's profile lists any contact information publicly — or is in the circles you're in, you'll have that user's information in your contact profile. This is one more reason to add a phone number or e-mail address in your Google profile.

✔ **Google Voice allows you to set phone settings for the contacts in each of your circles.** When you go into your Google Voice settings, a Groups and Circles tab lets you decide how calls are handled for each circle you've created. Because of Google+, your groups are automatically created for you. I expect this integration to go farther.

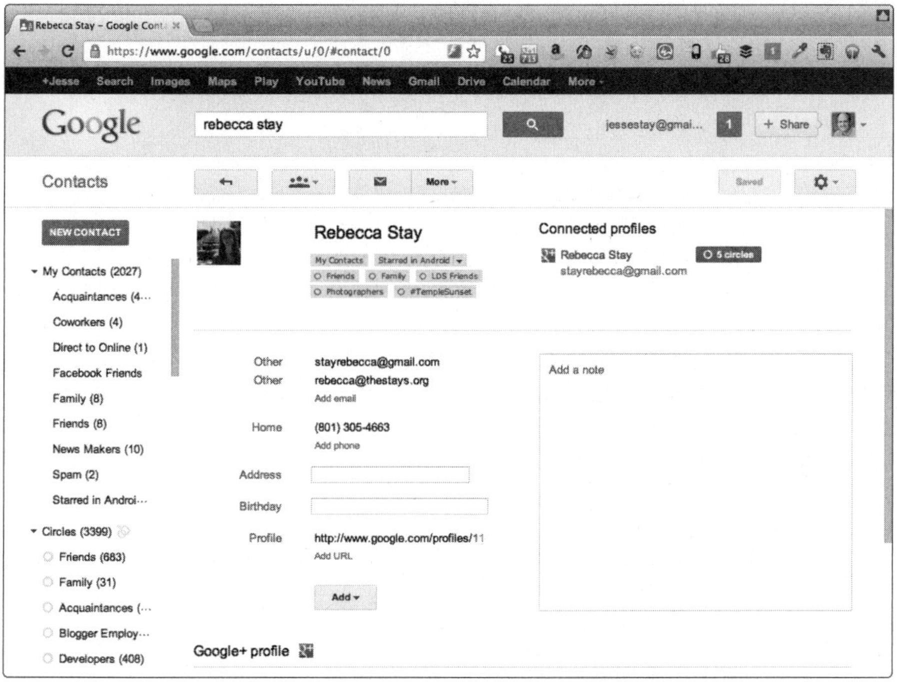

Figure 4-8:
Seeing a
particular
contact's
circles.

In Chapter 11, I talk a lot more thoroughly about strategies you can use with Google+ as a CRM tool. Here I just give you a working idea of where Google is going.

Improving employee collaboration with Google Apps

Google Apps allows businesses and corporations to host Google products in the cloud (another way of saying "on the Internet") under their own domains, for their employees. If you're like most corporations, there's a good chance you're using a mail product called Microsoft Exchange at the moment. (You may have heard of it, right?) Your own network usually hosts Exchange on servers owned by your company. Well, the Google alternative to Microsoft Exchange allows companies to host their data on Google's servers — under their own domains, without paying hosting costs or managing those servers and software — which provides several advantages:

- ✔ It gives the companies full control.
- ✔ It allows employees to log in to Gmail with their company e-mail addresses and receive all their company e-mail, calendars, and contacts in the Google interfaces they're most familiar with.

✔ It gives employees powerful Google search capabilities to use on top of all that data.

If you log in with your Google Apps account and go to `plus.google.com`, you can use Google+. You get some pretty neat features:

✔ **You can limit messages to just company employees.** If you want to keep your conversation private, you can use Google+ just as you would some of the other popular enterprise social network tools (such as Yammer or Salesforce Chatter). You just add your company domain as a circle and don't specify any other circles; Figure 4-9 shows you how to select your domain. When you do so, the message you post to that circle is visible to all your fellow employees — but to no one else. They will see your message in Google+, next to all the public people they have circled. They can narrow down to just your company and view updates from your company.

✔ **You can include public lists in conversations you're having with your fellow company employees.** When you add any of your circles to your company domain, both the employees and the public circles you specify can see your update.

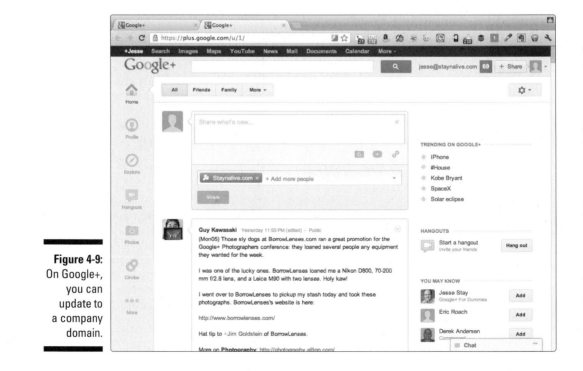

Figure 4-9:
On Google+, you can update to a company domain.

I like this feature because it gives you a way to bring customers (or other focus groups) into conversations you're having behind your firewall. You can do both your public and private communication all in the same interface.

✔ **You can integrate with Google Contacts.** The same deep integration you can get with Gmail and Contacts will work with company employees through the Mail product that comes with Google Apps (which looks just like Gmail). This enhances the corporate conversations you have behind your firewall by (a) showing you who you're talking with in Google Apps Mail and (b) giving you opportunities to follow them. It also allows you to organize conversations between employees much better.

Pairing YouTube and Google+

YouTube has integrated with Google+ quite deeply, and is moving more and more so through time. I mention various ways that Google has integrated YouTube into the Google+ experience. You can access Google+ right from YouTube itself.

Here are a couple of things you can do:

✔ **Share YouTube videos on Google+.** When you click the Like link on YouTube the Google+ Badge appears next to Facebook and Twitter. Just click the Google+ Badge to share the video directly to Google+.

✔ **Add YouTube videos to your Google+ Hangout.** When you click Share on YouTube, you can share the video with your friends via a Google+ Hangout. Just click the Google+ Hangout button shown in Figure 4-10. You're taken to a Google+ Hangout directly from YouTube, where you can specify with whom you'd like to watch the video.

Playing with advertising

Google's social ads are useful for businesses; they can allow people to +1 a link right from an advertisement on `www.google.com`. For example, if Samsung has an ad for the Galaxy Nexus on `www.google.com`, you can click the +1 button at the bottom of the ad to +1 the company.

Posting to your domain in Google+

If you use Google Apps for your business, you may want to post updates that coworkers only can read. To post such an update, follow these steps:

1. **Write your message.**

2. **Click Add Names, Circles, or E-mail Addresses in the circles box.**

   Or click Add More to add to the existing circles.

3. **Select your company's domain from the drop-down menu.**

In my example, I choose www. staynalive.com, the domain that hosts my e-mail address — jesse@ staynalive.com, as shown in this figure.

4. **Publish**.

You're all set! Your update will appear only to employees of your company.

Keep in mind that if you specify any other circles with your company domain, the update will also be visible to those circles — so be careful of who can see your update.

Turning on social ads does a couple of things:

- ✓ **It links your ad's +1s to a URL or a Google+ page.** When people +1 your ad, *their* friends see (in the Google search results) that they clicked the ad. Those results also get a higher ranking due to the increased number of +1s.

- ✓ **It allows people to see the friends who have liked the ad, increasing click-through and conversion due to social pressure.** Below the ad, people see pictures of friends who +1'd that URL or the ad itself. When they see that picture, it makes them want to click the ad as well.

I cover social ads thoroughly in Chapter 10. If you'd like even more information about integrating social ads, go to www.google.com/+/business.

Figure 4-10:
The Google+ Hangout button starts a Google+ Hangout.

Part II
Fishing Where the Fish Are

The 5th Wave   By Rich Tennant

"No, we're here to introduce Google Bloggers.
Bloggers. Not loggers..."

In this part . . .

Marketing seeks out customers in the environments where they're comfortable. Just like a fisherman, you don't create your own pond and wait for the fish to come; you go find the fish where they are — and then "fish where the fish are."

Google+ provides some great ways to fish for customers through `plus.google.com`. In this part, you see what your options are — and how you can get your brand in front of your customers in the Google environment.

Chapter 5

Outlining Your Strategy and Your Audience

*W*hen you get going with Google+, spend some time strategizing. How will you use the service? What are your goals? What are you trying to achieve? Does Google+ fit into that strategy? If so, how are you going to accomplish your goal with Google+?

Probably you already have a social media strategy for other social networks. Maybe you use specific tools for managing your presence. It's no less important to know what's available for Google+, and how to adapt your strategy for the network (if you need to change it at all).

In this chapter, I show you what tools are available, how to work Google+ into your existing strategy, and how you can create a new strategy that works well within Google+.

Strategizing for Social Media

Maybe you would like to improve customer service. Perhaps you need better promotion of a particular product. Maybe you're looking for more clicks on your website or more purchases of your products.

Whatever your purpose is, a proper social media strategy should follow this process:

1. Determine the problem(s).

2. Outline how social media can help solve the problems.

3. Identify the necessary tools.

4. Measure the results of your strategy.

5. Adapt your aproach according to learned results.

You can apply these tasks to just about any social network. In addition, you can integrate social network relationships into your own website, apps, and technology.

Social media in this case refers to any technology or tool that helps build relationships between people and allows them to more easily share information with each other. Social networks like Facebook, Twitter, or Google+ are not the only aspects of social media; you can find another valuable social-media resource in your own database and network of individuals. Always look within your own network first for what social networks you have; figure out how to build experiences that (in turn) build relationships among those individuals. Then look outside to see what other networks those individuals participate in; the idea is to determine how to bring those relationships into your own network. Google+ gives you a chance to focus on both the inside and outside networks that each Google user has.

Adding Google+ to Your Social Media Strategy

You might use Google+ in your social media strategy for many reasons; here are some typical examples:

- ✔ You need to rank better in search engines — Google in particular.

- ✔ You're trying to reach new audiences.

- ✔ Embracing trending terms could benefit buzz around your brand.

- ✔ You've decided live video (via Hangouts) is a great way to introduce your brand to your community.

No rule says you have to use Google+. Always use the best tool for the job.

The following sections cover the two most popular networks and lay out how your approach to them might differ from your Google+ strategy.

Looking it smack in the Facebook

Facebook has a lot of features in common with Google+:

✔ It has threaded comments. See Figure 5-1 for an example of a Google+ thread.

✔ It has a Like feature, which is similar to the +1.

✔ You can subscribe to people and add them to lists.

✔ Brands can have pages that represent their presence on the network.

Comments

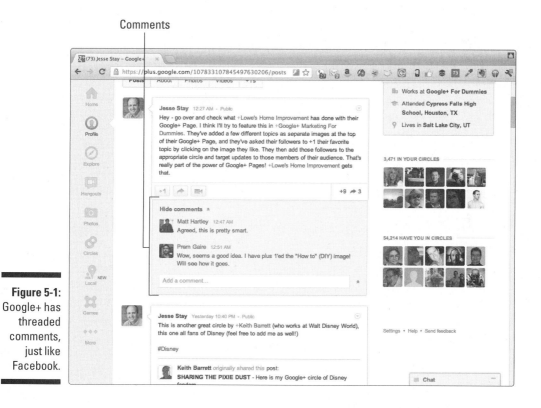

Figure 5-1:
Google+ has threaded comments, just like Facebook.

However, Facebook also has many differences you'll want to consider. Here are some differences between Facebook and Google+ that you should pay attention to:

✔ **Your Facebook audience may be different.** Google+ leans toward people with specific skill sets and professions (photographers, for example).

At least for right now, Google+ isn't the ideal place to target families and people who are related to each other. People tend to congregate with their closest friends and family on Facebook. On Google+, it's more about expanding beyond your core network and meeting new people. I anticipate that this situation will change over time as Google+ gets bigger. For now, take this difference into account as you develop your Google+ strategy.

✔ **Facebook doesn't have a rich public search function.** Google+ has a rich public search utility for status updates. Facebook lets you search public posts, but it doesn't focus on that experience. The entire Google+ experience thrives on this search, with trending terms front and center in the user experience.

Take advantage of this on Google+. Find ways to get your users all talking about one thing at a given time so the topic appears in trending terms (see Figure 5-2). Chapter 7 talks more about how to start conversations using search. Set saved searches (by clicking the Save This Search button at the upper right of any search results) for your brand and your name so you know when people are talking about you. This process just isn't nearly as easy in Facebook as it is on Google+.

Figure 5-2:
Google+
trending
terms work
nicely with
search.

✔ **Facebook relationships are mostly built around friends, not subscribers.** Facebook users can subscribe to others in a one-way relationship similar to Google+. Using the Like feature for Facebook Pages is similar to subscribing — but the core of the Facebook experience is built around two-way relationships. *Friending* on Facebook forces both parties to agree to subscribe to each other — which leads, I think, to more intimate relationships generally. The Facebook fans who Like your page — and toward whom you target ads — are likely to have much stronger relationships with each other. This may influence your targeting and messaging in a much different way than the slightly looser relationships of Google+.

At the same time, Google+ does allow Google+ Pages to circle people who circle them. This idea, which isn't available on Facebook, allows you to finely target your messages to specific audiences.

✔ **Facebook ads and analytics are more thorough than those of Google+.** As I write this, Google+ has been around about one year. Thus you can expect its social ads (via AdSense) to be a less fully developed capability than Facebook's.

Facebook's fine targeting of ads toward specific people and demographics is unmatched at the moment. You can target as finely as you like on Facebook. (I used to target ads to just my wife on her birthday. That's how targeted you can get.) Facebook has built many points where you can place your ads — very unobtrusively. Right now, Google+ mostly targets www.google.com (see Figure 5-3).

While Facebook has mastered the use of social ads, Google had AdWords (Google's ad platform) long before Facebook. AdWords lets you target ads not only on www.google.com, but also on other websites that have opted to share the revenue from such ads. Google has built social features into its ads (as explained in Chapter 10). I anticipate Google's solutions for social targeting will only get stronger. (So far, Google still makes more money on ads than Facebook does.)

To top it all off, Facebook has a very comprehensive analytics product called Insights. As the Facebook page admin, you can use Insights to see fine details about every post you make — broken down by demographic. Google+, at least for now, doesn't have such a comprehensive suite of analytics for its Pages product.

✔ **Facebook page management can be much more comprehensive.** On Facebook Pages you can see analytics (Insights) about each post. See Figure 5-4. You can integrate apps into the page experience. You can schedule posts. You can turn posts into ads. Each Facebook Page is also a timeline of stories throughout time, so the page itself is an experience. The list goes on.

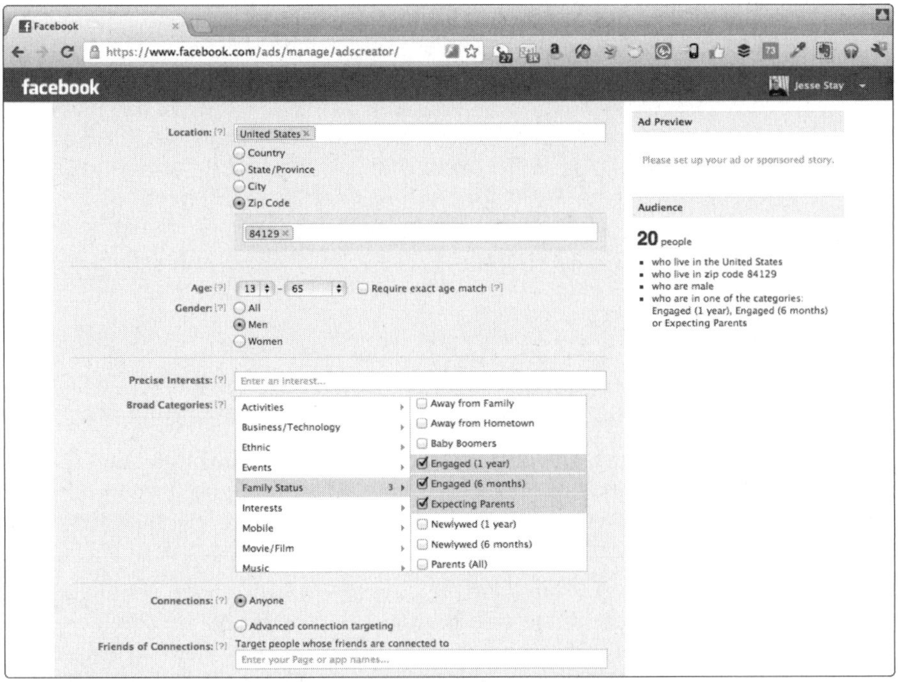

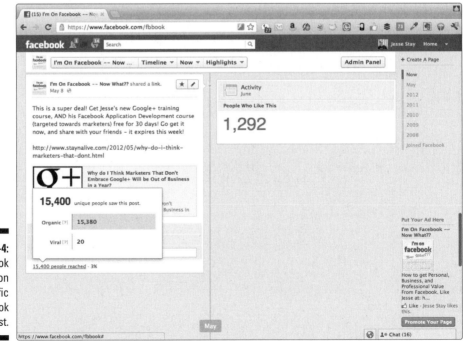

Figure 5-3:
Facebook
allows you
to target ads
very finely.

Figure 5-4:
Facebook
Insights on
a specific
Facebook
post.

It may not be to your benefit to focus as much on the Google+ brand page as it will be to focus on creating profiles for people within your company who use the service. Think of this as more of a LinkedIn-type approach: Your employees are using the service to network with each other and share information about what's going on within your company. If you use this approach , your Google+ strategy will be significantly different from your Facebook strategy.

Google+ is about people.

Flying in the face of Twitter

The quickest way to get a handle on how Twitter differs from Google+ is to start with what Twitter has in common with Google+:

✔ Both have a one-way subscription model for following people and things.

✔ Both offer strong public search across status updates and focus around trending topics and terms.

✔ Both attract news media, celebrities, and specific professions and networking professionals (and all their subsequent audiences).

✔ Both support lists and following topics by list.

You might find yourself comparing Twitter to Google+ benefits more often than I compare Facebook and Google+. Twitter and Google+ audiences are similar, catering well to pop culture (see Figure 5-5), news media, and their audiences. You may find yourself adapting your Twitter strategy to Google+ even more than you do for Facebook.

As you adapt your Twitter strategy for Google+, keep in mind the major differences and limitations. This may help you determine where Google+ will benefit you — and where it may even excel over Twitter. Here are a few differences:

✔ **Character limit.** Twitter's claim to fame is its 140-character limit. Because Google+ doesn't have this limit, you can write entire articles directly on Google+. That way your followers don't have to leave the site to read the message. This option isn't optimal for clicks or purchases, but it does help get your message out more effectively. Of course, Twitter's 140-character limit does force you to think in short bursts — which can make the messages you compose easier to consume.

Short text messages work great in international settings.

Figure 5-5:
Google+
caters
well to pop
culture,
as shown
in Britney
Spears's
profile.

✔ **Search dynamics.** Both Twitter and Google+ excel when it comes to search of public status updates. However, as you'd expect from a search engine company, Google+ has a few features Twitter doesn't. For instance, if you search for *Google* you'll see a bunch of updates mentioning Google. These results are the same for both Twitter and Google+.

Note, however, that Twitter shows only a search-results screen. Google+ search results show a *conversation* that you're taking part in (see Figure 5-6). I can post new updates on this screen, and even though they don't mention the word *Google* in the status update, because I posted them here, they will appear to everyone who's searching for *Google* on Google+. At the same time, images and videos are embedded in the search results on Google+. (On Twitter, you have to click an update to see them, and even then they don't always appear.)

✔ **Audience size and ability to influence trending terms.** As I write this, plus.google.com has fewer people using it than Twitter. That's just a fact you have to deal with, and you can use it to your advantage. After all, it's easier to become a big fish in a smaller pond.

Because `plus.google.com` doesn't have as many visitors, you may have an easier time getting people to talk about a particular topic so it appears in the trending terms on Google+. Getting something to trend on Google+ takes less effort than it does on Twitter. Spend some time strategizing about this approach (for pointers, check out Chapter 7), and you'll see more attention coming to your brand or campaign. Do it soon, though; I anticipate that before too long, Google+ trending terms will be much bigger than Twitter's.

✔ **Conversation organization (nothing like Conjunction Junction).** While 140-character status updates are a quick way to broadcast a message, you'll also find that a nice, organized conversation has its own advantages:

  • It can show everyone responding in one place.

  • Everyone has to see everyone else's responses, which can result in fewer trolls and fewer negative responses.

For Twitter, this is a great way to get (mostly) untainted feedback. When no one else is paying attention to the replies to your posts, commenters can be more honest — which is both good and bad. Google+ users know when they're replying to you publicly, and because all the comments are in a single, visible location, users are aware that other people might disagree with them.

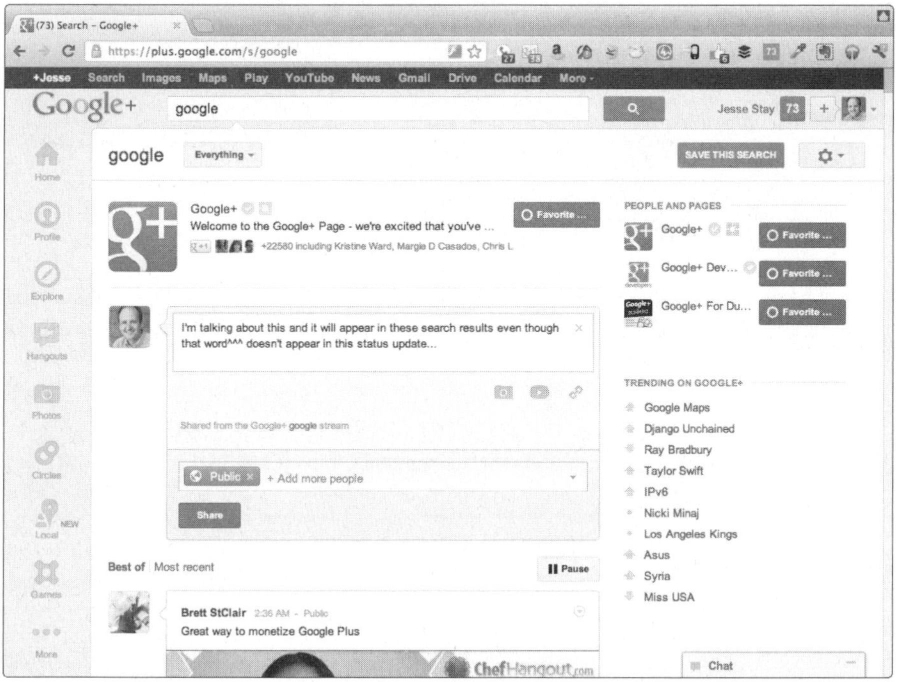

Figure 5-6: Google+ search is a conversation you're in.

✔ **Rich content.** Not every Twitter video or picture network or site is supported; see Figure 5-7. That's why Google+ works so well if you have content to share with subscribers or friends. Share an image and it appears with the post. Share a video, and it's embedded for anyone to watch — no clicking necessary. If you want to see the essence of this, download the Google+ mobile app: Beautiful content, not just text, is at the core of the Google+ experience.

Figure 5-7: Clicking a Twitter post can reveal an image.

Digging Into Your Google+ Toolbox

It's good to know what tools are available to help you manage your Google+ presence. Automate as much as you can while maintaining a personal approach to your Google+ presence. You can find tools to help you post more easily, moderate better, and track the success you have along the way.

Because Google+ is still new and trying to avoid spammers and too much brand focus, Google+ software allows only some vendors post updates to brand pages and personal accounts on behalf of users. This vendor software is mostly limited toward enterprise licenses, which can be pricey. You could pay over $1,000 a month to use one of those Google+ tools. This situation may change by the time you read this, but be warned.

Look at the tools you're considering to see whether they have the features to help you accomplish some essential tasks. Here are some of my favorite capabilities to look for:

- ✔ Schedule posts for the best times possible so you're not kept up late at night.

- ✔ Moderate the comments and assign commenters' problems to people in your organization.

- ✔ Sort the people you follow into circles so you can better organize what people are saying about you.

- ✔ Know when people are talking about your company or brand.

- ✔ Identify key analytics so you know how well posts are performing and where you can improve.

Social media management systems

A *social media management system* (a term coined by Altimeter Group) is a series of tools that helps social media community managers handle their presence online. The systems often focus on posting and moderating comments and replies around the posts that are shared from a company's or brand's major accounts. They make management as easy as possible; often they work in conjunction with social media analytics to identify how to improve as you develop your content strategy.

Commercial systems

As of this writing, only a few social media management systems (SMMS tools) work with Google+. Consider these brands, which only work with enterprise licensing:

- ✔ Hearsay Social at www.hearsaysocial.com

- ✔ Vitrue (now owned by Oracle) at www.vitrue.com

- ✔ Buddy Media (now owned by Salesforce) at www.buddymedia.com

- ✔ Involver (now owned by Oracle) at www.involver.com

- ✔ HootSuite at http://hootsuite.com/google+

- ✔ Context Optional (now Adobe Social, owned by Omniture/Adobe) at www.adobe.com/products/social.html

Try this approach:

1. Contact each SMMS platform.

2. Get a demo.

3. Compare the advantages.

Price and integration with other systems are the most interesting comparisons.

For instance, Adobe's Context Optional (Adobe Social) integrates with Adobe's existing social analytics product and aims to also integrate with their Site Catalyst site analytics product down the road. This approach to the product may be attractive if you already use Adobe. Same goes for Salesforce or Oracle. There will be features, as well as pricing models, associated with Hearsay Social, Involver, or HootSuite that you can't get with the other products. Research well and you'll find something that's perfect for your organization.

Free alternatives

If commercial systems are too expensive, you can use `plus.google.com` to manage your social media presence. The site can be good to start with, anyway, because it helps you adapt to Google+.

At the same time, consider a browser plug-in (an addition to your browser that improves your web browsing experience) or two for help. For instance, the Chrome extension Do Share lets you schedule posts in Google+. As long as your browser is open when the post is scheduled, Chrome will automatically share posts at your designated time (see Figure 5-8). Other plugins and extensions let you share to Facebook and Twitter. Search `www.google.com` for *Google+ Chrome extensions*.

Social media analytics solutions

Analytics are extremely important to your social marketing strategy. Before you implement something, make sure you can measure it.

With its the Insights product, Facebook has built analytics in to the heart of its experience. There are many tools for monitoring Twitter success and responsiveness as well. Google+ — at least right now — doesn't have a slew of analytics options, but here's what you have at your disposal:

✔ **Google Analytics.** If you integrate +1 buttons and Google+ Badges into your website, you can utilize Google Analytics to determine how much traffic is being generated on your website as a result of those elements. Be sure to read Chapter 13 for the scoop on how to do this.

✔ **Link tracking.** If you're on a budget, sites like `https://bit.ly` (see Figure 5-9) or Google's own `http://goo.gl` can help with shortening and tracking the clicks for a URL you share on Google+. More expensive tools (such as Adobe/Omniture's Site Catalyst) can track the number of clicks on any particular URL you share on Google+.

Never post any URL in plain format (without a link tracker) on Google+. Using a URL-tracking service such as `https://bit.ly` allows you to track every click that is generated from each post you make on the service. You can then go back and measure how many clicks you're generating as a result of posting on Google+. Some services let you track the purchases that occur from those clicks; make sure you're tracking those too if you can.

✔ **Campaign tracking.** Google Analytics and other site-analytics tools categorize links and referrals by specific keywords in the URL. You can then categorize your posts into campaigns, so you can focus on what types of campaigns produce what types of traffic and conversion on your website.

Campaign tracking can be a great way to *A/B test* (a marketing term for testing two scenarios to determine the best approach) different approaches, so you can see which types of posts can be more successful on Google+.

✔ **Spreadsheets for monitoring engagement.** When nothing else is available, the good old spreadsheet always comes to the rescue. Track things like the number of comments, +1s, and shares on each post. Categorize posts by campaign and use those as additional metrics to track success. Knowing the amount of engagement with a post and how it relates to the number of clicks or conversions can help you design new ways to form posts.

Don't just count direct click-throughs and conversions as an assumed success metric.

Often a conversation on a social network leads to people talking offline. Or it can get people thinking about your product, bringing brand awareness into the equation. This means people won't always click immediately but could become loyal customers later as a result of those conversations. This metric is hard to measure — and something I'm sure more social analytics tools will get better at monitoring in the future.

My general rule is to post once, measure twice. Always measure. There's no set formula for success other than measurement and use of analytics.

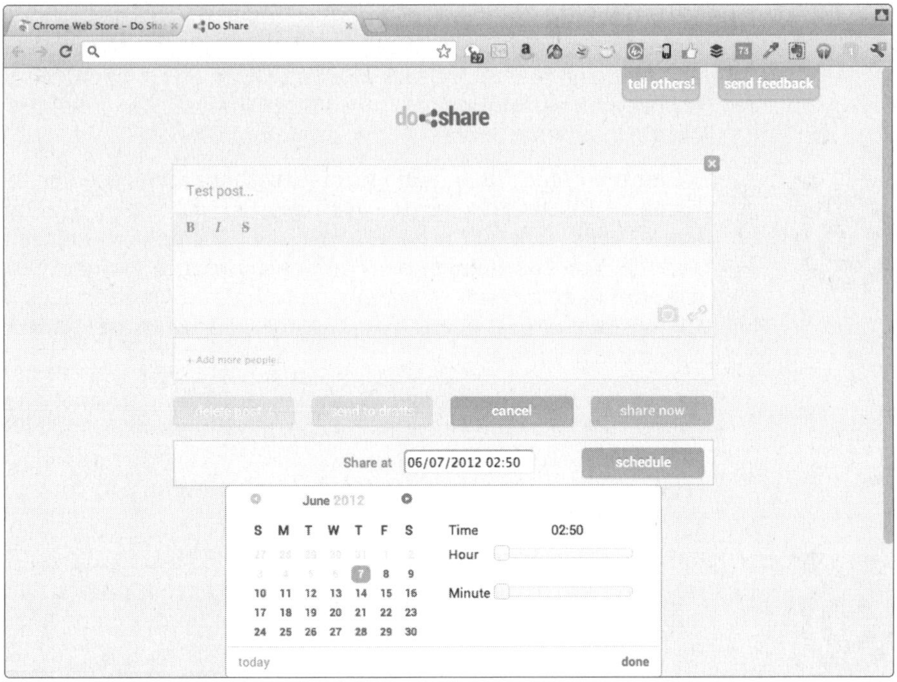

Figure 5-8:
Chrome's
Do Share
extension
lets you
schedule
posts.

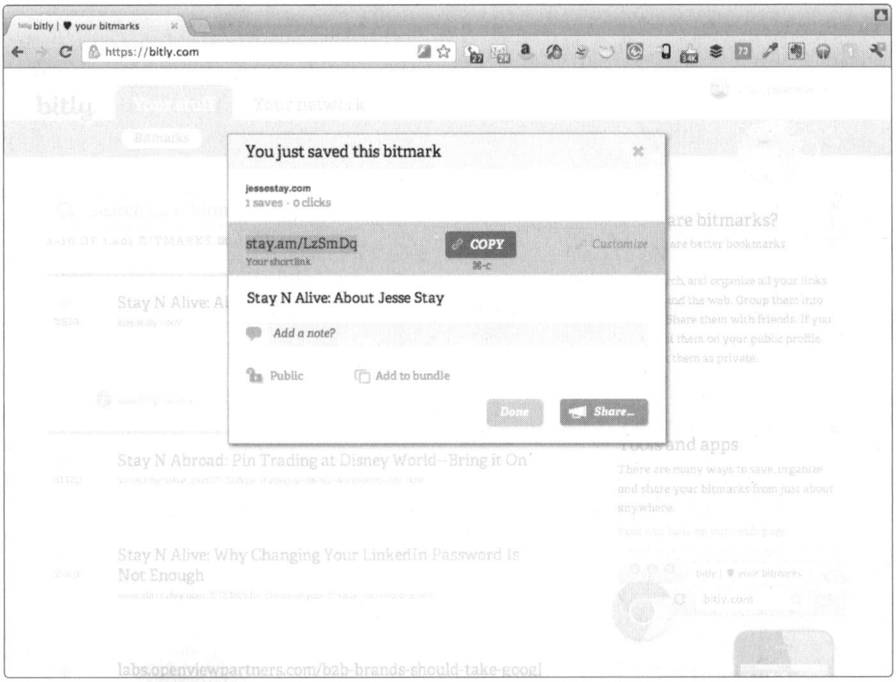

Figure 5-9:
Using
`https://`
`bit.`
`ly` for link
tracking.

Luring Your Existing Audience to Google

You've probably already established an audience elsewhere — and that can be a great place to promote and build awareness of your Google+ presence. There may be some benefits, too, such as increasing your `www.google.com` search ranking to getting your existing customers using the service, so think about how promoting Google+ to your customers can help your positioning.

Targeting your audience through SEO

Just using Google+ will naturally promote your brand to your audience. Following the tips in this book will put your brand in the Google Search Plus Your World results — and your audience will naturally learn about your presence on Google+ — so long as they're already Google users.

You may want to spend some time optimizing your presence on Google+ so that improving your search ranking on `www.google.com` happens automatically:

- ✔ **Adding +1 buttons throughout your site.** Every +1 naturally increases the ranking of your site when the friends of your audience add to your shares and +1s. As their friends use your site, they'll naturally see your site in `www.google.com` search results. It also encourages users to talk about your site on their own Google+ profiles.

- ✔ **Creating a Google+ Page and adding a Google+ Badge that links to that page.** Having the Badge on your website makes it obvious enough that you're on Google+. However, as your audience adds your page to their circles, other people will see your page in *their* circles. Using a Badge also provides an immediate opportunity for your Google+ Page to appear as a circle option when your website appears in `www.google.com` search results. See Figure 5-10 to see the Google+ Badge in action.

- ✔ **Adding authors to the content on your site and linking those authors to Google+ profiles.** As your users and customers search `www.google.com` for content related to your site, your content appears more prominent — *if* you've linked the content on your site to the content's authors. If you've done that, voilá — each author's big, bright, smiling face appears next to the search result. At the same time, several studies have shown that your content ranks a little higher on `www.google.com` as a result of this added level of authenticity.

- ✔ **Simple ads through AdWords targeting specific search terms.** As a last resort, you can create ads that target specific search terms to make your Google+ Page appear to those who are searching for those. For example, targeting the keyword *android* produces an ad linking to your Google+ Page for the Google Galaxy Nexus. This is a simple way to ensure that your Google+ Page always shows up at the top.

Figure 5-10:
Using a
Google+
Badge to
promote
your
Google+
Page on
your
website.

Cross-promoting from outside channels

Cross-promoting from your existing channels is always the best way to bring awareness to your Google+ presence or Google+ Page. As I mention in the previous section, be sure you have a Google+ Badge and +1 buttons on your website as a start.

Here are a my favorite ways to get your audience excited about your new Google+ Page:

- ✓ **Don't be afraid to mention on Facebook or Twitter that you have a Google+ presence.** The minute you create a Google+ Page, tell your Facebook and Twitter followers to come circle you over there. Chances are many of them already have Google+ accounts. You just gave them a reason to come and start using it more.

- ✓ **Include links on your existing social network profiles.** In the About, Links, or Info sections of your varying social networking profiles, include links to your Google+ Page as well. This section can be one of the first places people look to know you better.

✔ **Promote Google+ Hangouts on your other social networks, too.** Hangouts are a unique Google+ feature and strength. Hangouts can help get your other social network audiences using Google+ more, which can help your search rankings.

Be sure to share your Google+ Hangout (s) on each social network (see Chapter 9 for details).

✔ **Freely share links of interesting Google+ conversations, especially when they're directly related to Google+.** Don't hesitate to get a post's permalink and share it on other social networks. Some users may choose not to click through, but the people who have Google+ accounts will come look (and will, with any luck, participate).

✔ **Build campaigns that focus on Google+ strengths.** Getting your customers and users on Google+ can mean a higher search engine ranking for you. Google+ will draw them over if you try a few simple techniques:

  • Get them sharing a particular hashtag to talk about a particular event surrounding your brand over on Google+.

  • Do a special Google+ Hangout and invite fans from varying networks to participate.

  • Offer incentives and giveaways to encourage all this let's-go-check-out-Google+ behavior.

Chapter 6

Building Your Google+ Page Presence and Profile

Google+ is about people, but eventually you'll start promoting your company and your brand. To help you do so, Google+ has set up a place for brands to interact with their audiences and send messages about topics in which the audience might be interested.

Like a Facebook Page, your Google+ Page can send updates to followers. Note, however, that you can't compare a Google+ Page side by side with a Facebook Page and expect all the same features. You need to develop a strategy that is uniqe to Google+ and works perfectly for you and your brand.

Building It So They Will Come

After you've set up a personal profile and started getting used to Google+, look at the strong position you're in to start promoting your brand:

- ✔ You've discovered Google+ Hangouts.

- ✔ Your followers are aware of the brand.

- ✔ Your coworkers are using Google+.

- ✔ Your company is listed on your profile — especially in your employment history and in the tagline.

Each of these steps is important to your Google+ strategy.

After you reach this point, you have some further decisions to make:

- ✔ **Page name:** The name is important. Not only will the page name help you rank highly when people search for your page on `plus.google.com`, but it also helps you rank well on `www.google.com`.

- ✔ **Profile image:** Your profile image is how people will recognize your page; the image represents your brand in your followers' Google+ news feeds. By what image you want people to know you and your brand?

Don't change your profile image often. People get used to the image. Every time you change it, it gets harder for people to remember why they subscribed to you in the first place. Keep something recognizable that they can always know you by.

- ✔ **Images for the banner:** At the top of your Google+ Page, Google+ offers two options for the banner image:

  - Up to five square images

  - A single, much larger image

The cool thing with these profile images, compared to profiles on Facebook, is that these images can be animated GIFs. You can do some really cool things to get people's attention when they visit your page. See Figure 6-1 to see what Intel did with its page — using several animated GIFs to get subscribers' attention.

- ✔ **Tagline:** Your tag describes what your Google+ Page is about. Because it also helps your search visibility on `plus.google.com`, think carefully about what it will be. Your tagline may also lend a little boost to your ranking on `www.google.com`.

- ✔ **Administrators and moderators:** Who will post to your page? Who will moderate and answer comments? You can assign these roles when you create your Google+ Page.

- ✔ **Audience and messages:** You can target messages to different parts of your audience. You can assign members of your audience to circles. See the nearby sidebar about a company that has done this well: Intel.

Banner images

Figure 6-1:
Intel's
Google+
Page uses
animated
GIFs to
remind
people to
+1 their
images.

Setting up your page

If you're prepared for your Google+ Page, you're ready to set one up for your own use. After you read or review earlier sections of this chapter, you should be ready to go. Start by following these steps:

1. **Create a Google+ Page.**

   You can create a page in either of two ways:

   • Visit any Google+ Page (http://stay.am/gplusmarketingpage) and click Create a Google+ Page. Figure 6-2 shows the layout at the time of publication.

   • Go to www.google.com/+/business and click Create Your Google+ Page on the main page.

Case study: Intel and Lowe's

Intel has used Google+ in a very effective way. On its Google+ Page (`https://plus.google.com/116660275132722215045/posts`), the company has a series of animated graphics labeled with different topics. The GIF for each topic rotates, prompting the user to +1 that particular topic. When a user +1's a topic, Intel adds the user to a circle related to that topic. Intel then creates special content just for those subscribers and targets updates to those circles. Those users will always get content that's interesting to them.

Of course, this does require users to follow the page, so you need to add Intel to a circle of your own first if you want Intel to add you to the circle attached to the GIF you just liked. If you like what you see, you might also want to check out the Google+ Page for Lowe's Home Improvement (`https://plus.google.com/116595187804216119746/posts`). Lowe's is using a similar approach to get fans subscribing to their favorite content (as shown here).

Figure 6-2:
The Create
a Google+
Page in the
right margin
of other
Google+
Pages looks
like this.

2. **Pick a category.**

   You'll see categories like those shown in Figure 6-3:

   - Local Business or Place

   - Product or Brand

   - Company, Institution, or Organization

   - Arts, Entertainment, or Sports

   - Other

3. **Fill out the relevant information for your Google+ Page.**

   If it's a product or brand, select the following:

   - Page name

   - A website for your product or brand (optional)

   - An additional category (from the list in Step 2)

   - The age range your page is suitable for

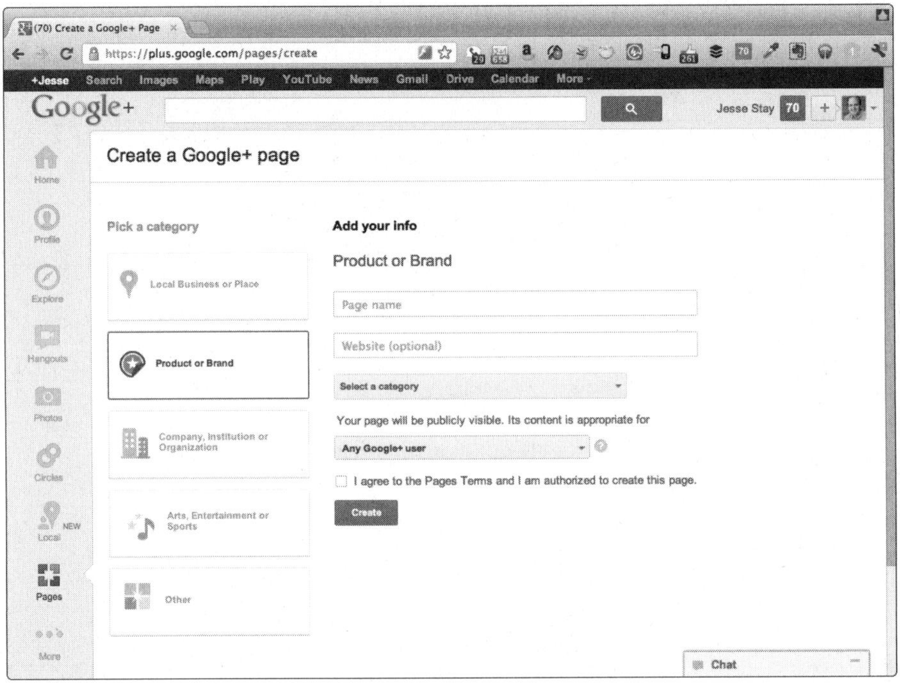

Figure 6-3:
Pick a
category
for your
Google+
page.

4. **Read the terms and check the box confirming you've read them.**

   Reading terms and conditions for social networks is very important. You need to know

   • How the network can use your data

   • When it can delete your data

   • Whether that data actually gets deleted

   • What might get your account suspended

   When in doubt, consult a lawyer. You need to be sure that the content you share does not put your brand in jeopardy under the terms that Google set forth — and you agreed to — when you created your Google+ Page.

5. **Fill out your page's public profile.**

   Complete your tagline and select the profile photo. The tagline is proven to be used by `plus.google.com` search to identify keywords that people might be searching for.

   Start your tagline with the most important keywords first. Because I want people to find me by Google+ as an author of Google+ books, I made sure my tagline started with *Google+*.

6. **Share your page with the world.**

   Post a status update and make it public by choosing the Public circle. Or click Finish so you can wait to post.

Getting to your page

After you've created your page, you'll probably wonder (repeatedly) how you found it the last time you published to the page. I can get lost finding my Google+ Pages and getting to the update screen.

When you log in to Google+, it defaults to your personal profile screen to update the service. Any update you make here will be from your personal profile.

You have a few ways, from your personal profile account and news feed, to find your page after you create it:

✔ **Click your name.** Your name is at the upper right of your news feed — in the "sandbar" (Google bar) at the top of Google+, next to your profile image. If you click your name, a drop-down menu lists all the Google+ Pages you manage. (You can see mine in Figure 6-4.) If you click your Google+ Page there, a new page (or browser tab, depending on your browser settings) offers a page for you to start posting to.

Figure 6-4: Select your Google+ Page from the drop-down menu below your name.

✔ **Search for the page.** This *is* Google, so when in doubt, search for it. Type the page name in the search box. Your page should come up in the drop-down menu or search results. Click the page to go to the Google+ Page you just created.

- By default, pages you visit (even those you created) appear as though you're just a visitor. You can't post to the page. When you comment, it's posted from your personal profile.

- If you're a page admin, a prompt at the top should say Switch to This Page (see Figure 6-5). Click Switch to This Page to go to a new mode. Now you can start posting *as the page* to your page's audience.

Be careful when you're in page administration mode; it's easy to accidentally post *as the page* when you mean to post *as yourself*. This can be an even bigger issue if you're managing a much larger brand page that has multiple admins or needs to maintain its reputation. Imagine if you posted a controversial opinion (politics or religion, anyone?) and you thought you were logged in to your personal profile — when in reality you were posting as the page. I've known people to get fired over such mistakes. If you're a page admin, *always* sit on your hands before clicking that Share button. Be absolutely sure you're posting as the entity you want to be.

Figure 6-5: Google+ prompts you if it sees that you're the admin of the page you're visiting.

✔ **Click the Pages link in the Google+ Navigation.** A Pages icon is in the main navigation area (next to your Home, Profile, Photos, and Circles icons). (See Figure 6-6.) When you click the Pages icon, you're taken to a list of Google+ Pages you manage. Click any of the pages to go to administrator mode.

Figure 6-6: Click the Pages link in Google+ Navigation.

Playing with Layout

When you're on a Google+ Page that you manage, you'll notice that it looks a lot like where you post to on your main Google+ profile.

While you're at it, notice these features that will help you navigate your Google+ Page:

✔ **Share what's new** This box works the same as the box you post to on your main profile. Here, however, is where you can post updates and target them to circles — as well as add images, videos, and links to your posts.

✔ **Your profile:** In the Google+ navigation area, you'll see the same profile icon and link. (Presently the area's on the left of the screen as s shown in Figure 6-7. It's been known to change places.) The main difference in admin mode is that if you click it, it takes you to a place where you can see and edit your public page presence on Google+. I go into more detail in the later section "Choosing a design."

✔ **Your photos:** As with your profile, you can store photos for the pages you manage. Clicking the Photos link in Google+ navigation takes you directly to the main profile images you selected when you set up your page. You can add more, especially if you have images you want to share with your audience. Think of this as a great place to share your weekly ads or pictures of employees and customers.

✔ **Circles:** Pages can add people *and* pages to circles. The main caveat is that to add people to a circle as a page, a person must follow your page first. I go into more detail on how this works in the later section "Managing the settings." To access this option, click the Circles link in Google+ navigation.

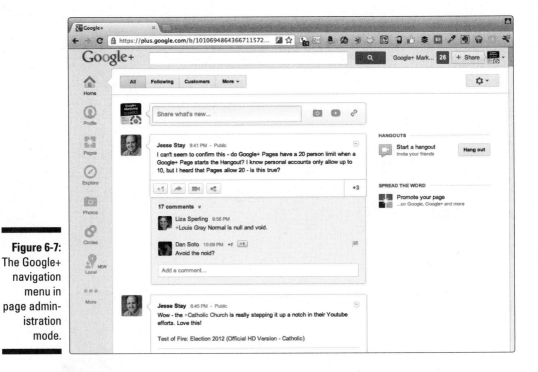

Figure 6-7:
The Google+
navigation
menu in
page admin-
istration
mode.

✔ **Local:** This link should be toward the bottom of your navigation on Google+. If you registered your page as a place, Google+ uses the address to identify a place for your brand. People can and find your location both on Google+ and in `www.google.com` search results and then leave reviews. Clicking the Local link in Google+ navigation lets you review what people are saying about your brand and the reviews they're making.

Posting to your page

Before you post your page, make sure you know how to post a message. Maybe just a simple Welcome message will do to test it.

To post a message on Google+ as a page administrator, follow these steps:

1. **Click the box that says Share What's New.**

   The box expands so you can enter text. You also get an area where you can add names, circles, and e-mail addresses.

   If you want to post just an image, video, or link, don't click the Share What's New box. Instead, click the camera, video (the little triangle in a box), or chain/link icon next to it. It will immediately prompt you to select an image, video, or link and attach it to the post.

2. **Type** Welcome! **or whatever message you want to share.**

   If you paste a link, it attaches to the message automatically, along with a preview of the page you're linking to. You can also add images and videos.

   You can tag individuals or pages in your posts, provided they're already following. Tagging an individual or page is a two-step process:

   a. *Type* +**your name** *(plus sign followed by your name)*.

      A drop-down menu appears and narrows down your options.

   b. *Click the name.*

      The name appears in a special format within your post. When users see this, they can mouse over the name and choose to follow, right from your post.

3. **Click the box titled + Add Names, Circles, or E-mail Addresses; choose an audience.**

   Usually you'll select Public. If you want to target your post, you can find details on how to do so in a later section, "Getting People into Your Page."

You can restrict how readers respond to your post. Click the down arrow next to the circle-selection box to do one or the other of these actions:

- *Disable comments.* I like to choose Disable Comments when I'm sharing other people's posts. That way people click through to the original post if they want to comment.

- *Lock the post.* This option prevents people from sharing or +1'ing it. (See Figure 6-8.)

4. **Make sure you know how you're posting: as yourself or as your page.**

   The "sandbar" (Google+ bar) at the top of Google+ shows the name and the profile image. If it's the name and profile image of your page, you're posting as your page. If it's your personal profile, you're posting as your personal profile.

5. **Click Share to post your message.**

   That's it! Your message will go live to your intended audience.

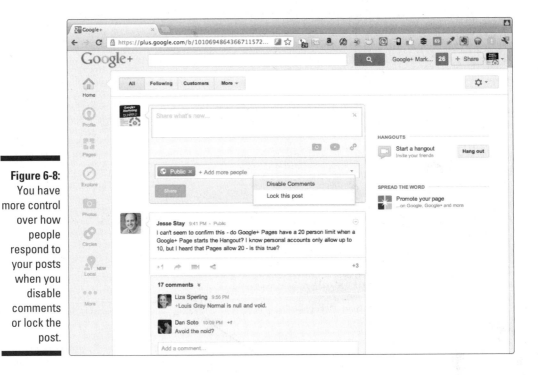

Figure 6-8:
You have more control over how people respond to your posts when you disable comments or lock the post.

Choosing a design

As with your personal profile, make sure your page's profile (your page's public image) is in pristine condition. Here's how:

1. **Go to your page's administration interface.**

2. **Click the Profile link in Google+ navigation.**

   This page will look a lot like your personal profile page, with fewer editing options. (See the section "Getting to your page," earlier in this chapter.)

3. **Click the Edit Page button at the top of the page.**

   You're now in profile edit mode (see Figure 6-9).

Figure 6-9: Profile edit mode for your page looks like this.

You can start editing a few parts of this page immediately. Click a section to edit it. Depending on your page category, you can edit these areas:

- ✔ **Cover photo.** To the left of the profile image, you can select one of these options:

    - One large 940 x 180-pixel cover photo that spans across and behind the profile photo

    - Five separate 110 x 110 photos that appear next to each other

    Any cover photo can be an animated GIF. This means you can have an animation that draws attention to the page or highlights features you want people to be aware of. (See Figure 6-1, earlier in this chapter, for an example of GIFs.)

    Don't make the animations annoying or you'll drive people away from your page.

- ✔ **Profile photo.** Clicking your profile photo lets you select a profile photo for your page. This image appears next to every post you make and shows up in the news feeds for people who subscribe to your page. This image is typically 250 x 250 pixels and can't be a GIF.

    Make this image as identifiable as possible for your brand.

- ✔ **URL.** Underneath your main profile image, you see a main URL for your page. The URL is taken from your Website field (selected later in this list) and can help establish authenticity for your brand (and Google+ Direct Connect, which enables `www.google.com` to allow others to circle your page from search results).

- ✔ **Tagline.** Earlier in this chapter, I show you how to decide on a tagline. Your tagline can help your Google+ search ranking (at `plus.google.com`), so pick something good. See Figure 6-10.

- ✔ **Introduction.** Here's where you describe your page a little more thoroughly than your tagline does. Spotlight your page and what it's about. Add links and format the text to look nice (make it bold, bullet it for lists, and so on).

    Consider including a link to basic ground rules for your visitors.

- ✔ **Contact info.** It's always good to have lots of ways for people to contact you. Choose one or more phone numbers, e-mail addresses, chat IDs, or street addresses.

- ✔ **Website.** This field links to the URL underneath your main profile image. This is an important field in identifying that you own that URL, because it tells visitors that the URL listed here is indeed yours. Then you can link your website back to your Google+ page and there's no doubt that both belong to you.

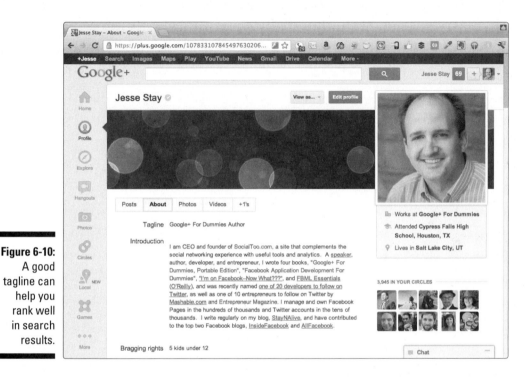

Figure 6-10:
A good
tagline can
help you
rank well
in search
results.

✔ **Links.** Your main website should be listed under the Website or URL fields. If you have other websites to point to, enter those here. These URLs will be less important, but be sure to label them so people know where the links go.

This area is a great place to put a privacy policy, terms of use, or similar set of links.

Managing the settings

Make sure your settings are tuned to your liking. To get to and edit your Google+ Page settings (see Figure 6-11), including privacy, take these steps:

1. **Go to your Google+ Page in administration mode (click the Home icon after you have logged in as your Google+ Page).**

2. **Click the gear icon in the upper right of your news feed.**

   A drop-down menu appears.

3. **Choose Settings.**

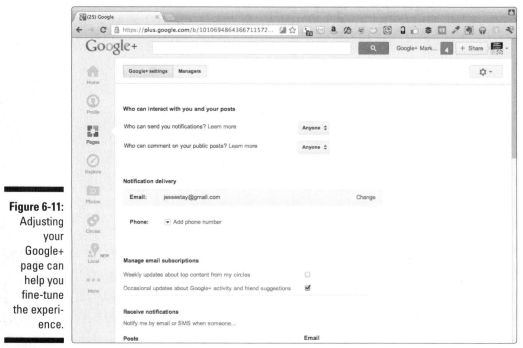

Figure 6-11:
Adjusting
your
Google+
page can
help you
fine-tune
the experi-
ence.

Follow these same steps when you're logged in via your profile and adjust very similar settings.

Go through each option and adjust to your preference. Sometimes the default may *not* be to your liking. Review each of these options:

- ✔ **The audience that can send you notifications:** You can get notifications from anyone, from anyone in your circles, just from circles, or from individuals.

- ✔ **The audience that can comment on your public posts:** If you want to be careful of spammers and trolls, fine-tuning this setting can help. The default, which is how I recommend you leave it, is set to Anyone. But you might experiment with reducing the audience to smaller groups of people, depending on your strategy. For example, limiting comments to your page's circles gives a feeling of exclusivity to those who participate in your page's posts. Users just can't see each other's comments until you circle them first.

- ✔ **The e-mail address (and/or phone number) where new notifications (comments, mentions, and so on) go for your page:** This address or number is where Google+ will send new notifications if you opt to receive them by e-mail. If you specify a phone number here, you'll receive notifications by text message.

✔ **What types of e-mail subscriptions you want to receive from Google:** Google can send basic newsletters to let you know what's happening on Google or in your circles on Google+. Read through the list and see whether anything interests you.

✔ **Whether you want to get an e-mail versus a notification (via the sandbar notification bubble) when people interact with your page's posts:** If you enable the e-mails, you get an e-message for each type of notification. You can decide to be notified only about certain types of mentions or similar triggers, as with these examples:

> • Someone adds your page to a circle.
>
> • Someone interacts with your photos or photos in which your page has been tagged.

I like to keep all notification options checked and then gradually uncheck them if my e-mail inbox gets overloaded.

✔ **How you want Google+ to manage photos as you upload them for your page:** Here you configure options such as whether Google+ will adds geographical location to your photos or tries automatically to detect people.

✔ **Enable privacy settings to determine who can see when your page is tagged by other people:** Go through the list, and think carefully about how you want to configure this and for what audience you want to configure it.

If you think your page could get tagged in an embarrassing photo, consider that possibility when you're choosing this setting.

Getting People into Your Page

As with Google+ profiles, circles are at the heart of Google+ pages. On Google+ pages you can target posts to the following:

✔ Public

✔ Individual circles

✔ Individual people

✔ E-mail addresses

You can target posts in a manner similar to how you post to your personal Google+ profile.

Google's No Touch policy

I've heard from a few Google employees that within the Google+ team that makes the product, it has what it calls a No Touch policy. They will never allow pages or brands to "touch" people who haven't first shown an interest in them through a circle of the page. Only when the user has circled the page can the page mention — or target posts to — a user.

This policy is why you can never add users to circles until they've first circled you. When a user stops circling your page, your page will automatically uncircle that user. The No Touch policy, which was built to help prevent spammy pages and apps from invading Google+, applies only to people. You can follow all the brands (other Google+ pages) you want.

There's one caveat: On Google+ pages, you can only circle people who have already circled you.

Adding people and pages to circles

As long as they've added you first, you can add anyone to your circles and then target posts and view lists of people according to the circles you've added them to. Targeting can be a very valuable way of ensuring posts you make are always relevant to the people you share them with. (For an example of how some companies use circles to target their posts, flip back to the "Case study: Intel and Lowe's" sidebar, earlier in this chapter.)

The more you can target content, the more applicable response you'll get to each post. If you don't target your posts, you're likely to get people who are — at worst — irritated at the content you shared (if they respond at all).

For instance, as a test, I purposely shared a religion-oriented post to a public audience to show how segmenting an audience may work better. Half the audience, of course, wanted nothing to do with the post. Could I have targeted this better? Perhaps I could have targeted it to an audience interested in religion or politics, instead of sharing with the public at large, if I wanted more comments or a more positive response. Or maybe I wanted a diverse discussion. It could work either way.

The following sections explain how to add people to circles.

Adding by mouse

You can add a person when these criteria apply: You're in page administration mode, a person is already following you, and there is an Add button below the profile picture when you mouse over the name. (If there is no Add button, they're not following you.) Here's the drill:

1. **Mouse over the name or click the Add button.**

2. **Check the box next to the circles you want to add them to; see Figure 6-12.**

   If you want to create a new circle for this person, select the link to create a new circle.

Adding by search

You can search for people who have followed you. You may just go through your list of your followers — or follow these steps:

1. **Type the name in the Google+ search box.**

2. **Go to the person's profile.**

3. **Click the Add button.**

4. **Follow the same steps in the previous section to add them to a circle.**

Figure 6-12: Add people to your page's circles by mousing over their names.

Targeting posts to individuals, circles, and e-mail addresses

After you've added a few people to your page circles, try targeting a post or two to those circles.

To target a post to a circle, individual, or e-mail address, follow these steps:

1. **Click the Share What's New box.**

   A dialog box opens.

   - If it's your first time, the text reads Add Names, Circles, or E-mail Addresses.

   - If you've previously posted to Google+, the last circle selection you chose is chosen again.

2. **Click Add Names, Circles, or E-mail Addresses.**

   If a circle is already listed, either remove it or click + Add More People.

   A drop-down menu shows your circles, as well as an option to share — publicly or to all your circles.

3. **Select the recipients.**

   You can select recipients by

   - Selecting circles that you've created

   - Typing either the names or e-mail addresses of individuals who follow your page

4. **Write your post.**

5. **Click Share.**

   You just targeted your first post!

Building your audience with other tools

Posting frequently and measuring response are the best ways to build your audience. The better the content you share, and the more of it you share, the more people will +1 and share your content — and the more people will discover you.

TIP

If posting regularly and targeting posts where you can isn't helping you build your audience appropriately on Google+, try these options:

- **Use people to share your page.** You'll always see the best response on Google+ if you focus on people more than you do your brand. Get your employees and your Google+ customers out there promoting your new Google+ page. The more they talk about it, the more their friends will want to have it in their circles. Your page audience will naturally grow and become a natural complement to your existing audience.

- **Engage your audience.** If they've already added your page to their circles, build a relationship with people. Highlight your most passionate or influential fans in some way. The more you can establish a meaningful relationship with your fans and customers, the more they'll stick around and share your page with their friends.

- **Start a Hangout or two.** Hangouts are a great way to engage your audience and build awareness around your page. Since Hangouts appear on the side of Google+ amongst the friends in the Hangout, invite a few influencers to your Hangout and then broadcast the Hangout via the On Air feature. A large audience has the potential of discovering the Hangout your page started — which naturally leads to them discovering your page.

- **Integrate Google+ Badges in your website.** Adding to your website a Badge (that you can find at `www.google.com/+/business`) that links back to your Google+ page can be a great way of leveraging your existing website audience. (I cover Badges in detail in Chapter 12.) Take advantage of your existing channels as much as you can to promote your new Google+ page.

- **Consider a Google AdWords advertisement of your page.** Google isn't pushing this capability a lot right now, but I don't see why you couldn't do it. Consider creating a Google Ad Words campaign. You pay to advertise your Google+ Page for select keywords. Of course, you'll want to measure whether this converts well for you. If it doesn't accomplish your goals, you may not want to spend much money on this approach.

Chapter 7

Building a Search Strategy

S earch is at the heart of everything Google does. It's the company's crown jewel. Google started with search, and it's what they do best.

Many may agree with me that Google is no longer a search company, but look at what has made them a favorite for many:

✔ Gmail is popular because you don't need folders to find old e-mail — you just search for it.

✔ Google Reader became popular because it was a great way to archive old news and find it again later — through search.

✔ Google Contacts is one of the best ways to search through large contact lists.

Google+ succeeds, and will continue to succeed, because search is at the heart of the experience. The greatest value you get out of Google+ happens because of search both within and without the product.

Showing How Google+ Can Affect Google Search

Building a strong presence on Google+ naturally affects your presence on Google as a whole; the essence of Google+ is Google itself. The improvement is two-way: Improve your presence on Google, and you improve your Google+ experience.

Everything you do on Google+ (`plus.google.com`) can affect what happens on Google.com search. Each one of the following activities can affect your ranking on Google search as a direct result of your using Google+:

- **Just posting to the Public:** Google indexes any text, link, image, or video you post to the public. For other Google+ users, these posts appear in their normal search results through Google Search Plus Your World. The more people sign up for Google+ — and the more people you connect with on Google+ — the more likely they are to find your posts through simple Google.com search.

- **Sharing a link to the Public:** Google thrives on links; they are what holds the web together. In Google Search Plus Your World, Google+ users see ranked search results that appear based on the number of shares, +1s, and comments that those URLs have. You can even share and +1 the links right from Google search results. Therefore, whenever you share a link to the public on Google+, you add to that URL's authority on Google among your friends who use Google+. Who knows — someday this effect may apply to all Google search results.

- **+1'ing someone's share or post:** Similar to shares, +1s can also affect the ranking of a link in your Google search results. The more +1s, the better it will rank, because that shows some level of popularity in comparison to other links that match the keywords you're searching for (see Figure 7-1).

Seek +1s for your posts. The URLs for those posts get better traction.

- **Commenting on someone's post:** The number of comments on a post can also affect how a post ranks in Google.com search results.

Figure 7-1:
In Google search results, you can now see your friends who have +1'd URLs.

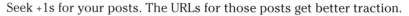

Welcome to Facebook - Log In, Sign Up or Learn More
www.facebook.com/
Facebook is a social utility that connects people with friends and others who work, study and live around them. People use Facebook to keep up with friends, ...
You, Chris Lang, Aaron Curtis and 68 other people +1'd this

- **Naming your Google+ Page appropriately:** Since the title of any website has a big impact on how that website ranks for certain keywords, the title of a Google+ Page can also affect how that page ranks in Google.com search results.

  Google+ Pages are public — they get indexed too.

  As Google+ Pages are integrated into Google Search Plus Your World, you can circle and +1 those pages right from Google.com search results. Those results become more prominent on Google.com; you can use feature to ensure that your brand is front and center in search results.

- **Adding a good tagline for your personal or page's profile:** A tagline strongly affects not only your ranking in Google+ search, but also how Google.com ranks your profile or page in a traditional Google.com search. (My profile shows an example in Figure 7-2.) A good tagline can mean that your page appears ahead of similar pages with the same name as yours but no focus in the tagline.

Figure 7-2: My profile tagline starts with *Google+,* so people who search for Google+ will see it first.

✔ **Installing a Google+ Badge on your website:** It's pretty clear from my tests that the more you can link your website with a Google+ profile, the higher it ranks in traditional Google.com search results. This is especially the case as you're competing for valuable real estate against similarly ranked websites that aren't on Google+ or haven't linked properly.

Installing a Google+ Badge from `www.google.com/+/business` will ensure visitors to your website know that Google+ Page is yours, but at the same time it also tells Google that it's yours, which gives your website a level of authenticity that other websites don't have.

✔ **Adding your website to your Google+ personal or page profile:** Just as you need to have a Google+ Page Badge linked from your website that tells Google where your Google+ Page is, having a link from your Google+ Page will tell Google where your website is. If the two point to each other, that gives a level of authenticity to not just Google, but your users and customers as well — ensuring that everyone knows this website is yours and that the Google+ Page is linked to it. This, in turn, improves your ranking and experience on Google.com itself.

✔ **Linking the byline of your articles on your website to your Google+ profile:** Here's an example: I linked the byline of articles from my blog over to my Google+ Profile, which produces a couple of useful effects:

  • *For every article on my blog by me, the search result on Google.com stands out a little more than the others because it has my picture and name right next to it.* Google automatically reads this connection and adds your picture from Google+ as the author. Figure 7-3 shows an example of what shows up on Google.com.

  • *Google appears to rank articles that have actual, verified authors a little higher than articles that don't.* This means your articles will also rank higher as a result of this link. Be sure to check out Chapter 12 for how to make this link happen.

You actually don't have to link directly to your Google+ profile. There is a certain format you can add to profile pages you've built on your website that will tell Google where the profile image is, what the name is, and more so Google can properly parse the content into the Google.com search results. However, if you don't in some way link that profile on your website to a Google+ profile, it's a lot harder for Google to identify you as a real person writing those articles. Your content should still rank higher if you can find some way to link articles on your blog to an actual Google+ profile. Play around with that; see how it affects your ranking — then report in this book's Google Group at `http://stay.am/gplusmarketinggroup`.

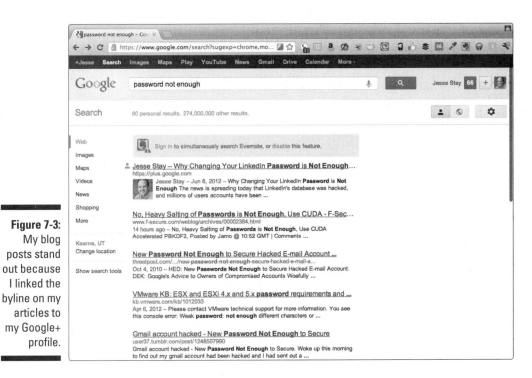

Figure 7-3:
My blog posts stand out because I linked the byline on my articles to my Google+ profile.

Reaping the effect of engagement

With Google+, Google.com is benefiting more and more from engagement, not just links.

Google used to rely on links to identify a story's importance and indicate how high the story should rank in the search results for particular keywords. If I searched for *dummy,* for example, Google would look at every article that had the word *dummy* in it, look for every article about *dummies,* and then look at each article's search ranking to determine the order in which to list the search results.

An article's search ranking is influenced by a number of factors — most notably the number of websites that link to the article's URL and the keywords identifying that URL. Those with the greatest search ranking end up ranking higher in search results — the idea being that you will always get the results that are most relevant to you when you are searching, because more websites have shown interest in that URL by linking to it.

With Google+, that changes. Not only do links affect the ranking of a site, but the number of people interacting, commenting, and +1'ing a site can also affect its ranking. *Social* is the new SEO. Clearly, you're ahead of the game if you can get people on your Google+ profile and pages to engage positively with you and with each other — and you can do so in two ways:

✔ **In the organic search results:** Sites and articles with more +1s and shares on Google+ can rank naturally higher than sites and articles that have a similar search ranking but don't have the same engagement. Be sure to test this and you may see similar results. This is affected even without users logged in to Google.

✔ **In Google's Search Plus Your World:** Google inserts articles that have been +1'd and shared by your friends in search results (see Figure 7-4). With this feature, the more +1s, comments, and shares an article or website has on Google+, the better it ranks among the friends of those who have +1'd or shared those URLs. This boost means your site will be seen by more people.

Bottom line: Engagement helps propel you to a better search ranking.

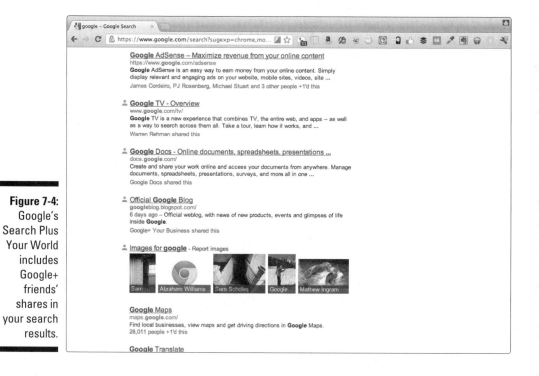

Figure 7-4: Google's Search Plus Your World includes Google+ friends' shares in your search results.

What is engagement?

As a marketer, you'll hear the word *engagement* used quite frequently with reference to social media. *Engagement* is what you do to attract your fans' attention and encourage them to respond to you — and what they do in response. On a Google+ or Facebook Page, you engage fans by finding ways to get them to comment, +1, or share your post. Sometimes just clicking a link or playing a video can be considered engagement.

In short, engagement can be anything you do to get your customers *doing* things to accomplish your goals.

✔ On Facebook, your goal for engagement is generally to get people commenting and liking posts so that your posts are more likely to appear in *their* friends' news feeds (on Facebook, when you like or comment on something, your friends see that in their news feeds).

✔ On Google+, every post automatically appears in the news feed — so getting people to comment on or +1 posts on Google+ may not give you the same boost that it does on Facebook. Also, the comments people make as they comment — or the +1s people make — don't appear explicitly, as they do on Facebook.

Of course, getting followers to comment and +1 your posts does have an effect. Remember that the power of Google+ *is* Google. Everything you make happen on Google+ affects other Google products in some way.

✔ In the case of comments and +1s and even shares, those "actions" cause your posts to appear more prominently in Google.com search for those individuals' friends. This can be a very powerful way to get your website to rank well in Google.

✔ The more you get your followers to comment, +1, and share your page, the better relationship you build with them and the more they'll come back.

On Google+, you'll want to engage your followers by asking them questions to get them to comment. Consider things like fill-in-the-blank posts or even multiple choice polls that you let people add their own options to. Or just say, "+1 this post if you agree." You'll quickly find that just asking your followers to respond yields much better results than if you assume they know what to do. That's the essence of engagement on Google+.

There are infinite ways to get your followers and customers on Google+ to engage with your Google+ Page or the personal profiles of your employees, and content authors. Here are a couple of my favorites:

✔ **Ask a question.** Find questions that get your audience wanting to answer. If you can find questions that tug at the heartstrings or that will get your audience agreeing or disagreeing with each other, you'll typically have more comments. More comments typically lead to more +1s and shares. More of all those can potentially even get your post in the What's Hot section of Google+, which brings even more attention to your posts.

✔ **Use classic "test" questions.** Think back to high school or college (my default answer for most of life's questions). Remember the tests you took — multiple-choice, fill-in-the-blank (see Figure 7-5), and true-or-false. These types of questions can all get people responding. What I've found is that even on true-or-false questions, people never want to accept just true or false answers. They often want to explain why they said what they did, or show why the answer isn't cut and dried (nothing ever is). Also consider open-ended questions — the more you can get people to think and open up, the more conversation will ensue.

✔ **Describe in "x" words.** This is a fun approach — "In three words, describe what you think about x." You'll find people like to be creative, and enjoy showing off for their friends. Use this human characteristic to your advantage, and make posting a game for your followers.

✔ **Post pictures and videos.** Typically, posts with pictures, videos, and multimedia to draw your audience's attention do better than plain text. People are very visual, especially on Google+, which focuses so much on photography and images. You may consider Google's own meme generator for adding catchy text to your images that people can share (see the sidebar "Google's Meme Generator").

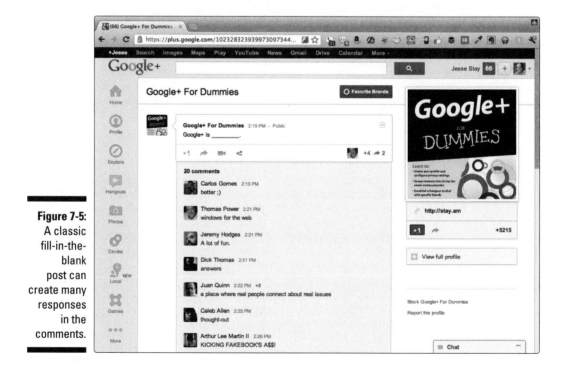

Figure 7-5:
A classic fill-in-the-blank post can create many responses in the comments.

✔ **Tie your brand to current events.** Relevance and timeliness are so important in social media. The more timely and relevant your message to your audience, the more they're going to respond and share. If there is a current event you can tie into, find ways to fit your brand into that event. Stay respectful and classy, but this can be a great way to stay on top of current events. Follow Google+'s trending terms if you're ever uncertain, and tie your posts to those — there are always eyes on trending terms.

✔ ***Ask*** **your followers to do what you want them to do.** When in doubt, ask. Most of the time your subscribers don't know what to do when you post. Sometimes just a "+1 if you agree!" can get more people to +1 your posts than if you just assume that folks who like your post will know to click that +1 button.

Don't be afraid to ask them to +1, comment, or share your posts (or whatever you want them to do).

✔ **Set up scavenger hunts.** I've seen quite a few people on Google+ utilize online scavenger hunts on Google+. The goal is to set a list of things they have to find and post on Google+, and then either tag your page or account, or utilize a hashtag (see Chapter 3 for in-depth information) or common term that others can search for. Because you're behind the scavenger hunt, people naturally come back to you to find out what all their friends are doing and why they keep posting about your scavenger hunt.

Above all, make sure you're always tracking the response to each post. Google+, as I write this, doesn't include any response-tracking tools (as Facebook does) — but you can still use a spreadsheet to track the methods you use in each post, and how many comments, +1s, and shares result from your efforts. Then you can adapt your approach in response to your success rate.

Tracking link clicks by using an analytics tool such as Adobe/Omniture SiteCatalyst, Google Analytics, or bit.ly can tell you how many people click your posts as a result of your efforts. You may also consider some additional tracking to identify how many sales (*conversions* of fans to customers, which is covered in Chapter 13) actually occur as a result of your approach to posting.

Google's Meme Generator

Google has its own Meme Generator that you can use to add catchy text to your image and create more engaging posts that get people commenting, sharing, and +1'ing.

To start it, just drag an image or upload an image to the posting box on Google+, and click Add Text below the uploaded image.

Google will pop up a dialog box for you to add text to the image. Follow the directions and you've got your own meme.

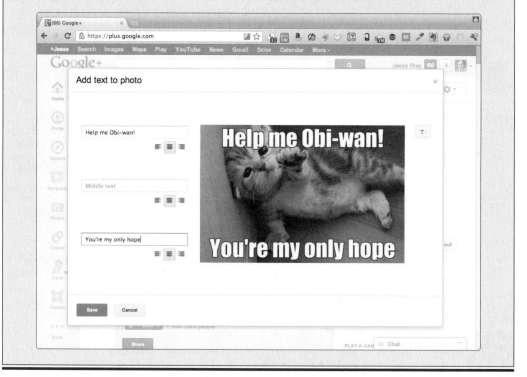

Harnessing the power of +1

On Google+, the +1 isn't quite the same as what people would think of its equivalent on Facebook to be: the Facebook Like button.

On Facebook, the Like button not only tells the person who posted that you like the post, but it also posts your like in your friends' news streams, and other friends can discover and like the post and join in on the conversation.

At the same time, the Like button on websites turns each website into its own virtual Facebook Page, allowing the admins of that page to post messages to those who have liked that URL. That just isn't the case with the Google +1 Badge — at least not as I write this.

On Google+, while very similar, there are two different types of +1 buttons.

Posts

Next to each post or item on Google+ is a +1 button (see Figure 7-6). When users +1 your post, they're indicating to you, the post owner, that they agree with you, or acknowledge that you posted something interesting. Unlike the equivalent feature on Facebook, that +1 doesn't share to all their friends' news feeds that they +1'd your post.

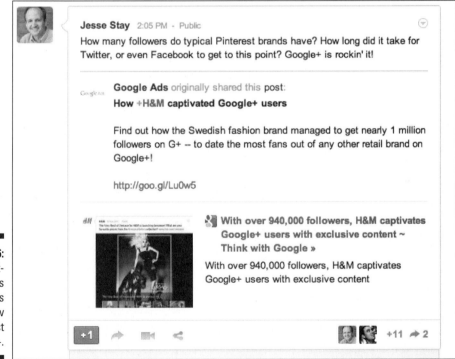

Figure 7-6:
The +1 button for posts appears right below each post on Google+.

One thing the +1 button for posts does do, however, is increase the ranking of a post in Google Search Plus Your World rankings. It also may start improving the ranking of normal, non-social search results on Google.com in the future. On Google+, the +1 button is how you can tell your friends who've logged in to Google.com that you like an article or post.

In addition, your +1s are archived on a link on your profile — you may find some benefit in that feature as a way to bookmark posts and articles.

Websites

You may recall that the +1 button is how you get your friends logged in to Google.com (not Google+) to know you +1'd or showed interest in a post or URL. That's where the +1 button for websites is most valuable.

Because +1s can improve your results on Google.com, it's to your advantage to put +1 buttons everywhere you can. Google gives website owners +1 Badges they can add to every page of a website to accomplish this task (see Figure 7-7). Keep in mind that the main purpose of putting +1 buttons everywhere is not so much to get people discussing your website on Google+ as it is to boost your website's rank in Google Search results.

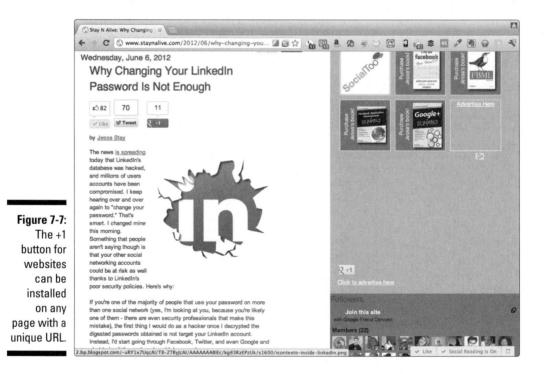

Figure 7-7: The +1 button for websites can be installed on any page with a unique URL.

Then, naturally, because a Share dialog box pops up when your users click +1, your users can *choose* to start a conversation around your website. See Chapter 12 and I'll go into how to install the +1 button in much more detail.

When people click the +1 button on your website, it automatically pops up a dialog box that prompts them to also create a post based on that URL and share it to Google+. So there's not really much need to add Share buttons all over your site — as always, however, test this assertion and see for yourself. If adding more Share buttons will improve your shot at attaining what you want to achieve on your website, go for it. Be sure to read Chapter 13 for more on how you can measure these results.

You can get all the code you need to add Google+ +1 buttons to your website at `www.google.com/+/business`. It's as simple as filling out a form there and copying and pasting the HTML they give you into your website.

Google Search Plus Your World

Before Google+, Google.com was where users could find the most relevant search results, optimized by the best algorithm Google could find, for what they were searching for. Now it includes results that it thinks your friends want you to see, based on the search terms you enter. With Google+, the search experience is much less lonely and much more social.

Google Search Plus Your World is Google's brand for socializing the Google.com experience. It includes several different additions to Google Search, much of which will probably change and improve over time. Here are the most notable additions:

- **Articles your friends have +1'd and shared related to the terms you're searching for:** Google now ranks the URLs and articles your friends have +1'd and shared right inside Google.com search results. A combination of how relevant the URL is, along with how many people have +1'd or shared the article, determines how high that URL appears on your search results. Now, in addition to traditional SEO, you'll want to get people sharing and +1'ing your website as well.

- **Posts your friends have +1'd and shared related to the terms you are searching for:** In addition to URLs and articles, posts that your friends have shared on Google+ will start appearing in Google search results (see Figure 7-8).

  As a marketer, you should also start optimizing your posts on Google+ to rank well on the keywords you want.

- **Pages and people:** In some cases, people or pages related to your Google search will appear in the right column of Google, with the option for you to circle them. For instance, if I search for *Google,* I see relevant Google-related Google+ Pages appear in the right column.

Figure 7-8:
When I
search for
H&M, posts
with *H&M*
in them
appear in
my search
results.

✔ **Metadata taken from Google+ to improve the look and feel:** If you include the proper tags on your website to identify a Google+ profile behind the content on your website, Google.com search results will return the profile image — and the name of the author behind the content on your site. It also provides the option to circle the individual, right inside Google.com search results.

✔ **The option to +1 right in the search results:** As on your website and in posts, if you +1 an article in Google.com search results, your +1 gets tabulated in deciding future search results for your Google+ friends. This means that encouraging your followers to +1 search results can also help you rank higher on Google.

✔ **The option to circle your favorite brands right from Google search results:** If you're searching for a brand that has a Google+ Page, depending on how long they've been around and what their follower count is, you may see the brand at the upper right of your search results (see Figure 7-9). As on Google+, you can circle that brand right from Google.com search results.

You can turn off Google's social features by clicking the little globe icon (next to the icon of the person's head at the upper right) to turn off Google's personal search (see Figure 7-10).

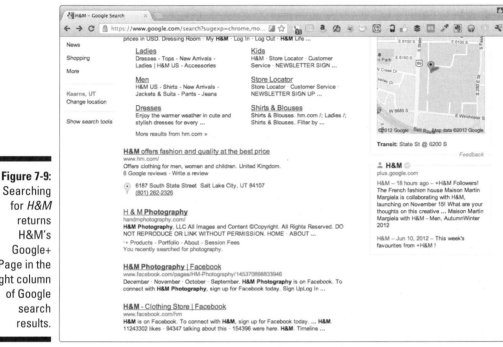

Figure 7-9:
Searching
for *H&M*
returns
H&M's
Google+
Page in the
right column
of Google
search
results.

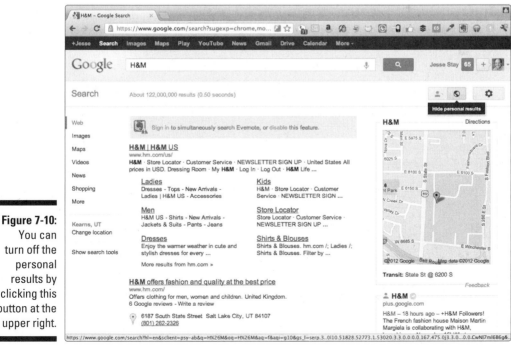

Figure 7-10:
You can
turn off the
personal
results by
clicking this
button at the
upper right.

Optimizing your profile for search

Your Google+ profile is pretty important for ensuring you rank well in Google.com search results. As with optimizing your website for search you'll want to optimize your Google+ profile as well.

There are a few parts of the profile you'll want to make sure you pay attention to as you are optimizing your Google+ profile — these are the best guidelines I know:

- ✔ **Make sure your page has a name that people will search for.** If you want to rank well when people search for *chocolate chip cookies,* it probably won't help you to have *Mrs. Fields* in your title. Make sure your title also has the words *chocolate chip cookies* in it, preferably toward the start of the title rather than the end. Your page will rank better the more closely it matches the search terms for which you want to rank well.

- ✔ **Put important keywords at the start of your tagline.** Time will tell whether your tagline affects your Google.com search results, but your tagline does affect your Google+ search results. Make sure that critical search terms occur toward the beginning of the tagline for your page or profile.

- ✔ **Fill out your employment and education information (for personal profiles).** This is important so that when people search for your company name they can find the employees who work there, especially those who are also their friends. If I search for *Microsoft,* for example, I'm likely to see a list of Google+ profiles belonging to those in my circles who work for Microsoft.

- ✔ **Pick a recognizable picture.** Your picture is what appears if your website is configured to show authors of articles. Making sure you have a recognizable picture ensures you or your brand is recognized immediately when it appears in search results. The more recognizable your image, the more people's eyes will be drawn to *your* search results, regardless of where you rank on the page (see Figure 7-11).

Optimizing your posts for search

After your profile is optimized (as mentioned earlier in this chapter), you'll benefit from optimizing the posts you make on your page. This is an ongoing process, and you'll want to constantly test the success of your posts. Make sure you're not just testing your posts for comments and +1s, but also for the Google+ rank that your posts attain among individual users' friends. This approach can be tricky, but with a little experience you'll become a pro at it. Here are a few tips for optimizing your posts on Google+:

✔ **Use keywords you want people to find you by, even when no link is present.** Make sure the keywords you want to rank for are listed in your posts. Focus on creative ways to do this without making it obvious. Keep your posts personal while focusing on search as much as you can. Always remember that people come first on Google+; don't neglect that.

✔ **Engage your followers as much as you can.** The more you can get your followers to +1, comment, and share your posts, the better you'll rank on Google search. Engage your followers to do this by following the steps I lay out earlier in this chapter, in the section "Reaping the effect of engagement."

✔ **Encourage fans to +1 you on Google.com as well.** A good Google+ strategy involves some training as well. Don't be afraid to encourage your followers to +1 your site's returned articles from searches on Google as well.

Figure 7-11: Can you tell which article I wrote in these search results?

Your fans can find all the articles on your site by doing a Google search for *site:yoursite.com* (replacing *yoursite.com* with your site's domain). This will return a list of every page on your site that Google has indexed. Encourage your fans to go through this list and +1 their favorites. If it moves you, ask them to share the pages that move them. But be sure to measure their response — some people may get annoyed with too many prompts to help you.

Formatting your website for Google Search Plus Your World

When you have Google+ all optimized and ready to be indexed by Google, you'll want to spend some time optimizing your own website for Google. Okay, this book isn't focused on SEO (Search Engine Optimization), so you may want to consult with an SEO professional for good tips on this established web-marketing technique. However, if you want to just optimize your website with what you've done on Google+, here are some ways to do so (most of these I cover in detail in Chapter 12, so I'll keep it simple here):

✔ **Utilize snippets:** If you go to www.google.com/+/business, you'll find a form you can fill out that gives you *snippets* (pieces of HTML code to place in your website). Use them to format your website's content when it appears in Google+ posts and in Google search results (see Figure 7-12). This format is called Microdata; I share a few examples in Chapter 12.

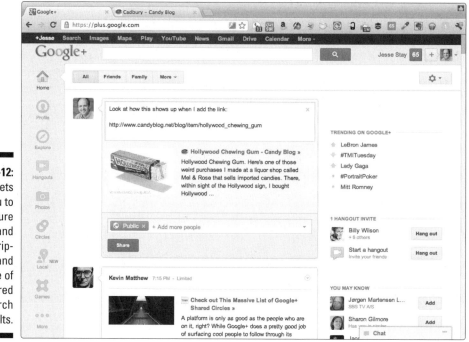

Figure 7-12: Snippets allow you to configure the title and description and image of links shared on search results.

If you're familiar with Facebook's Open Graph Protocol (see my book *Facebook Application Development For Dummies* [John Wiley & Sons, Inc.] for a good overview), the good news is that Google+ also recognizes Open Graph Protocol. Therefore, if you've already optimized for Facebook, there's a good chance your site is already configured and optimized for Google+.

✔ **Google+ Page Badges:** Badges allow you to tell Google what your Google+ Page is for your website. This, in turn, allows Google to enable Direct Connect for your website and page, which Google enables for only a select number of pages at the moment (one of them is H&M's page, featured earlier in this chapter). With Direct Connect, Google will allow people to circle your page right from Google.com search results; your brand, in turn, will stand out more when people are searching for similar terms.

✔ **+1 buttons:** I've made this point throughout this chapter, but having a +1 button on every page of your site can significantly help your site's ranking among the sites that other Google+ users search for on Google.com.

✔ **Use** `author` **tags.** Adding a simple `"rel='author'"` option to the bylines of articles on your website, and linking them (via the `href` attribute) to their authors' Google+ profiles will make your articles stand out much more strongly among other search results (as I show you, in detail, in Chapter 12).

Chapter 8

Focusing on Real People and Relationships

In This Chapter

▶ Learning to build relationships

▶ Finding ways to serve

▶ Opening up to your audience

As I contemplated the content for this book, I realized that a social networking topic needed a look at what has brought me a lot of success over the years: a focus on relationships. Google+ is so thoroughly about people that relationships are especially critical there.

Entire books — lots of them — are devoted to the interpersonal topics I cover in this chapter. I'll do my best to squeeze what I know into about 12 pages, and with any luck, you can apply this information productively to your own efforts. Most importantly, marketing is about relationships; it can become a robotic chore if you aren't invested enough in it. With social media marketing, make sure you don't forget the "social" part of your job — as a marketer, you grow your audience that way.

Winning Friends and Influencing Profiles

The age-old methods of building relationships have not disappeared just because so much social interaction happens in virtual reality now. Always remember that social networks are not destinations, nor are they a replacement for reality. Social networks are simply tools for helping you to build relationships with people you probably wouldn't have had contact with otherwise. The more you learn to use these tools in new, creative ways, the better you'll be at building relationships with people — many more people.

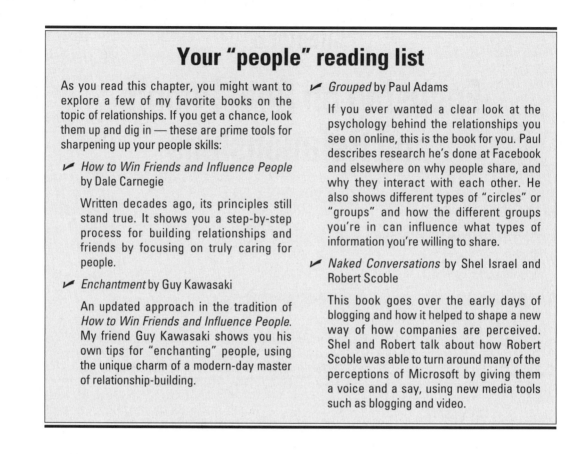

Your "people" reading list

As you read this chapter, you might want to explore a few of my favorite books on the topic of relationships. If you get a chance, look them up and dig in — these are prime tools for sharpening up your people skills:

✔ *How to Win Friends and Influence People* by Dale Carnegie

Written decades ago, its principles still stand true. It shows you a step-by-step process for building relationships and friends by focusing on truly caring for people.

✔ *Enchantment* by Guy Kawasaki

An updated approach in the tradition of *How to Win Friends and Influence People.* My friend Guy Kawasaki shows you his own tips for "enchanting" people, using the unique charm of a modern-day master of relationship-building.

✔ *Grouped* by Paul Adams

If you ever wanted a clear look at the psychology behind the relationships you see on online, this is the book for you. Paul describes research he's done at Facebook and elsewhere on why people share, and why they interact with each other. He also shows different types of "circles" or "groups" and how the different groups you're in can influence what types of information you're willing to share.

✔ *Naked Conversations* by Shel Israel and Robert Scoble

This book goes over the early days of blogging and how it helped to shape a new way of how companies are perceived. Shel and Robert talk about how Robert Scoble was able to turn around many of the perceptions of Microsoft by giving them a voice and a say, using new media tools such as blogging and video.

As you study this book, learn as much as you can. As you learn new tools and approaches to using Google+, always ask yourself, "How can I use this tool to better build relationships with others?" By taking this approach you'll come up with creative ways for building a relationship with your audience that you may have never had before. The best brands (think Disney, *Star Wars,* Ford Motor Company, Harry Potter) have a unique relationship with their customers and those they interact with.

Caring genuinely about people

A person who comes to your brand as a customer or a follower should never be just a "customer" or a "follower" in your eyes. Each one is a real person with a real life, real feelings, and real needs. The more you can think of your customers and followers as real people, the more you can start to care for them. It's important to stay in touch with that caring; just going through the motions won't cut it.

The more you try to truly care for those you interact with online, both as an individual and as a brand, the more they'll feel that caring and respond to it, which builds loyalty toward you. A major advantage of social networking is that you can do all this online, with much larger groups of people at a time, than is possible in face-to-face life.

Here's a list of some strong ways to show that you care. Remember, these can't just be empty gestures — they have to be genuine and real efforts.

- ✔ **Get better at remembering names.** When you interact with someone online, remember his or her name; then, if you ever meet the person in real life, your interaction will have that much more meaning. At the same time, when you meet people in real life, seek to tie that real-life interaction with who they are virtually so you know whom you're dealing with. There's nothing more awkward than forgetting someone's name when you're interacting with him or her.

- ✔ **Note down birthdays, and wish each person you interact with a happy birthday (see Figure 8-1).** In a recently launched feature, Google even tells you the birthdays of your friends via a little notification that appears in the upper-right of many Google products. To me, this offers a unique opportunity: Seek to find out your followers' and customers' birthdays. Maybe you notice their friends wishing them Happy Birthday. Maybe they've given a birth date to you through a web form or by other means. When you have this information, don't lose it. Then, when those birthdays come around the following year, be ready with a Happy Birthday greeting.

   Keeping track of birthdays can get difficult with a large audience. Try to do as many as you can personally — maybe prioritize them so that the people you genuinely know in real life get your personal response. Then, perhaps, hire an assistant to help you with the rest, knowing that you *would* genuinely wish them a Happy Birthday if you could. The less you can automate, the more special they'll feel.

- ✔ **Remember when people mention needs they have in life — seek to help them.** I thrive on this concept. As most folks do, I have a set of talents I'm aware of that I can offer on behalf of people who have needs I can meet — and I jump on the opportunity. This is a great way to keep relationships with your audience, but it's also a great way to connect with *influencers* (people with a large audience) as well.

- ✔ **Seek ways to discover the talents of the people you interact with and connect them with the needs of others you interact with.** Being a connector and facilitator puts you in the middle — right where you want to be. When you find ways to connect the talents of your audience, both sides of the connection look to you as the one who facilitated the relationship. This doesn't always bring fame and fortune (which isn't the point anyway), but it does strengthen the relationships you've built with that audience. Seek to provide opportunities for your audience to network with each other; introduce them to each other. They'll look to you for that in the future, and that makes you all the more influential.

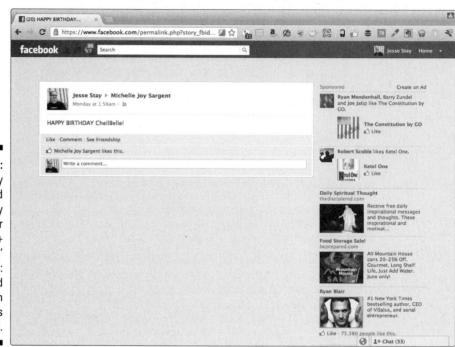

✔ **Say "thank you."** Those two words can have a powerful effect on people. Publicly thank people when they help you. Make it a point to show appreciation to the members of your audience who are helping out you or your brand. Send them private messages when the public approach doesn't make sense, just to let them know you acknowledge their contribution. When people feel appreciated, they put more effort into that relationship.

✔ **Be open about your own needs.** When you don't open up yourself, your audience and those you interact with can't learn to trust you and be open with you. The more you share about yourself, the more you build trust with those you interact with. Of course, there is such thing as TMI (too much information), so respect the limits of privacy and consideration. With a balanced approach to openness, you come across as much more real to those you interact with. As a result, they share more and you get a clearer sense of the needs you can help with. Most importantly, opening up makes you more interesting to them.

✔ **Try to remember conversations.** When you have one-on-one conversations with people — in real life, in private conversations, in online comments, or wherever — try to remember who they were and what you talked about. When a conversation comes around again, bring up the previous conversation so the person knows you were paying attention. It's a way to show you care.

✔ **Seek to make people feel special and unique.** This is the most important tip in this list. No matter who you are, treat everyone as if they're important, intelligent, and worth your time. In social media, they pretty much are. If you treat people like the potentials they have and can become, they'll remember your example and look back to you as they grow. At the same time, they'll turn to you when they need to feel special again.

Showing interest in people

When you interact with people both online and offline, the number-one rule is to show genuine interest in them. Try to truly care about them. Seek to put yourself in their shoes so you can understand where they're coming from.

Developing that interest is a natural way to strengthen your relationship with people. The more people you do this with, the more effective you'll be. Find ways to communicate to your followers and customers that you truly care. Make sure you really do.

Seizing Opportunity

Opportunity is everywhere. You just have to look for it. Especially on Google+ and other social networks, it's easy to find people in your audience, or among your friends, who have needs you can help with. Seize this opportunity to find the needs of your friends and help in any way you can.

Searching for service

Service is one of the most meaningful ways you can build relationships with others. You'll benefit most as a marketer if you seek out ways to serve. Let me share an example:

I started out as a software developer — it's a set of skills that I still hone by creating programs that make my life easier. In the early days of Twitter, I noticed that a lot of my friends were following me, and following everyone who followed me every day was getting to be a repetitive task. So I wrote a script to auto-follow anyone who followed me first.

Guy Kawasaki, Apple's former evangelist, author of many best-selling books, and a man with a great audience of followers (see Figure 8-2), was one of the people I followed — I respected his advice and loved his experience. I was also fascinated with him and wanted to learn more about him.

Figure 8-2:
Guy
Kawasaki
is a prime
example of
someone
who uses
genuine
relation-
ships to
build an
audience.

One day Guy shared in his Twitter stream that he was looking for an automatic tool that would enable him to follow the many people who were following him on Twitter. I sympathized with him — and I had just the tool. Immediately I responded and offered to let him use the script I had recently created. There was one problem. though — it was just a script, not quite user-friendly yet, and it would be tough for Guy to use it.

From that point, I decided to build a website out of it that Guy could use. I approached Guy and built the site — and from that, my service `SocialToo. com` was created. Guy and I have remained friends ever since, and he was even willing to be an advisor to my company. He helps me out every so often, and I help him out — it's a true friend relationship, and it all started with an opportunity to genuinely serve. You can use this same technique as you're trying to influence people and build relationships between yourself, your brand, and your followers.

There are other ways you can serve as well. Here are a few ideas you can try out on Google+, for yourself personally and for your brand:

✔ **Match donations to +1s (or circles).** I've seen a few brands do this — "For every +1 we get, we'll donate $1 to x charity." This approach is win–win — your followers get their friends +1'ing and circling your Google+ page, and you get to donate to the charity of your choice. You could up the ante even more by randomly picking one of your followers' favorite charities. Or maybe you can get your followers to submit creative videos on why a specific charity should be the one you donate to — you get the point. The possibilities are endless.

✔ **Offer discounts.** Discounts are a great way to capture the interest of those following you, and it serves them because they save money. Offer discounts and deals on your profile exclusively to Google+ users, and you'll see a much stronger relationship built between yourself and your followers.

✔ **A phone call can make a big difference.** See a follower in need? Maybe it's an irate customer who needs attention ASAP. Either way, a simple phone call from someone at your company, preferably someone of influence, can make all the difference. If you don't have the follower's phone number, most users on Google+ have an option to contact them through their profiles — send an e-mail and start the conversation there.

✔ **Recognize customers and followers making a difference.** Nothing makes someone feel better than being recognized publicly in front of their peers. Celebrate your followers and customers who are making a difference. Offer rewards for their efforts to help other followers and customers of yours. Doing so encourages more people to help each other and in turn builds a strong relationship between you and your followers and others you deal with.

✔ **Use your audience to build the audience of others.** If you've already got a big audience, seek out people who are making a difference, or people who impress you or have been doing great things for your brand. Then tell your audience to go follow them by adding them to their circles. This is a great way to serve your most loyal followers. Add your favorites to a circle, and share the circle; I've found that shared circles really help a person's audience grow. I enjoy when I share a list of my favorite people to my audience, seeing the responses on each of their streams asking why their follower counts are going up all of a sudden, and having their friends tell them I suggested them.

Finding your hidden talent

What strengths do you have to offer? That is what you should be seeking if you don't already know. Start with yourself as an individual. What are your talents? What do you like to do? How can you help others?

Then look at your brand and do the same. What are the benefits your brand can bring to others? How can your brand serve others in unique ways that other brands can't? Are there people in your company who can also contribute?

Once you've answered these questions, find ways to identify and contact people in your audience whom you can apply your talents towards helping. Help others know what your strengths are so they can tell their friends.

"Spreading the word" is a great use for Google+ Hangouts. Share, via live video, the things you can offer. There are (for instance) some musicians on Google+ who do mini-concerts for their Google+ fans. In that sense, they serve others' needs with the gift of music. Many have built quite an audience as a result of this effort.

Opening the Covers

The more I learn in life, the more I realize that transparency leads to much more effective results than secrecy. As I open up to people and share what I do, respecting others' privacy and security at the same time, people begin to see that I'm a real person and not just a brand.

People don't like brands as substitutes for human beings. Brands are objects. They have no feelings. They don't talk back to you. They're just bland objects with no personality. They're untouchable and unresponsive.

When you open up the covers and put real people and lives behind the brand, it turns your brand into a real company full of real people. It makes your brand more about people than it is about itself. People can associate with other people. They might wear a brand on a T-shirt or buy a mug with a logo on it but can't associate with a brand unless it also connects them to people.

Promoting your company from within

Seek to involve your employees as much as possible in promoting your brand. Let your employees talk, and feature them more than you do the brand image itself. Make them a reflection of the brand; Disney (for example) calls all its employees "cast members." You'll notice that even a big company like Google does this by letting their employees be the ones who personally announce products on Google+.

On Google+, there are multiple ways you can start to make your brand more about people than about the brand itself — here are a few ideas:

✔ **Use Google+ Hangouts to have Q&A hours.** Google actually uses this approach on its own behalf, opening a weekly Hangout where developers can get in and ask questions and interact with their API team for questions (see Figure 8-3).

You could do the same with your customers, giving your customers an opportunity to meet real people in the company. Michael Dell, CEO of Dell Computer, Inc., does this on occasion to see what his customers think. Only 10 people at a time can join, so that provides a limit to keep you from getting overwhelmed, and you can always stream the Hangouts through Google's Hangouts On Air, which is available to everyone.

✔ **Make sure your employees have accounts on Google+ (get them a copy of this book).** Domo, a company founded by Josh James (founder of Omniture), requires its employees to have certain social media accounts in order to be employed. Employees are given free rein to use their accounts, with the goal of familiarizing employees with social networking. You may or may not choose to do this, but I argue a Google+ account is one of the most important accounts your employees can have to help promote the company. If you're interested in Google search, this is the way to do it — most important, it gives your customers a chance to get to know your company's employees.

✔ **Share circles of your favorite followers.** This is a great way to make your followers feel good. Reward and promote good behavior, and good behavior will occur.

✔ **Share circles of your employees.** You should probably have a circle or two of your employees on Google+. Maybe you separate the circles by department. This will allow those on Google+ to get to know the people behind your brand, and show that there are actually human beings working behind the scenes.

✔ **Use YouTube to do regular updates of how your products are made and what your employees are doing.** Video is a great way to do behind-the-scenes updates on what people are doing in your company. Robert Scoble started doing this for Microsoft in the early days of the Internet. He created a podcast and started blogging and sharing, via video, what other Microsoft employees were doing to improve the products. This was over ten years ago, and people at the company thought he was crazy. However, what he did restored a lot of Microsoft's image and made them a brand that people could associate with.

✔ **Utilize Blogger.com to post longer-form text updates about your company as well as new products.** Like video, a blog can be a highly effective way to "write the news the way you want" — and provide longer-form content for your customers, and those following your brand, to subscribe to. Hosting your own blog using tools like Blogger.com allows you to create the news, which brings me to the next section.

Figure 8-3:
The Google+ Developer Relations team holds weekly Hangouts to interact with developers.

Becoming the news

For about as long as media have been with us, brands have relied on what news outlets said about them. They sent out press releases when new products were launched or when new news within the company came out, and then sat back and hoped that the press would interpret those releases positively and cover the news in a way that helped (or at least didn't hurt) their business. All that suspense is no longer needed with social media.

Using social media, businesses can now create their own news, custom-tailored to present what they do and make in the best light. No need to rely so much on the audiences of major news outlets. These days, especially using tools such as Google+, you can build your own audience that is friendly to your brand — and deliver your news the way you want it presented. Then, no matter who writes about you, readers can always come back to the source and have access to exactly what you intended to say.

In addition to creating the news, you are guiding a conversation. Now, when a news outlet misquotes or misinterprets what you've said, you can reply, in real time, with the correct information. This is powerful and means even a bad article about your brand can be corrected in minutes. You are now in control.

There are multiple tools you can use to "become the news" — that is, take control of the news about your business, service, or product. Many of these tools are even more powerful when you use them in tandem with Google+. Here are some examples:

- ✔ **Use Blogger.com to create content; then use Google+ to discuss it.** Long-form content certainly isn't dead. People are just discussing it on social networks like Google+ now. Use Google+ as a way to respond and guide the conversation that is happening surrounding your long-form messages. Post regular updates of new products and announcements to your Blogger.com blog, and share that information to Google+ for further discussion. Make sure people understand the message you present, and have employees pay attention to the discussion so they can answer when misperceptions occur.

- ✔ **Utilize an enticing content strategy to engage your audience and build even more followers as a result.** Chapter 7 shows you these techniques. Engagement is what builds audience. The greater the audience you build, the less you need the general media to distribute your message. What I've found is if you build a strong enough audience and a strong product, the media will start following your social media channels for updates. You won't need to send out press releases anymore, and you'll become the public source of everything written about you.

- ✔ **Use YouTube video to give your executives a voice; then get them responding in the comments on Google+.** This is tough to accomplish. Many executives aren't totally familiar with social media, and that's okay. Help them to understand that these are tools that give them more of a voice, and allow them to respond faster than they could before. Therefore, if they say something they'd rather take back, fortunately they can take it back much faster than they could before. They can save face, in real time via social media. Google+ is a great place to do this because you can link their quotes to your blog and get your articles ranking higher as a result.

REMEMBER

Tools help people do things faster and better. A common argument that I hear from executives and those who represent them is that they don't have time to add social media to their existing workflows. My solution to this problem is to remember that social media is a communications tool (among other things, of course). Executives who need to communicate better, for example, should look at their existing communication strategies, consult you, and determine how social media can help them reach more people even faster. Used effectively, this strategy should *save* them time, not take away from it.

Case study: Domino's Pizza

Domino's Pizza really engaged its fans and customers by getting its executives involved on social media channels when faced with a PR controversy. A fictional incident at one of their restaurants, one that didn't put the company in a good light, led to a negative (but popular) YouTube video getting shared around the Internet and going viral. Domino's was faced with a groundswell of irate customers who were fooled into believing that the video was authentic.

Domino's and their executives took active steps to get the company's reputation back:

✔ Immediately Domino's released a YouTube video of the company president responding to the negative videos, saying that the company was taking action, acknowledging the seriousness of the issue, and laying out how the company was going to resolve it

✔ Soon a new YouTube video introduced the Domino's head chef, again affirming the company's commitment to top-quality pizza and asking customers who were passionate about the brand to share their own images of the pizza they were ordering.

Before long, images of Domino's pizza were flooding the web, turning a bad situation into a positive marketing experience. This outcome was all because the company got its executives involved in a very personal way, and they were able to respond quickly.

Chapter 9

Utilizing Hangouts to Share Your Brand

. . . .

In This Chapter

▶ Getting the hang of Google+ Hangouts

▶ Building an approach to using Hangouts for business

▶ Studying examples of successful Hangouts

. . . .

*O*ne of the most useful parts of Google+ is a simple tool that many companies charge hundreds of dollars a month for others to use to communicate. Google does it for free on its public site for consumers — and also free as a feature of Google Apps for businesses. The tool is video chat, in this case allowing up to ten Google+ users at a time (and an unlimited number of people watching if you choose the On Air option) to chat via webcam or video together. This simple method of communication has brought many people together, face to face, who would never have met otherwise. And where you find people sharing interests and getting to know each other — in real life or in cyberspace — there you find opportunities as a marketer.

Exploring Google+ Hangouts

In essence, Google+ Hangouts offer a consistent, attractive online space where you can connect with people you know — and build relationships with people you don't yet know — in a way that text and chat just can't accomplish. Google+ Hangouts have several features that go well beyond other competing chat products:

> ✔ **Chat, via video, with up to ten people at a time (nine other than yourself).** The most defining feature of a Hangout is that you can pick up to nine other friends on Google+ and talk to them face to face (see Figure 9-1). The person currently speaking gets the focus in a big video in the middle, and soon you're having a conversation with nine others as well — from anywhere in the world.

Figure 9-1:
Chatting
with nine of
your friends
on Google+.

✔ **Watch videos, participate in apps, and have fun together.** In addition
to the people you contact in a Hangout, you can have videos, and other
apps that people participate in. You can watch a video on YouTube
with others, for instance — and maybe trade satirical comments about
it if it's a bad movie — or play a game with friends. It's all possible in a
Google+ Hangout if you're running the right app.

Apps in Hangouts can give you a way to hold focus groups around
videos or other experiences you create. For example, you can select a
YouTube video, get the group to watch it, and ask for opinions live as
you watch it. The possibilities are endless.

✔ **Broadcast your chat for the world to see.** Google+ Hangouts have a
feature called On Air, which allows groups of up to ten people who are
chatting through video to broadcast that conversation to the world. The
conversation can be viewed live on Google+ or on YouTube, or archived
for later watching. I share some examples of this approach in this
chapter (see the later section "Broadcasting a Black Eyed Peas concert").

Starting your first Google+ Hangout

The best way to understand Google+ Hangouts is to start one yourself. Creating a Hangout is quite simple — here are some steps to get you started:

1. **Click the Hangouts button at the left of the Google Plus page and then click the Start a Hangout button to the right on the page.**

   You can also just click the Start a Hangout button in the right column of your News Feed (see Figure 9-2).

   A window pops up, giving you the option to add some more information before you start. If this is your first time, you might also be asked to install a plugin. In that case, follow the instructions, and you'll return to this step in no time.

2. **Choose which circles or people you want to invite to your Hangout.**

   This is the cool part of Hangouts — you get to select exactly who you want to invite. Select Your Circles if you want to invite anyone you've circled, or type in individual names of people to invite. You can always bite the bullet and just invite everyone by choosing Public as well — just keep in mind that your Hangout may fill up really fast (which might be a good thing).

3. **Select a name for your Hangout.**

   When people are looking under the Hangouts section in Google+ for Hangouts occurring in their circles, this is the name they will see. They can also search for Hangouts, and your Hangout will appear if it fits in their search query.

4. **Decide if you want to publish your Hangout to the world with Hangouts On Air (see Figure 9-3).**

   After you've selected who you want to have *in* the Hangout, you can decide whether you want the world to be able to *watch* the Hangout. When this is enabled, your Hangout shows up in the streams belonging to the friends of anyone who's watching. The Hangout will link to YouTube, and anyone can watch as you and those you invited chat live "on air."

   Below this option are other choices, including whether to allow minors to watch the Hangout. If you're talking about adult topics, you might want (or even need, depending on what the laws require where you are) to check this box.

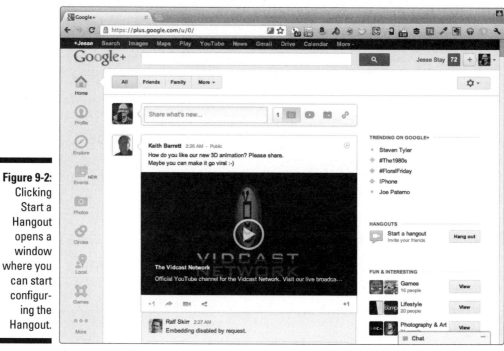

Figure 9-2:
Clicking
Start a
Hangout
opens a
window
where you
can start
configur-
ing the
Hangout.

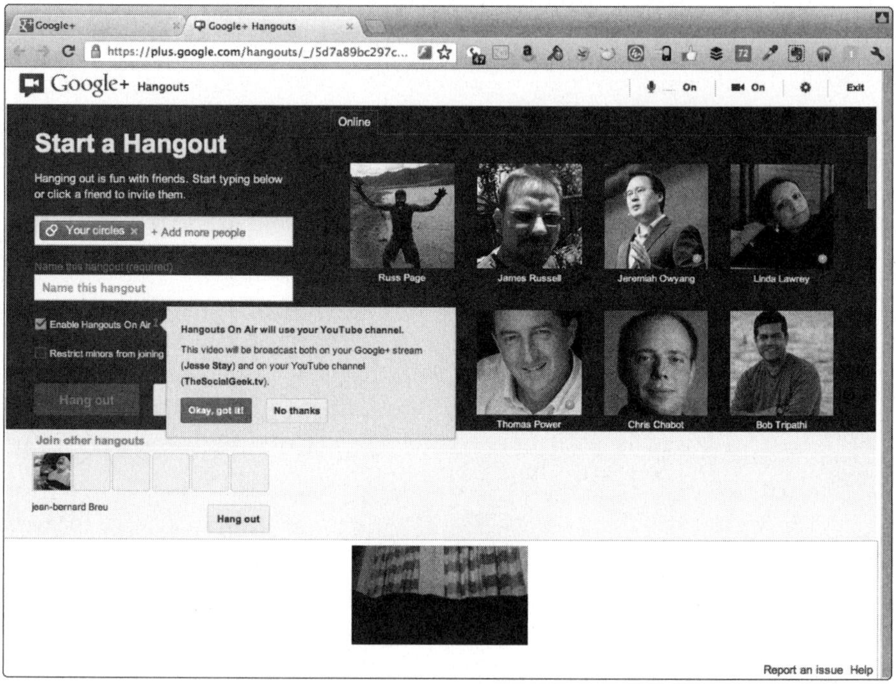

Figure 9-3:
Checking
this box
enables
Hangouts
On Air.

5. Click Hang Out.

Check your hair, do your makeup, adjust your glasses, and then just click the Hang Out button. Doing so invites your friends to the Hangout, and they'll see the Hangout in their streams. Soon, friends who want to join you in the Hangout will start joining your Hangout and participating in the conversation with you.

You can also start a Hangout *as your brand*. To do so, you switch to your brand's account by clicking your name, selecting your Google+ page name, and then following the steps in this section when the new window appears. Just note that your own computer's camera will be used; make sure that the people you want to represent the brand are the people in front of that camera.

Your Brand Hangout then shows up as "Your Google+ Page Name hung out with x people" in the news feeds of people following your Google+ page. Visitors to the Hangout see, in the Hangout video, the people you've chosen to represent your brand.

The Hangouts feature procedures that I've laid out could change if Google+ ever changes its design. If that happens and you're lost, just go to this book's Google Groups page at `http://stay.am/gplusmarketinggroup` for the lowdown on what's up.

Looking deeper into the value of Hangouts

So what's the big deal about another video-chat product? Dozens of them are on the market — Skype, Facebook, Microsoft Live Messenger — even Xbox has its own video chat. The value of Google+ Hangouts to you as a marketer is in not only the number of people participating in video chat at once, but many other factors as well.

Varying factors contribute to why Google+ Hangouts are so powerful. Here are just a few:

- ✔ **Every Google+ Hangout is embedded right in the feed.** Every Google+ Hangout started shows up in the Google+ news feed — right along with every other update on Google+ (see Figure 9-4). So when your friends (and the other people you're interested in) start their own Hangouts, you have the opportunity to join and get to know them better. Hangouts offer an easy way to discover opportunities to meet people face to face.

- ✔ **Hangouts can target specific circles and people to chat.** Each Hangout you start gives you the opportunity to choose who can participate in the Hangout. You can invite the entire public to your Hangout or just specific people. My friend Leo Laporte, host of TWIT.tv, uses circles in Hangouts to invite influential media and web personalities to participate in his podcasts. He then records and broadcasts these conversations for the rest of the world to see.

Figure 9-4:
Hangouts appear in the news feeds of the friends of those participating.

✔ **Hangouts are all about collaboration.** Each and every Google+ Hangout is built around a large onscreen canvas, with pictures of the individual participants below. The canvas usually fills up with the person currently talking, but you can also use apps, watch videos, or even share your desktop to get others collaborating with you on what you're working on. All those participating can work together face to face, no matter where they are in the world.

✔ **Hangouts help you build relationships.** As you collaborate with the other chat participants, you're also building relationships. As you use Google+ more — and start to participate in Hangouts — you'll find that Google+ has its own unique, tight-knit community. One reason for this closeness is that many of those who participate have seen each other face to face — and have built relationships through participation in Hangouts. Many people have built their followings by getting to know other people individually through Google+. Everyone has a story — and Google+ Hangouts are a golden opportunity to find out the story of each person you interact with and meet new people in the process.

✔ **Google+ Hangouts have deep integration with YouTube.** As mentioned in the previous section, you can use Google+ Hangouts to watch videos with your friends (see Figure 9-5). Built into each Hangout is the capability to watch any YouTube video — just click the YouTube button at the top of the Hangout, and click Allow to allow the YouTube Gadget. Then select the video and click Play, and everyone will be watching it with you. In addition, when you choose to broadcast your Hangouts to the world, they stream live (or recorded) over YouTube as people visit them to watch. So you get to make contact with a wider community of hundreds of millions of people on YouTube as well, bringing even more eyes to your Hangout — and to your brand — in the process.

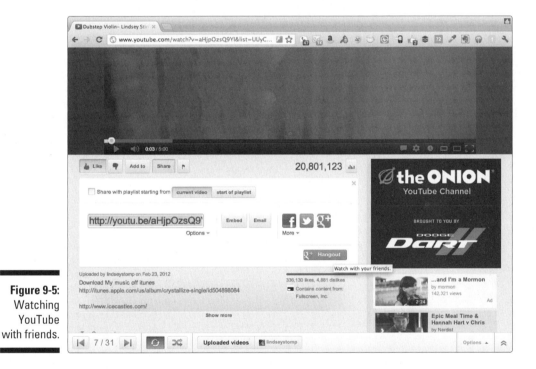

Figure 9-5:
Watching
YouTube
with friends.

Getting to know your customers

Because Google+ Hangouts are natural ways to build relationships and get to know new people, they also offer marketers or businesses a large-scale — but friendly — opportunity to get to know their customers.

As mentioned in the "Starting your first Google+ Hangout" section, earlier in this chapter, you can also start a Google+ Hangout not only as a person, but also as your brand. Whether you log in under your personal account or under your brand's account is up to you. Here are some ways you can personalize the interaction by introducing your customers to the people behind your brand:

✔ **Have weekly "office hours" where your customers can come ask questions and get to know your team.** The Google+ Developer Relations team reaches out to their professional community this way. Having weekly hours during which your customers can come and ask questions can become an indispensable customer-service tool, as well as a way to build up your reputation with your chosen community. Bring in people who can answer your customers' questions and get action on problems. Try to get your executives involved in this process as much as you can.

✔ **Invite fans of yours who you know are passionate about your brand.** Get them talking about your brand with others; broadcast the conversations live via Hangouts On Air. When people who don't work for a company that I like talk about how much they like that company, there's nothing more convincing. Get your most passionate customers to join in a Hangout and talk about topics related to your brand. Maybe you send them a sample to open and try out on air. It's a hands-on way to "be there" with those fans and to pass along their enthusiasm to others.

✔ **Invite your CEO and other executives to participate and answer questions.** With social media, it's all about people. Google+ Hangouts give you the opportunity to unveil and showcase your brand, and there's nothing like live, one-on-one conversations with those who actually run or own the company to bring drive and excitement into the conversation. Get your CEO and other executives involved in the conversation. Michael Dell does so for Dell Computer, for example. Let your customers talk to the execs and ask them questions. Have someone moderate the conversation with your exec as the host to keep out spammers and trolls. Have a PR issue? Arrange for the news publication in question to join a Hangout that you start and correct any misperceptions live, on the air. Google+ Hangouts give you the power to ensure that all your customers know where you stand, getting the word straight from those who make the decisions.

✔ **Search for Hangouts that are related to your brand's vision and goals, and get your employees to participate and get involved in those conversations.** Just ask your fans to start their own Hangouts, and make sure you can easily find them in some way. Then get your employees to go through the Hangouts your fans created one by one and chat with your customers and most passionate fans. (A later section, "Meeting fans with Hangouts," describes how the popular DJ Kaskade pulled off this bit of magic.)

Another way to approach the quest for instances of your brand is to just search for keywords related to the brand (see Figure 9-6) and find Hangouts where people are talking about things related to the brand. Then you can get your employees to join in the conversations that are pertinent to your brand. To do so, just search for the keyword, and then, from the Everyone drop-down list, select Hangouts.

Search text   Search button

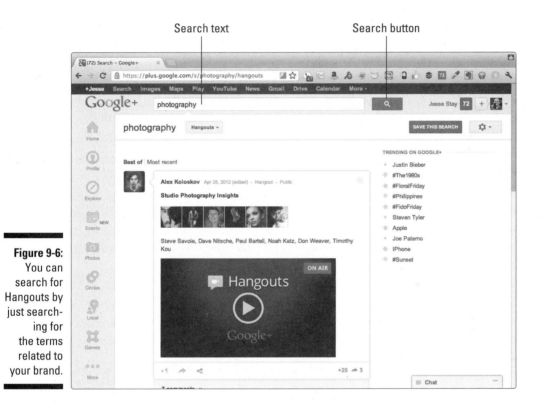

Figure 9-6:
You can
search for
Hangouts by
just search-
ing for
the terms
related to
your brand.

Building a Marketing Strategy for Hangouts

You can use Hangouts in various ways to grow your audience or build relationships with your customers. Here are a couple of examples of techniques you could be using to strategize Google+ Hangouts most effectively.

Educating others — the panel

If you're looking to help others learn what you want them to know about your brand, one effective way to educate customers (or potential customers) is to fill up those ten slots of video chat in a Hangout with a panel of experts who can discuss your brand in all its glory, nuance, and indispensability.

One way I've found to build an effective online marketing strategy is to identify what real-life situations could be simplified or localized using the technology I have available. With this particular approach in Google+ Hangouts, I look to conferences and meetups where a panel of individuals speaks about a specified topic. A moderator sets the tone for the conversation, and each member of the panel is given the opportunity to share his or her thoughts and discuss the topics at hand. Imagine the benefit if all those thoughts, discussions, and topics were about your brand.

The basics: Set up a Google+ Hangout, bring in ten people who know their stuff (especially about your brand), and assign one of them to be a moderator. This person keeps control of the Hangout and plays producer for your broadcast. Turn on Hangouts On Air so the conversation is broadcast, and share it to your audience. Then discuss up a storm.

If you want to go beyond just a simple panel, you can try these approaches:

✔ **Allow the audience to ask questions of panel members as you share your Hangout.** When you share your Hangout on Google+, your fans will be able to comment on the post and participate in the conversation. Don't neglect this potential gold mine of customer interest. Use these comment areas as places to engage fans during the Hangout; get them asking questions (see Figure 9-7).

✔ **Bring in people of influence related to your brand.** The more interesting the people, the more people will pay attention. If your CEO is well known, bring him or her into the panel. Another approach is to even bring in competing brands and start a conversation just around the topics your brand is most interested in. This panel could be a great way to have a constructive conversation or even debate around a particular topic. Perhaps you've set some ground rules ahead of time, or you have a moderator to keep the peace.

✔ **Schedule your panel Hangout ahead of time.** Your fans will add your Hangout to their schedules if you just let them know ahead of time that it's happening. Panelists are especially important; the more interesting the panelists, the more people you get watching the Hangout when it goes live.

Figure 9-7:
Don't
neglect
the con-
versations
happening
in your
share of the
Hangout
when it
goes live.

Try not to share Hangouts impromptu — let your audience know ahead of time, and you'll have a much better turnout.

✔ **Consider leaving a few open slots in the Hangout so fans can participate with the panel.** There's nothing more personal and authentic than having real customers sharing their enthusiasm for the brand or participating in the conversation. Let your fans fill a couple of slots in the panelists and maybe even rotate in and out with new fans. This personalizes your panel and makes it look like you're paying attention to your fans and customers as the panel is occurring. That leads to the next section — participatory Hangouts.

Meeting others — participatory Hangouts

Google+ Hangouts are about building relationships with people — in particular, your customers. However you use the advantages of Hangouts, the main goal should always be to meet your customers and give them as many opportunities as possible to participate and be a part of the team for your brand. Here are a few tips:

✔ **Send select groups of customers some sample products to try out in the Hangouts you host.** I'd love to see more brands embracing this technique. The secret to a good social media campaign, in my opinion, is when you don't have to call in the heavy-hitter influencers, and you can get your existing fans and their friends all sharing good stuff about your brand with each other. You can reach many more millions of people by embracing the crowd from the bottom up (by having millions of your customers all talking about your brand with their hundreds of friends) instead of going from the top down (by having a few influencers share with their millions of followers).

Try sending several lucky fans some samples of your products to try out, with the stipulation that they do the trial in a Google+ Hangout that you organize. Set the date and time for each, and get all of them opening and trying out your products at the same time on air (or you could have them do so on separate occasions or in sequence). Broadcast this trying-out to your fans, and voilà — instantly you've made contact with a much larger public audience of normal, everyday customers who may be watching alongside and can associate with people just like themselves. In addition, you're having normal, everyday people share their thoughts about your product live, on air, for all your customers and potential customers to see. This approach of affecting hundreds to millions of your common customers is, if you can do it right, so much more powerful than sending products to only a few influencers.

✔ **Create "office hours" for customers to meet your employees.** You should provide support opportunities for your customers using Hangouts. This is a great way to let your customers interact face to face with employees of your company and truly get their questions answered. Just set up a time once or twice a week for customers to join a Hangout with your employees, where they can ask you questions directly (see Figure 9-8).

Use this as an opportunity to give tours of your office. Show the viewers who works there. Bring in your executives if possible. Truly try to open the curtain on your brand as much as you can so your customers can see that your organization is run by real people just like your customers. This approach makes your brand easier for viewers to identify with.

✔ **Make sure your employees are controlling the show.** It's vital that you're not just putting on a PR front for your organization or brand. Bring in the real employees behind your brand as you host your Google+ Hangouts. Bring in the executives. Find the most interesting people in the company, and let them host the Hangouts. Those who generate customer interest can get more people interacting with your brand.

✔ **"Show off" your customers as much as you can.** There's nothing more complimentary to a customer than to have the companies he's passionate about "show him off" to other customers of the brand. People like attention. They like to get recognized when they deserve it.

Find opportunities to bring your customers into as many conversations as you can. (Check out the way the Black Eyed Peas used this technique, later in the chapter.) If you're broadcasting to a large audience, let some of your customers be in the broadcast to that audience. The audience then feels like "one of their own" is there with you, and it makes your broadcast much more personal for each person watching.

Broadcasting to your audience — performing live Hangouts

Typically, most of your Hangouts will include you and nine other customers or followers. These aren't always broadcast to the world, but make sure you allow the world to peek in; let your brand's loyalists take turns participating with you. If you need a much bigger audience, you should consider turning on the Google+ Hangouts On Air feature to broadcast your Hangout to the world.

Google+ Hangouts On Air allow you to take your Hangout of up to ten people (you, a group of other employees, or any other customers you want to participate in the conversation), and broadcast that Hangout to the world. The Hangout shows up in your news feed, and any of your fans can click through and watch the Hangout live, on air, over YouTube.

Figure 9-8:
The Google+ Developer Relations team hosts weekly Hangouts of their own.

Google+ Hangouts On Air have provide some invaluable benefits:

- ✓ **Your audience is unlimited.** There are no limits to Google+ Hangouts On Air (other than age limits if you choose not to broadcast to minors). Every Hangout On Air is broadcast to the entire public.

- ✓ **You can record your Hangout.** Each Hangout On Air is automatically recorded and posted to YouTube.

- ✓ **You get some of the added benefits of YouTube.** Your Hangouts On Air videos all get broadcast right on the YouTube site, and you can link them to your existing YouTube channel. This handy feature can pump up the content on your YouTube channel and give you the additional capability of having live conversations within your YouTube channel (see Figure 9-9). Better yet, you can embed your videos in blogs and other websites, just as you can any other YouTube video.

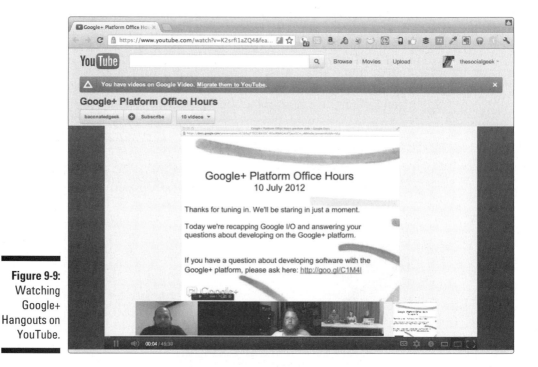

Figure 9-9: Watching Google+ Hangouts on YouTube.

Hanging out with the stars

No, not those stars — the ones you can see when you look up. One of my most memorable Hangouts to watch was during the transit of Venus across the sun in 2012. Astronomy enthusiast Fraser Cain organized a Hangout with various amateur astronomers so they could all watch the transit of Venus together, as shown here.

Each participant in the Hangout had his or her own telescope or watching gear set up. One person had a really nice telescope. Another had a rigged a pair of binoculars set up to project a shadow on a wall And anyone who wanted could watch the Hangout live, as Venus was traveling across the sun.

When the clouds covered the sun, I wasn't at an ideal observation point, so I didn't have the opportunity to watch this rare event in person. But I did get to see it via Google+ Hangouts On Air — live — and even take it with me on my mobile device as I traveled that day.

I didn't miss a thing!

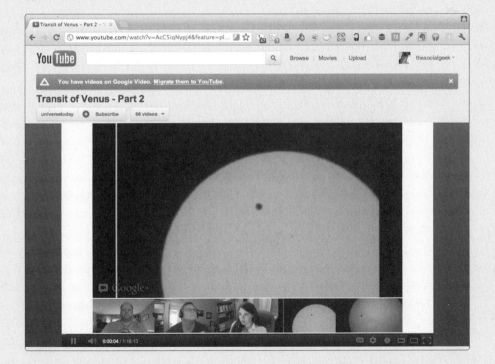

Learning Hangouts Through Tips and Examples

I am constantly asked, in my presentations and conversations with others, whether there are any spectacular success stories on Google+. You know, considering that the platform is so young, one would expect only a few such stories to emerge in just a year's time. But watch this space. Google+ Hangouts in particular have seen success not only in growing an audience, but in building relationships and growing sales as a result. Nothing speaks better about the power of a product than real-life examples. Read on.

Broadcasting a Black Eyed Peas concert

In late 2011, not long after Google+ launched, the lead singer for the Black Eyed Peas, Will.i.am, immediately made good use of the site. Hosting several Hangouts with his fans, he broadcast one of the Black Eyed Peas concerts to fans. He didn't just broadcast it, though — he let eight other lucky fans join in the Hangout, and *they* broadcast the Hangout live, not only to the band's audience on Google+, but also on the big screen of their concert in New York City (see Figure 9-10). You can imagine the number of fans just waiting for their turn to participate in *that* Hangout.

Will.i.am used several techniques that I think are noteworthy enough that I mention them throughout the book:

- **He used his personal account (+will.i.am) to promote his brand.** Will.i.am recognized that Google+ is about people, not brands as brands, and used that focus to his advantage: He used his own account to promote the Black Eyed Peas. Granted, the Google+ Pages feature wasn't around at the time, but keep in mind that sometimes the personal accounts of those behind your brand can be at least as powerful as the brand pages themselves.

- **He allowed his customers and fans to be a part of his brand and promoted them to his own audience.** By allowing his fans to participate in the Hangout and displaying them onscreen at the band's concert, he put his customers first. He made his fans a part of the brand experience, making them feel just as much a part of the team as he was. This face-to-face opportunity to be a part of the brand only sharpened the personal dimension of his concert.

✔ **He brought out members of his brand — the band members themselves — to interact with those in his audience.** By broadcasting the concert and letting his band members interact with fans in the Hangout during the concert, people saw Black Eyed Peas as more than just a impersonal brand. Their fans got to know the individuals behind the music — those who make the concerts happen and the music itself happen. In return, the audience got to feel like they were a part of the band itself.

Figure 9-10:
Black Eyed
Peas
hosting
one of their
concerts in
a Google+
Hangout.

Enlightening through the Dalai Lama and Desmond Tutu

In an epic meeting of spirituality, a Google+ Hangout was organized allowing the Dalai Lama (whom some believe to be Buddha himself) and Desmond Tutu, archbishop of the Church of England, to have a face-to-face conversation — across the world. In the Hangout, the two talked peace, religion, and spirituality in an amazing meeting of two very humble spiritual minds (see Figure 9-11).

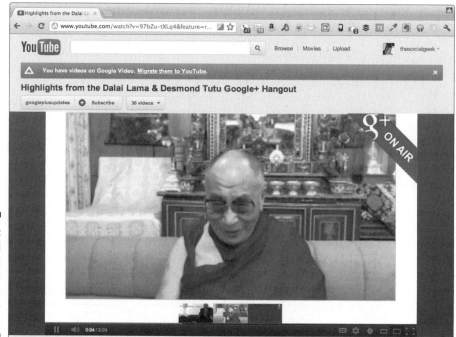

Figure 9-11:
The Dalai
Lama and
Desmond
Tutu chat in
a Google+
Hangout.

In this case, an incredible opportunity was given — and broadcast to the world, where two highly influential and hard-to-reach leaders were made accessible — to each other, and for others to watch and learn from. The remoteness of each leader's location provided a great chance to use Google+ Hangouts and Hangouts On Air to allow the world to watch the conversation as it happened in real time. Your organization can apply similar principles by bringing together thought leaders related to your brand or field of expertise and getting them talking about interesting topics with one another. When you're the facilitator, your customers go through you to watch such interesting conversations.

Meeting fans with Hangouts

One of the most unique uses of Google+ Hangouts occurred before Google allowed anyone to access Google+ Hangouts On Air. Kaskade, the popular DJ, liked to use Google+ to interact with his fans — and did so from the very beginning of Google+. One day he decided to figure out a way around the ten-person limit for Hangouts and posted a message to his fans that specified a time frame and asked them to share the URLs to their own Hangouts during that time frame (see Figure 9-12). Kaskade then proceeded to join as many of his fans' Hangouts as he could while they were all accessible, giving his fans an opportunity, one by one, to get to know him.

Figure 9-12: Kaskade offered to join his fans' Hangouts instead of relying on the ten-person limit.

Kaskade used several strategies with this approach:

✔ He spent time trying to relate and get to know his customers (or fans) by building conversations with them in Hangouts.

✔ He kept the experience personal, using his real self over his brand itself to promote his brand.

✔ He put his customers first by actually joining each individual Hangout of each fan who participated.

Building a nation with President Obama

In 2012, just after the State of the Union address, U.S. President Barack Obama provided an opportunity for students all over the nation to ask him questions about the address. These questions took place live, transmitted to the world via Google+ Hangouts On Air; they covered topics that ranged from the economy to job growth to war.

The Hangout brought in five U.S. citizens (one was a sort of composite citizen — a high school class of six people) to participate in the conversation and was led by a moderator from Google and, of course, President Obama. Citizens of the United States were given the opportunity to submit questions via YouTube; their favorites were featured for the president to answer. Participants in the Google+ Hangout were also given the chance to ask their own questions (see Figure 9-13).

Figure 9-13: President Obama having a conversation with citizens of the United States.

This Google+ Hangout accomplished several things:

✔ **It gave average citizens of the United States the opportunity to participate in a conversation with their president.** Citizens from all over the nation were able to submit their questions via YouTube. Choosing a few of these from YouTube provided a feeling that the voice of the people was being heard by President Obama.

✔ **It let average citizens speak face to face with their president.** The participants in the Hangout could ask real questions of the president. Not every one of them voted for him in the past election; they could voice their frustrations and disagreements, and the president could answer them face to face. The conversation felt unfiltered by the media, putting President Obama on the same level as those he was talking with.

✔ **It let the president talk face to face with the American people.** Perhaps the greatest benefit to this conversation was that the president was a live voice instead of a recorded broadcast. Some of the filtering effect of the media went away; President Obama himself was controlling the conversation and could respond directly to those he was talking to.

✔ **It gave the White House control of the conversation.** In this new medium, the White House was unfiltered by newspapers and cable news networks — and had more thorough control of the message.

Making things with Make.com

In 2012, the popular magazine and movement *Make* (owned by O'Reilly) decided to launch a week of making things. The event targeted teenagers and their parents wanting to learn how to build fun things and get the creative juices flowing. I even brought my son into the event to participate and build our own things that week.

What I especially liked about the Make event was that they used Google+ Hangouts to show people — live — how to make the things they were sharing (Figure 9-14 shows them making a device in a Hangout). People participating could also participate in the Hangouts and get help with their projects. This one-on-one interaction through Hangouts was like walking side by side with those participating, helping each participant make the particular project of the day along the way. It's a terrific example of the "office hours" concept I mention in the earlier section "Meeting others — participatory Hangouts."

Figure 9-14:
A demo of building a project for a Google+ event, shown on Make.

Chocolate tasting with your customers

Chocolate-maker Cadbury UK, perhaps one of the most popular Google+ brands at the time of this writing, used samples of their products to get their customers to demo their products for them. The chocolate-maker let a select group of their customers do a live tasting of their latest chocolate product in a Google+ Hangout for their customers to see live on air (see Figure 9-15).

Cadbury UK randomly selected participants and sent them all three of their yet-to-be-released candy bars. Participants, and fans, were then allowed to vote for their favorite candy bars. They finally chose the winning candy bar and shared that with their fans. Fans were involved in the entire process.

Some great techniques were applied here:

✔ Customers were given control by letting them choose their favorite candy bar.

✔ Fans felt included because they were a part of the chocolate test.

✔ Normal fans were put in the same place as influencers (people with a large audience), making each of them feel important.

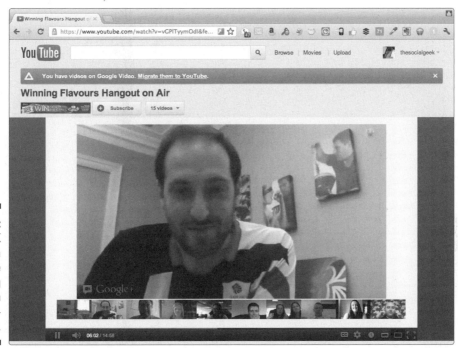

Figure 9-15:
Cadbury UK
holding a
chocolate
tasting
through
Google+
Hangouts.

Part III

Going from Fisher to Fish-Farmer

The 5th Wave   By Rich Tennant

"It was supposed to be a simple sleep potion. That's why you can't always trust the information you get off of 'Wiccapedia.'"

In this part . . .

*J*ust as Part II shows how to build your brand by using Google+ to "fish where the fish are" — so Part III shows what to do after you've attracted that plethora of new customers, traffic, and sales to your website or app.

Here's where you take it to the next level: promoting your brand and marketing your products by cultivating customers in one consistent place. Instead of going out to where your fish are, how about creating a farm where your fish can congregate — and keeping track of the fish swimming in your pond?

Through simple integration with your website and in your own apps and digital products, you can bring the power of Google+ into your own products. First and foremost, you can make your products social through Google+ — by linking Google+ Pages and Profiles to your content and bringing people's circles into your user experience. As a marketer, you're moving from fishing to farming!

Chapter 10

Advertising with Social Ads

Social advertising is a new phenomenon to emerge in the last decade. Starting with Facebook, the World Wide Web provided new ways to advertise products, services, and ideas to *targeted demographics* (groups of people with a clear marketing angle in common). This approach departed from that of earlier ad products like Google AdWords, which allowed ad managers to target ads by websites and keywords — but not by people.

Facebook ads gave marketers a new option — completely automated — not only to target ads at specific people and their close friends and family, but also to see that interaction with each ad. You can bet that Google saw a new competitor in the market and felt the need to respond.

Google has released a relatively simple competitor to Facebook's ad product: AdWords . Called *social extensions,* this product allows Google to integrate the offerings of `plus.google.com` with ads that appear in Google search, as well as with AdSense on websites. Now you can increase the interaction and click-through rates on your ads, as well as go after better conversion for each ad (because of the linking of a prospective customer's friends) and take advantage of the social influence factors that bring your site up higher in the search results of each person who sees your ads.

Google AdWords itself can, and does, take up many other books, but here's where I cover the essentials of using AdWords to build a social campaign that will improve your ad ranking and help your site in the long run.

Looking to Google Social Ads

Google *social ads,* as I call them, are ways to turn your traditional Google AdWords ads into social endorsements from the friends of those who see them. Social ads can appear anywhere you see a Google ad — including any website integrated with Google AdSense or a Google.com search.

Each ad comes with its own +1 button and a list of profile images (in the case of display ads) or names (in the case of text ads) of other people in your Google+ circles who have clicked +1 on that ad (see Figure 10-1). The cool part is that you can also link ads to Google+ Pages. Doing so links the +1s for the ad to a Google+ Page — which greatly increases the chance that your visitors will see their friends in the list of those +1s for the ad. Those +1s are integrated automatically with the targeted landing page for the ad. Then that landing page has a much greater chance of appearing not only with +1s, but also with an Add to Circles endorsement in Google.com search results (and other places where Google+ is integrated). Google has said that enabling social extensions (now the default on Google AdWords) significantly improves an ad's click-through rate compared to ads that don't turn it on.

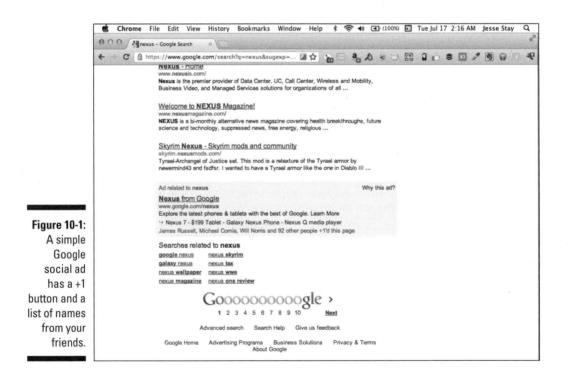

Figure 10-1:
A simple Google social ad has a +1 button and a list of names from your friends.

The workflow of Google+ social ads from the user standpoint works like this:

1. The text ad appears on Google.com or an AdSense-integrated site.

2. Option 1 — the text ad: In *text ads* (ads that have some sort of text enticing the user to click), the user sees the names of friends in the ad, and as a result feels inspired to click +1 on the ad. The user's name now appears in the list of people who have +1'd, and the circle continues.

3. Option 2 — the display ad: In *display ads* (ads that have pictures that you can click), the user sees pictures of friends in the ad and as a result feels inspired to click the ad — and maybe to purchase a product as well. While the user is there, he or she clicks the +1 button on your website. Now a picture of the user appears in the list of people who have +1'd, and the circle continues.

4. While the user is on your website, because you've implemented a Google+ Badge that links to your Google+ Page (see Figure 10-2), the user also circles your Google+ Page and starts to get updates from you, for free. The endorsements grow; your chances of appearing in Google. com search results — and other places where Google+ is integrated — improve significantly.

Badge

Figure 10-2:
A simple Google+ Badge on a website (like this one on Mashable) can improve the visibility of your site in search results.

Creating Google social ads

To create a Google social ad, you start by creating a simple Google AdWords ad. Many services and companies are available online to help with this process — you may want to shop around — but for now, going to adwords. google.com to manage and create your social ads is a good way to get started. You need a Google account, and you should have previously logged in to Google AdWords to do this:

1. **Go to** adwords.google.com.

   A screen appears, showing any ads you've previously created; you can go in and track stats for each campaign (see Figure 10-3).

2. **Click the New Campaign button to create your new ad campaign.**

   A form appears for creating your campaign. Go through it and learn what each option does for you.

   Click the question marks if you want to learn more about anything on the page.

3. **Fill out the form.**

   Okay, an exhaustive list of the best options to choose is beyond the scope of this book — but take some time to get to know what you can do here. Fill out the form in the way that works for you — and test your results.

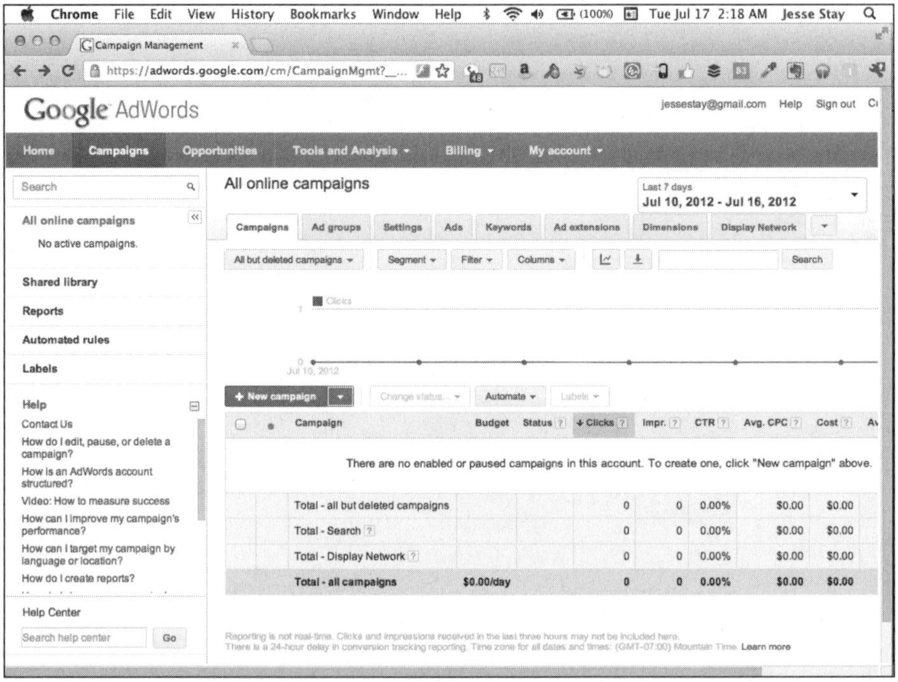

Figure 10-3:
Clicking
the New
Campaign
button.

4. **Check the box next to Increase the Social Relevance of My Ads by Associating Them with My Google+ Page.**

   Doing so gives you the option to specify the Google+ Page you want to associate with (as shown in Figure 10-4). (Refer to the later section "Linking your Google+ Page to your ads" for details of how this works.)

   If you've previously associated a Google+ Page with your ads, you're shown a drop-down list of previously used Google+ Pages. Select the one you'd like to associate with this campaign, or select Create New Extension instead.

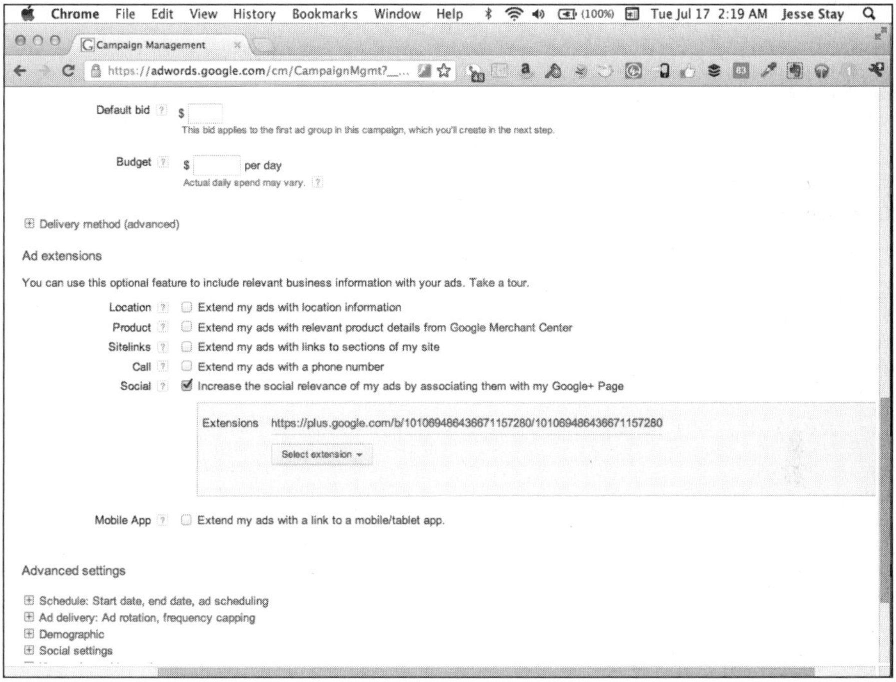

Figure 10-4: Increasing the social relevance by adding a Google+ Page to your campaign.

5. **Go to your Google+ Page; copy the URL for the page.**

   To find your Google+ Page, you can either search for it, or click your name on plus.google.com and select your Google+ Page from the drop-down list. Then copy the URL it brings you to — this will be the URL of the page's profile (the Posts or Home URL should also work, though). Paste the URL to your Google+ Page into the text field, right where it prompts you to put it.

6. **Click Save and Continue.**

   This will take you to a page where you can start configuring what your ad looks like.

7. **On the following page, fill out the form to customize your ad's appearance; select keywords if appropriate; and then click Save Ad Group.**

   Fill out this form to the best of your ability, and make sure you Like what's there. Let Google recommend a few keywords, or choose your own, one per line. (I made the mistake of using commas to separate my keywords and got an error message.)

   After you click Save Ad Group, your ad is submitted for approval and will start showing up on Google search results or on the websites you configured.

This procedure may change over time. Don't forget to refer to this book's Google Group at `http://stay.am/gplusmarketinggroup` if you have questions.

Linking your Google+ Page to your ads

Associating a Google+ Page is a great way to bring more likes and get more people following your brand's presence on Google+. By adding a Google+ Page to your ad, you are enabling all +1s on that ad to also +1 your Google+ Page. In addition — and importantly — any existing +1s you have on your Google+ Page are added automatically to your ad. (Figure 10-5 shows where to find the +1s on your Google+ Page.) As a result, people who see the ad will see that their friends have +1'd the ad as well. (If the ad is related and connected to a Google+ Page, it will reflect the Google+ Page that they +1'd.)

Linking your website with your Google+ Page brings the benefit of associating a Google+ Page to your ad. The best way to do this is with a Google+ Badge. When you have a website associated with your ad, and people click it, they'll see the Google+ Badge and will be able to circle and +1 your page right from your own website. Then, because every +1 on your ad equates to a +1 on your Google+ Page, and because that Google+ Page has been linked to your website, your website also gets a +1 — improving the chances of your website appearing in Google search results. This cumulative effect is how social ads use social touch points to influence the Google.com search ranking for your website. You can do so to best advantage by associating a Google+ Page with your ads.

In the previous section on creating Google+ social ads I show you how to do this in detail. To summarize, just select Increase the Social Relevance of My Ads By Associating Them with My Google+ Page and insert your Google+ Page URL in the field provided.

Figure 10-5:
You can find the +1s for your Google+ Page below the profile picture of your page's Profile section.

Linking your Google+ Page to your website

Once you've linked your ad to your Google+ Page, you should really consider also linking your Google+ Page to your website. You can do this through a small snippet of code Google gives you or a Google+ Badge for your Google+ Page that you can put anywhere on your website.

To link with code (which just tells Google+ that the Google+ Page is owned by your website), follow these instructions:

1. **Log in as your Google+ Page by clicking your name in the upper-right of plus.google.com and selecting your Google+ Page from the drop-down list.**

   At this point you should be able to post as your Google+ Page, and you'll be on the news feed for your page.

2. **Go to your Profile section for your page via the links on the left.**

   This will take you to the profile page for your Google+ Page.

3. **Select the Edit Profile button in the upper-right (or somewhere at the top, depending on your screen resolution).**

   Now you'll be in edit mode for your profile.

4. **Make sure you've entered your website in your page's profile, and click the Link Website button (see Figure 10-6).**

   To add a website, just click the website field for your page's profile, and you'll be able to add a link for your website. The Link Website button is on the right and will initiate a dialog on top of the page that gives you a code snippet you can copy and paste into your website (see Figure 10-7).

5. **Copy and paste the code where you want it to go in the HTML for your website.**

   By default this shows up as an <a> tag that you can paste as a link anywhere on your website. If you don't want this visible to visitors, just interchange the a with link so it's a <link> tag instead of an <a> tag, and leave all the other attributes there. You can then place it in your website's <head> section where the average visitor won't see it.

After you follow the steps just given and associate your website with your Google+ Page, the page is eligible to have a verified check mark appear next to its name. That check mark signifies that Google has verified your Google+ Page as being owned by the website it represents (see Figure 10-8). This technique is highly recommended if you want your visitors on Google+ to know for sure it's run by the company it represents. When you're eligible for this status, work with a Google account rep to place the actual check mark next to your page name. This feature is usually only available to people with large ad accounts, so if that's not you, you're out of luck for now.

Figure 10-6:
The Link
Website
button
appears
next to your
website link
under Edit
Profile.

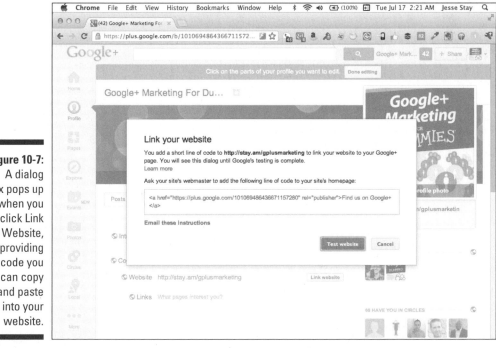

Figure 10-7:
A dialog
box pops up
when you
click Link
Website,
providing
code you
can copy
and paste
into your
website.

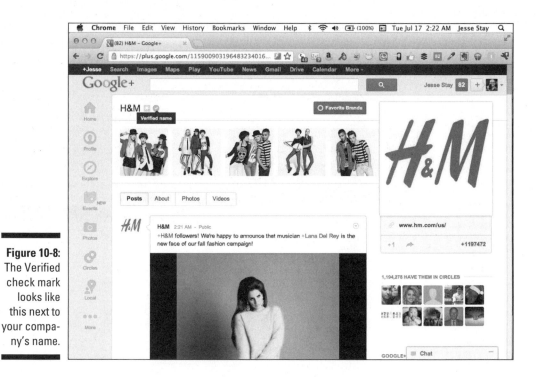

Figure 10-8:
The Verified
check mark
looks like
this next to
your compa-
ny's name.

My personal recommendation is that if you can choose the Google+ Badge, as opposed to the link to your Google+ Page, do it so that people can circle your Google+ Page directly from your website and know that it's there. In either circumstance, you still need to do the previous steps — but setting up the Badge does it for you. To set up your Google+ Badge, these steps should get you going:

1. **Go to** `https://developers.google.com/+/plugins/badge`.

   On this page, you see a form you can fill out to get the HTML code you need to paste into your website (see Figure 10-9).

2. **Select the Google+ Page you want to associate your website with in the drop-down list on the form.**

3. **Configure the design of your Badge.**

   As I write this, you have the option of choosing an icon, a small Badge, or the standard-size Badge. Select each option to get a preview of what it looks like; then select the one that fits your website best. If you want, you can dive into the Advanced Options below the form, but by default you should have everything you need here.

4. Copy the code and paste it into your website HTML.

When the form's filled out, copy all the HTML that's in the box on the right and paste it where you want the Badge to go on your website. The result is a Google+ Badge that you can integrate well with the design of your site.

Figure 10-9:
The form
you fill out
to get your
Badge code
looks like
this.

Linking between your Google+ Page and your website

Linking your Google+ Page to your website and your website to your Google+ Page will help your ranking in Google.com search results. However, it has several other benefits as well. Here are my favorites:

✔ **People are able to know that it is your Google+ Page.** They look at your website and see that you endorse the fact that you have a Google+ Page; linking the two also puts a little Verified check mark next to your Google+ Page's name. This check mark appears next to the name everywhere your Google+ Page appears throughout the Google experience.

✔ **Direct Connect makes your site more prominent in the Google search recommendations.** Direct Connect is a relatively unknown feature of Google+ that causes recommendations for Google+ Pages to show up when you type a plus sign (+) followed by a search term in the Google.com search box. The only way to get this feature to work is to link your website and your Google+ Page. Google is gradually adding sites that do this to their list of Direct Connect–enabled Google+ Pages.

✔ **Your Google+ Page is more likely to appear with the latest posts that you have posted to the page and more in the sidebar of search results (see Figure 10-10 for H&M's example).** For select Google+ Pages, depending on the number of followers and the relevancy of the search results and social endorsements, you may see a dedicated section in the sidebar of Google.com search results just for the related Google+ Page. These results usually include a link to the page, information about the page, as well as the latest posts from that page — bringing more attention to your Google+ Page and, in return, a larger audience.

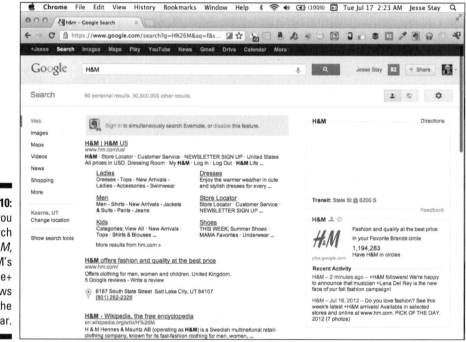

Figure 10-10: When you search for *H&M*, H&M's Google+ Page shows up in the sidebar.

Creating an Effective Google+ Ad Campaign Strategy

Let's talk strategy. How can you leverage Google social ads to be most effective and take advantage of the social extension you added? Adding +1 buttons and letting people see their friends in the ad campaigns you create is a strong start. All these tools should be in your overall campaign strategy. Read on to find out how you can maximize the benefits.

Using ads to engage your viewers

The first step to building a good strategy for your Google social ads is to think about engagement. How are you going to engage those who see your ads, and how are you going to entice them to click through and end up at your website? What is your purpose — are you looking for more purchases of a particular product? Do you want more fans of your Google+ Page? Or maybe you just want a person to refer more friends to your brand or your product's landing page.

Figure out the answers to those questions, and they can help you figure out how to build your ad. Here are my favorites:

- ✔ **Use your ad to tell your viewers what you want them to do.** As with a typical post on Google+, be sure you use a call to action to tell your viewers what you want them to do with your ad. If you want them to click it and buy something, try to get that message through. If you want them to just +1 the ad, use text that calls for a positive response (such as "+1 if you like chocolate").

  For display ads, find images and videos that reflect similar messaging. You'll be surprised to find that your audience doesn't necessarily know what you want them to do when they see your ad. Sometimes, just a little nudge can push them in the right direction.

- ✔ **Recognize that your fans are now seeing your Google+ Page with your ad.** Because your ad has a +1 button attached to it by default, and you know you benefit by having people click that +1 button, entice those who see the ad to click the button. +1 buttons don't cost anything when people click them. (Only the ads themselves cost money when people click.) They increase the +1s for your Google+ Page and website — and the additional endorsements make your ad even more interesting. Encourage people to click that +1 button.

✔ **Recognize that your fans are now seeing their friends with your ad.**
As with the +1 button, if a person's friends have clicked +1 on a particular Google+ Page that's associated with your ad, their names or profile images will show up with that ad. Maybe some text along the lines of "See, your friends want you to click" could help your campaign.

Thinking socially with ads

This is my bread and butter. How can you now turn your ad campaigns into social experiences in which your visitors are continuing what they just saw on the ad? By "thinking socially," as I call it, you can integrate the Google+ experience into your own website, continuing an experience that integrates the list of friends they saw in your ad. Here are my favorite tips:

✔ **Integrate a Google+ login button.** The technical nuts and bolts of this process are beyond the scope of this book, but point your developer to `https://developers.google.com/+/history/#authorizing_the_user` to find out how to integrate a Sign In with Google+ login button that authorizes the user and gets the information you need to start building a social experience (see Figure 10-11).

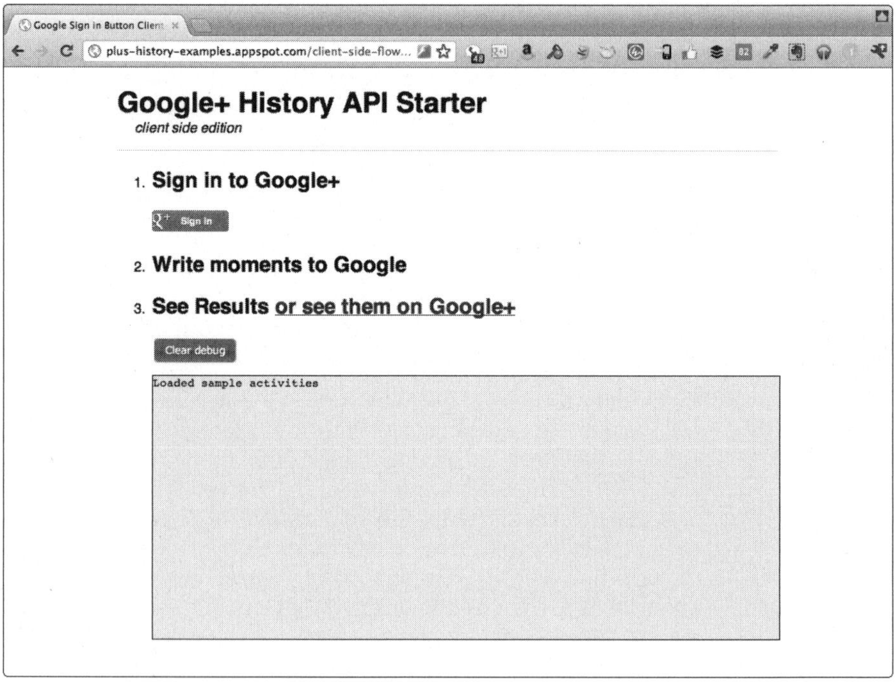

Figure 10-11:
The Sign
In with
Google+
button looks
like this.

When a user is authorized, you can pull information from his or her Google+ profile and start to find things such as people circled and posts made, provided the user has given you permission to do so. You can also automatically start publishing to a pre-established queue (named History) that users can select to publish to their circles. As I write this chapter, the History feature is available only to developers, so you may not see it immediately without developing an app.

✔ **Find the logged-in person's friends, and determine which of them have +1'd or circled your page.**

(a) After the users are logged in, you can continue the experience they just saw in the ad by detecting who they've circled; you do so by making calls with the developer API, or Application Programming Interface. (Again, you'll likely want to bring in a developer for this step.) Then go through the people who have circled or +1'd your Google+ Page and determine whether any of the people *they* circled have also interacted with your Google+ Page.

(b) As soon as you know who has circled whom, you can start to build social experiences out of that information. Entice those folks to +1 or circle your page through a Google+ Page Badge as a way to join their friends who have done so. Help them feel that they are not alone in the process of purchase or of conversion from visitor to customer.

✔ **Determine which of those friends purchased your products, or converted to a sale or within your business goals.** Among your authenticated visitors' friends, look to see who has purchased products or (if it's not a purchase) has completed the conversion process. Use that list to entice users to do the same. Show a list of their friends who have purchased products. Or show the products purchased by their friends. Maybe you don't show which friends purchased which products, but just let them know that some of their friends purchased a particular product. Seeing their friends' names and images in Google social ads makes them want to follow suit.

✔ **Entice visitors of your website to share with their friends.** When your visitors have completed what you want them to do, entice them to share that fact with their friends. You can do so in a couple of ways:

• You can encourage them to click a +1 button or Share button (found at `https://developers.google.com/+/plugins`).

• You can automatically push items to a special queue called History that Google has set up. History is not yet available to the general public, so you may not see it. However, developers can start testing it. It's still in testing mode, so I suggest seeing what your developer can do with it, because it will likely evolve by the time you read this chapter. Depending on its state, your visitors can choose which items they want to share with their circles.

In contrast to how Facebook handles sharing, the Google+ team has developed a non-automated approach. They don't want developers to be able to specify the automatic sharing of posts to Google+; the idea is to prevent spamming. Google+ History, a specialized queue (presently in testing, but it should be live when you read this), gives users a way to selectively approve the items that apps offer for them to share with their friends. Users can go in, select posts from your website, and select the circles they want to see those posts. This way, nothing ever goes out accidentally to the wrong friends.

Chapter 11

Building Relationships Through Google CRM

. . . .

In This Chapter

▶ Getting a handle on how Google+ integrates with CRM

▶ Figuring out where to integrate with CRM

▶ Adding Google Apps to your Google+ CRM strategy

. . . .

Customer Relationship Management, or CRM as it's usually called, can be one of your greatest tools as a marketer for making contact with customers, keeping their interest, and knowing how best to help them. If you're in sales, CRM helps you close the deal by knowing previous contact you had with each customer. If you're in customer support, CRM help you better solve customers' problems by providing a record of what's been done to address those problems.

Whatever your position, it's always helpful to know as much as you can about each customer you work with, as well as each individual you're talking to. That's where CRM comes in — and Google+ can make the process of getting to know those you interact with much easier.

Seeing Google+ As a Giant CRM Tool

Google+ is much more than just plus.google.com. Google+ is just a social layer that spans across all Google products. It helps you build relationships with your customers and those you interact with.

For openers, as you interact with individuals on Google+, you're adding data to the giant Google CRM database called Google Contacts. Every time you circle someone on Google+, you add that person to Google Contacts. This means every interaction you have with that individual through Google products will only improve the data you have on that individual.

Building and tracking relationships through Google+, Google Contacts, and Gmail

The best way to illustrate how Google+ works as a CRM tool is to show you the process of data being added to a contact as you interact with the same person on each Google product. Here's what it looks like:

1. You post something on your Google+ page, and a random customer — call him Joe — comments on your post, saying he has a problem with your product.

2. You circle Joe with your personal Google+ account and give him an e-mail address where he can contact you.

3. Once Joe is circled, he appears in your Google Contacts under Circles, with the circle you added him to. Any information he has chosen to share publicly will also appear in this contact, which may already include an e-mail address or phone number.

4. Joe e-mails you, and you receive his e-mail in Gmail. Next to the e-mail you see a Google+ contact for him, along with the option to circle him.

   If you chose not to circle him earlier on, circling him now adds him to your contacts, complete with the e-mail address he just used to e-mail you.

5. If his e-mail wasn't listed in his Google profile, and you circled him in Gmail, he'll now have two contacts — one with the e-mail and one without. You can merge the two records in Contacts, so that now Joe's record in Google Contacts has an e-mail address associated with his Google+ profile.

6. Let's say you decide to schedule a phone call to Joe. You've set up a phone number in Google Voice; you give him that number. You've set it up so that people in your "customers" circle, which he's in, are sent to a custom message in your Google Voice voicemail. You get the message about the problem, and realize it's from Joe.

7. To call Joe, you pick up your Android phone, take the number from Google Voice, and choose to add it to your contacts — but since Joe is already in your contacts (which integrate seamlessly with Android through Google Voice), you opt to add him to your existing Google+ contact. At this point, that same record for his Google+ profile has an e-mail address *and* phone number associated with it. You decide to add him to a new circle of people you've previously talked to in person, so you can recognize him the next time you see him online.

8. When Joe's problem is resolved, you move on and continue posting on your Google+ page. Joe comments again. You click his Google+ profile and see immediately that he's been added to your "previously contacted" circle, and you also have an e-mail and phone number associated with his contact record in Google. You send him an e-mail thanking him for his comment and asking how his previous problem worked out. Now you have a happy customer — and a solid relationship.

In this scenario, I used a customer-service example to show how Google+ can be used for CRM, but you can also apply it readily to networking, sales, or other business needs. Using Google+, you can track your relationships as you build them — throughout each customer's Google experience.

Learning the different pieces of Google+ CRM

To really understand Google+ CRM, consider all the places Google+ integrates a user's experience of Google itself. The power of Google+ is in all the touch points throughout the entire Google experience — and in how they all interact with each other — letting your Google+ profile follow you wherever you go.

There are literally hundreds of touch points for Google products integrating with the Google+ profile. Here's a closer look at the most important . . . .

The Google+ profile itself

This is really the center of the entire Google+ CRM experience. As you edit your Google+ profile you can choose how you want the information on your profile to appear to people who circle you — which includes what will appear in Google Contacts for those people. If you set this to Public, everyone who circles you will see the information you make public. If you set it so only certain circles can see it, only those in your circles will see it in their Google Contacts.

On the About page of each profile you visit, if that individual is already in your contacts, you can see what you have on that individual in your contacts (see Figure 11-1). If there are notes attached, you'll see them here. You can stay up to date in each customer relationship by developing a simple habit: going to the profile's About page and looking at the Google Contacts information farther down the page (if it's available).

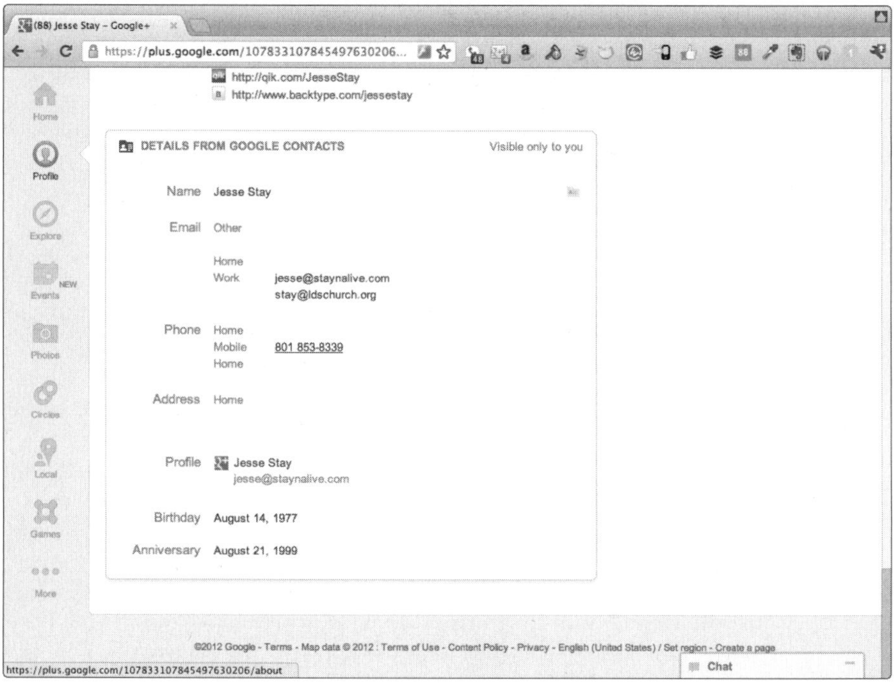

Figure 11-1:
Each profile on Google+ will show whether someone is in your contacts, and (if so) what information you have on that individual.

Gmail

As you e-mail and interact with people in Gmail, they're added to your Google Contacts automatically whenever you send them e-mail. Every time you receive an e-mail from someone who has associated an e-mail address with his or her Google+ account, you'll see that Google+ account appear to the right of the message. Then you can circle the person or click the name to view the Google+ profile (see Figure 11-2). This gives you additional opportunities to categorize those you communicate with for future reference, as well as learn more about them as you interact with them.

If, say, Joanne's e-mail address isn't associated with a Google+ profile, you can still add her e-mail address to a circle. If she ever adds the address to her Google+ profile, the address you circled becomes a real Google+ profile automatically. In the meantime, you can still share messages from Google+ with her through the e-mail address you circled.

The Google+ record in the right column of Gmail will also show you her latest posts on Google+. If you select the Show Details link below her name and info, you can see all recent conversations you've had with her on Gmail itself (see Figure 11-3). Each record, if available, shows the Google+ profile picture and any additional data made available.

Figure 11-2:
You can add each contact made in Gmail to your circles, even if your contacts haven't yet added their e-mail addresses to their Google+ profiles.

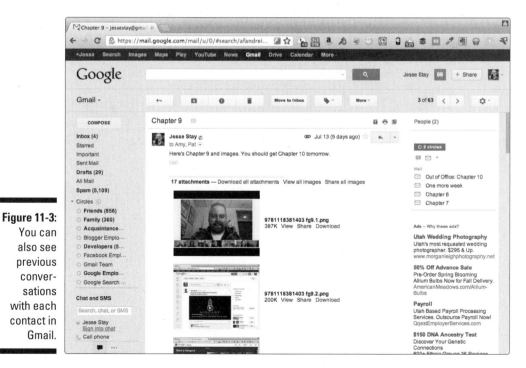

Figure 11-3:
You can also see previous conversations with each contact in Gmail.

Google+ notifications work seamlessly with Gmail. You can respond, +1, and share all from within Gmail (see Figure 11-4). Posts update in real time, showing new comments right inside Gmail. I send all my notifications on Google+ to e-mail for this reason: Doing so gives me a searchable database of all my conversations with different individuals that I can reference later if I ever need more data about someone I've interacted with.

TIP

If people are not added to your contacts automatically when you send them e-mail, be sure to select When I Send a Message to a New Person, Add Them to Other Contacts So That I Can Auto-Complete to Them Next Time under your Gmail settings on the main General tab (toward the bottom of the page).

TIP

Opting to receive your notifications as e-mail (not just in the little red notification box in the Google "sandbar" at the top) gives you a searchable database of all your conversations in the future. If you come across an individual and want to know what conversations you've had with that individual, just search for his or her name. Gmail also shows you other threads and conversations you've had with this person if you click Show Details in the little Google+ box in the upper-right column of Gmail next to an e-mail from that person.

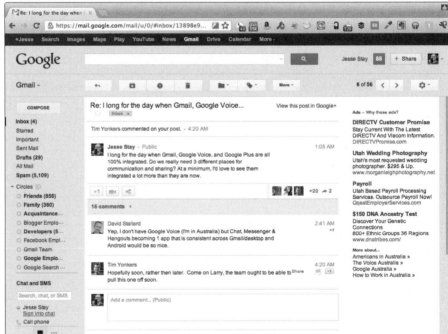

Figure 11-4: You can respond to conversations right inside Gmail; all are indexed for you to search later.

Google Contacts

Besides the Google+ profile, Google Contacts serves as a place to store all your relationships. With each Google contact you can leave notes, adding information as you get it. As I mentioned, this data also shows up on the individual's Google+ profile if you've associated the two.

Inside Google Contacts, you'll also see associated Google+ profile for the listed individuals (see Figure 11-5). These profiles can provide additional information, such as where they work or where they've previously worked, intros they've provided about themselves, and other places they've lived.

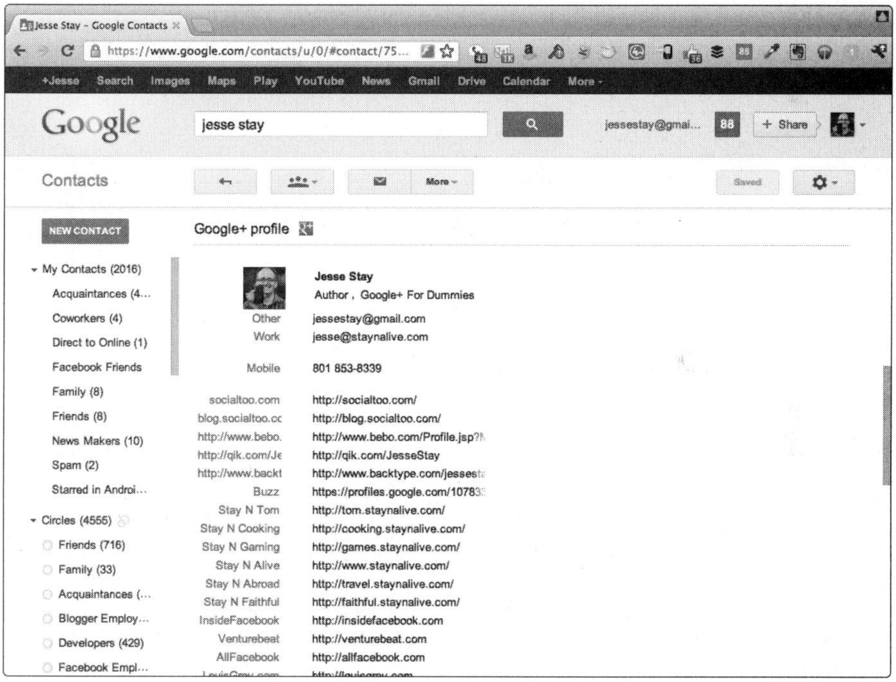

Figure 11-5:
Each Google Contact will show the associated Google+ profile if there is one available for that individual.

As you have similar names but different contact info, and you begin to discover that they're the same name, you can merge those Google contacts into one contact for one individual. This combines even more information and puts all that data alongside the person's Google profile.

Now, everywhere you see that individual's Google profile on the web, you can click it and have access to a plethora of information about the individual, as well as to any notes you've taken about that relationship. Go back to Gmail and you can also see all your conversations with the individual.

Access Google Contacts at `http://contacts.google.com` or by clicking anyone's name in Gmail or Google Voice.

Google Voice.

Many of the tips I gave for Gmail can also apply to Google Voice. Google Voice (`http://voice.google.com`) is the "switchboard" for determining how calls get routed and what numbers they should go through. Google Voice also integrates with both Google Contacts and Google+.

If someone in a particular Google+ circle calls you on Google Voice, you can select which voice message to provide in reply (see Figure 11-6). You can also choose whether you want your phones to even ring before switching the incoming call to voicemail. This feature is an opportunity to give your customers the information you want them to have, whenever they call — whether or not you're in — so they don't give up on trying to contact you.

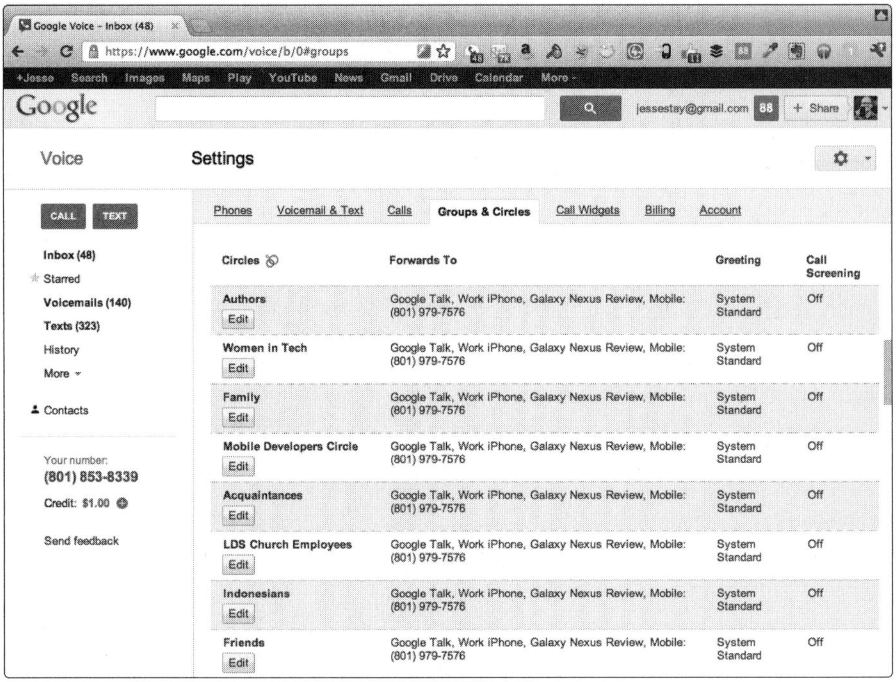

Figure 11-6:
Selecting what voice-mail to ring for certain circles allows you to ensure that each person gets an appropriate message.

Because Google Voice integrates with Google Contacts, you can also get Google profile data about each person calling you. Although Google has not yet integrated the CRM functionality of Gmail with Google Voice, you can click through to any name and see the caller's record in Google Contacts. Having that additional information about the caller and how you've interacted with him or her can help make the call useful on both ends.

As you find people in Google+, check Google Voice for previous voicemails, calls, or text messages from each individual you circle. You can record calls, and Google Voice also transcribes text messages and voicemails for future reference (I never delete these; that way I can search them later). You may also want to send these transcriptions to your e-mail so that you can have one central place to search whenever you want to look up information on an individual.

Android

Using an Android device with Google+ provides even more CRM opportunities. For instance, I can search for any name by just typing or saying it into the universal search box in Android. If multiple names pop up, I can go through, edit the name right on the device, and even choose to merge fields. Android also shows the Google+ profile and all other contacts for that particular name; you can merge that profile with all similar contacts.

If you've given Android your Google account credentials, it links your Android contacts automatically with your Google Contacts. Then editing a contact on Android also edits the same contact automatically on Google Contacts. Under this arrangement, using Android gives you automatic access to all the contact data you've already stored on Google+, including profiles — a CRM treasure trove.

Android also integrates seamlessly with Google Voice; after you install the Google Voice app and go through its setup, you can receive calls straight from your Google Voice number, receive voicemails, and call your callers back, all without revealing the original number of your Android device. (If you have an iPhone instead, check out the accompanying sidebar.)

"What if I have an iPhone?"

Although the Google Voice app isn't nearly as integrated with iOS as it is with Android, you can install it on your iPhone and still get some (limited) functionality tied to Google Contacts.

In fact, I usually replace the phone app on my iPhone with the Google Voice app in the main dock at the bottom of the screen.

There really are some huge advantages to using Android when you're trying to get the "fully integrated experience" from Google. If you're looking for the best integrated experience for Android, I recommend the latest Nexus products. Currently, it's the Galaxy Nexus by Samsung, which Google intended as the flagship product for determining what the Google experience is like on a mobile phone. Most other phones alter the experience quite a bit. If you're a fan and user of Google products, you'll usually be satisfied by going the Nexus route. To see what phones are available, go to `http://www.google.com/nexus/#/`.

Google Chat

Google Chat spans both Google+ and Gmail as way to switch quickly from e-mail to real-time chats with the people you're interacting with. You can chat over a video stream or via text, getting quickly in touch with someone you see either on Google+ or on Gmail if you (or your customer) should ever need a quick answer.

In addition, you can choose to save your chat histories, which then become accessible in Gmail. To make the appropriate Gmail settings, select Chat⇨Save Chat History (as shown in Figure 11-7) and configure any other options as needed. Saving your chat histories gives you a handy resource, as does pushing all your notifications to Gmail (described earlier in this chapter): Gmail becomes an even richer storehouse of data about your contacts.

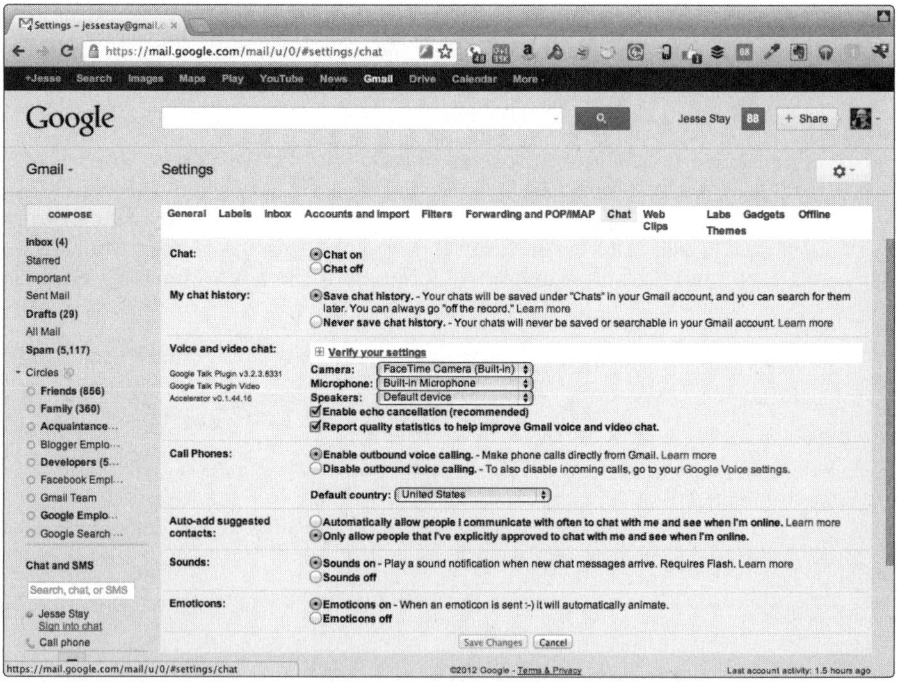

Figure 11-7: Setting Google Chat to save each chat to history in your Gmail settings.

Although Google Chat is fine for starting spontaneous conversations, not everyone is always available to chat. In addition, pinging someone to chat can come across as an interruption; use it carefully. In general, unless a chat's been agreed upon beforehand, I like to e-mail the individual first and schedule a time to chat. In general, treat a Google chat (text or video) just as you would a phone call or a meeting — schedule it in advance if you need to say any more than just a couple of things. Efficiency is courtesy here.

Google+ Events

The ultimate way to seal any online relationship is to meet in real life. Google has provided Google+ Events to encourage just that. Try to attend Google+ Events as much as you can — this is a great opportunity to HIRL (or Hangout In Real Life) with the people you're interacting with on Google+. Then, after the event, go to the Google+ Event page: Make sure you circle, and leave notes in your contacts for, each individual you met at the event (see Figure 11-8). You may also consider sending each of them an e-mail through Gmail to thank them for the opportunity to meet (adding yet another record to that contact in Gmail). Consider tagging the people you met, as well as yourself, in the photos if the Google+ Events party mode has been turned on and photos are (or were) shared. Doing so gives you a photo record of your interaction. I talk about events, party mode, and more in Chapter 1.

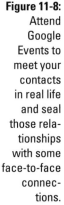

Figure 11-8: Attend Google Events to meet your contacts in real life and seal those relationships with some face-to-face connections.

Google+ Hangouts

If you can't meet in real life, consider a Hangout or two. As you join Google+ Hangouts, this is an opportunity to record interactions with each person you "hung out" with. For each person you interact with who joins the Hangout, mouse over that person's videos and names, and make sure you've added him or her to a circle. Also, be sure you leave a note about each person in your Google Contact records; remind yourself of how you met these folks. Then, after the Hangout, go send them thank-you notes in Gmail to add one more record of your interactions with them to your contact information.

Working with Google Contacts — adding, editing, and merging your contacts

Google Contacts (accessible through `http://contacts.google.com`), along with the Google profile, are really the heart of the Google+ CRM experience. Understanding how these work and how you can integrate each of these into every experience on Google is important. Google Contacts is really the database for every contact you make on Google+, so you should understand how to use it.

Be sure to master these three simple tasks when working with Google Contacts: creating contacts, editing contacts, and merging contacts.

When you can do those three things easily, you can completely manage your Google Contact experience in every product that utilizes Google Contacts.

Creating a contact

There are several ways to create a contact in Google. Contacts are created automatically when you send e-mail in Gmail (and have the appropriate settings set up to do so). You can add them through Google Voice or Gmail and other Google products when you see an e-mail address or phone number that isn't yet in your contacts (this is usually accompanied by an Add to Contacts link next to the number or e-mail address). Or you can go to `contacts.google.com` and create one from scratch there.

To create a contact from scratch (this applies in various ways to the other methods mentioned, too), follow these steps:

1. **Go to** `contacts.google.com`**.**

   A list of all your contacts appears. Play around and learn what's available here.

2. **Click the big red New Contact button.**

   As I write this, the button appears in the upper-left part of Google Contacts. That may change in the future as Google changes its interface.

3. **Add all the information you can.**

   On the page that follows, you can enter all the information you may have about your new contact, such as a profile image, e-mail address, phone number, address, or notes about meetings.

4. **Click Save Now.**

   Your contacts are saved automatically as you add information, but you can also explicitly click the Save Now button to save your information at any time. Either way, your contact is saved and in your database.

If you add just one piece of information that someone already has in his or her public Google+ profile, the other blanks in your contact information on that person fill in automatically (see Figure 11-9). To try out this feature, enter **Jesse Stay** as the name and then add `jesse@staynalive.com` as the e-mail address. Immediately, my Google+ profile picture and other public information will be added to your contact without your having to add anything else. Save the contact, and you've got me in your contacts for speaking engagements and future consulting opportunities.

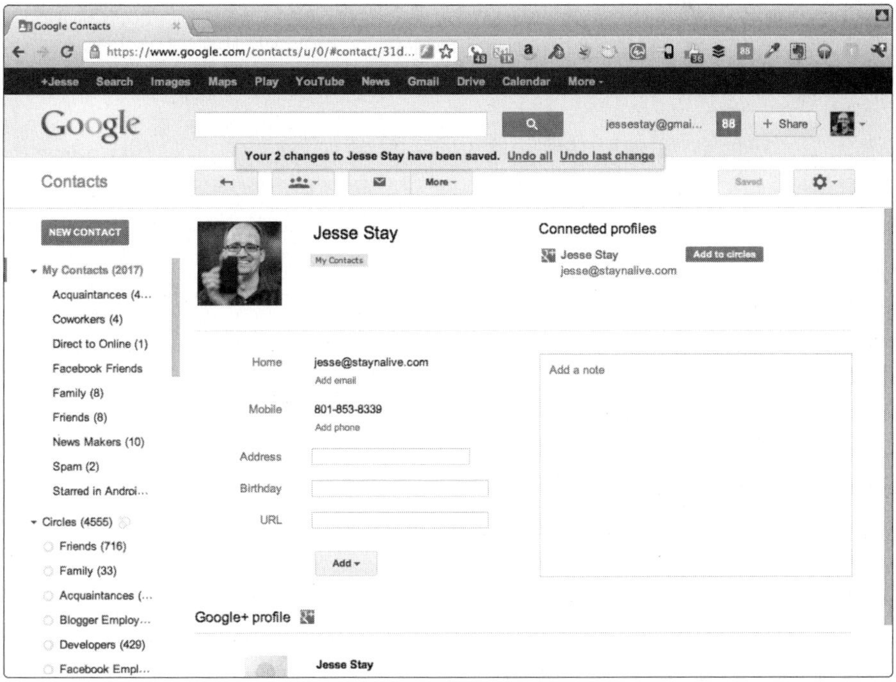

Figure 11-9: Adding the e-mail address of any Google profile adds public information from that person's profile to your contact.

Editing a contact

Now that you've created a contact, it's good to learn how to edit a contact in Google Contacts. This is even easier. Here's how:

1. **Search for any contact.**

   You can either search or go through them one by one from `contacts.google.com`.

2. **Click the contact.**

   Clicking the contact should open up that contact's details.

3. **Click any area you want to edit.**

   There are no Edit buttons on this page. Just click where you want to edit.

   You can't edit the stuff under the Google profile information section. The individual who owns that profile is the only one that can edit that section (by editing his or her Google profile).

4. **Change the field you want to edit.**

   Just type — it's that simple. Press Enter when you're done, if you like.

5. **Click Save Now.**

   As with creating a contact entry, editing a contact entry will automatically save your changes. If, for some reason, it doesn't, you can also click the Save Now button. (If the entry is already saved, the button will say *Saved* and won't be clickable.)

Merging contacts

Merging contacts is the third of the three major tasks you need to know how to do in Google Contacts to be an expert.

You can let Google automatically merge duplicate contacts by clicking the More drop-down list in Google Contacts and selecting Find and Merge Duplicates (see Figure 11-10). However, I've found letting Google do this automatically causes too many problems for my liking; I try to do it manually as much as possible.

Here's how you merge more than one contact:

1. **Check the check box next to more than one contact you would like to merge.**

As you're searching for names, and you see more than one of the same name (or similar names), check the box next to each one you think is the same.

2. **Click the More drop-down arrow and select Merge Contacts.**

You're taken to the Merged Contacts page. Google takes all the information from all the contacts you chose and combines them into one large profile.

3. **Edit the merged contact to look the way you want it to be.**

There will likely be old — or wrong — information that was stored incorrectly in the other duplicate contacts here, so delete anything that's wrong, and make sure the contact is clean. Your changes will be saved automatically. Now you should have just one contact that will always link to the correct Google+ profile when you're in various Google products.

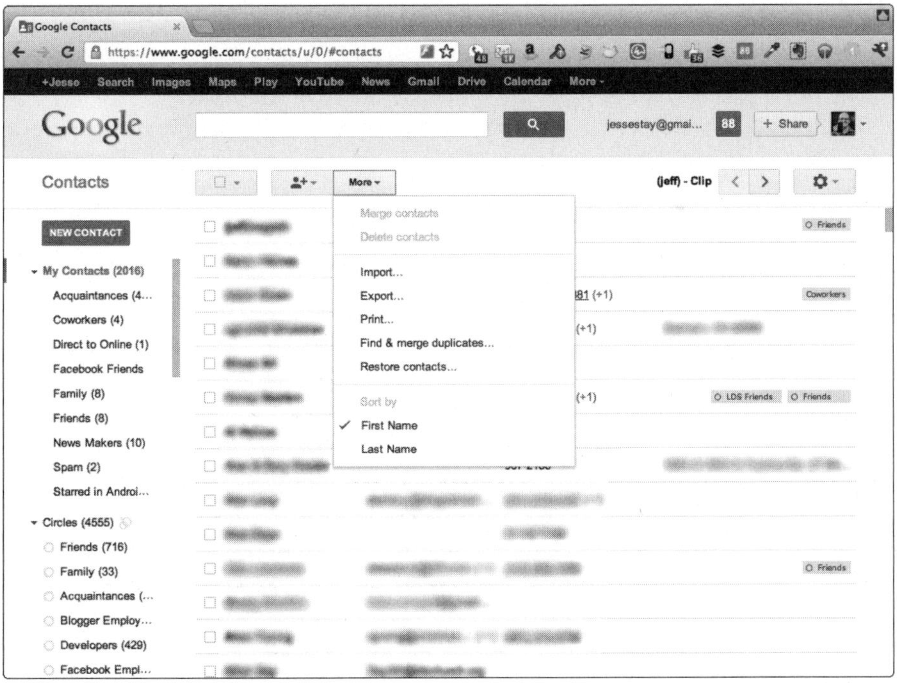

Figure 11-10: Clicking the More option allows you to select the Find and Merge Duplicates option if you want to automate the process.

Integrating Your CRM Strategy into Google Apps Using Google+

It's worth recalling that Google+ has potentially hundreds of integration points throughout Google products. Here's a nice one for the marketer: Google has enabled Google+ to work within Google Apps.

Google+ for Google Apps presents some unique opportunities for your business to integrate Google+ into your own company's network. Perhaps the most notable feature of Google+ for Google Apps is that you can target messages to just your domain — in this way only those in your Google Apps domain can see your message. This is useful for when you want to have communication inside your own company that uses a common platform.

The advantage to using Google+ over, say, Yammer (which offers similar capabilities) is that Google+ for Google Apps offers you these options:

- ✔ You can target messages to just your company employees (by targeting just the domain).
- ✔ You can make those messages visible to people outside your company as well.

These capabilities provide some unique opportunities for bringing outside folks — especially customers — into internal conversations. I detail those advantages in the rest of this chapter.

Google Apps

Google Apps allows businesses, educational institutions, and nonprofit organizations to use the various Google products under their own domain. So instead of going to Gmail.com to get your e-mail, you can go to yourdomain.com and you'll be presented with an interface just like Gmail, but using your company's own domain.

Instead of `yourusername@gmail.com`, you can now have `yourusername@yourdomainname.com`. Google has also extended this to Google+, as I explain in this section, allowing you to send messages to just those other people who are using your Google Apps domain.

Using Google+ for Google Apps Effectively

For a close look at how Google+ for Google Apps works, follow these steps:

1. **Go to** `http://plus.google.com` **and log in with your Google Apps e-mail and password.**

   If you're logged in to your traditional Google account, log out or switch accounts.

   You end up on a news feed just like the one for your traditional Google account (you may need to configure this feed if it's new). You should see updates from other employees under your domain by default, but you can also find people outside your network and circle them; then you'll start seeing them here as well.

2. **Make your first post.**

   To do so, click the post box just as you would for a normal Google+ post. Enter the text for your post, and (as you would for a normal Google+ account) select a circle or two in which you want your post published.

   The difference here is that now you'll see your company domain in the drop-down list of circles (see Figure 11-11).

   • Select this domain, and only those other people using your Google Apps domain can see your updates.

   • Add other circles, and others can see your update.

3. **Click Share to publish your post to your intended audience.**

Turning virtual connections into real-life events

The goal of everything you do on Google+ should be to make lesser-known contacts into better-known contacts. Face-to-face interaction is the epitome of this type of strategy.

Figure 11-11:
Selecting
your domain
from the
circles
drop-down
list.

When you're dealing with communications inside your company (as you would for Google+) for Google Apps, face-to-face interaction is still the goal, especially if you're in a large organization where it's hard to get to know everyone. Some companies can get mired in red tape, departmental divisions, and other bureaucratic barriers. Opening communication across departments and throughout the company can improve teamwork, efficiency, and business processes. Assuming your company is set up with Google Apps, you can do this online magic easily by making posts targeted to your company's domain on Google+.

Here are my favorite guidelines:

✔ **Start conversations that foster solving problems across departments.** Especially in larger organizations, departments have some difficulty talking with each other. Work can be duplicated, bogged down, or not even implemented. To unclog cooperation across departments, start conversations that get departments talking to each other. You can start with posts that target just your domain, and get employees talking and solving problems together. Any employee in the company can do this.

✔ **Use circles to organize employees.** Just as you can organize your normal Google+ friends in circles, so you can organize those in your organization into circles — and integrate them into contacts. Then the whole CRM process (everything I've shared with you in this chapter) becomes a tool for internal business communication. You can get to know the people you work with and find ways to solve their needs better.

✔ **Utilize Google+ Events to get employees sharing at company events.** Google+ Events, especially with party mode turned on, can get employees sharing information within the company. When they're attending events together, they'll find it easier to remember each other and to share memories of your event. (That's where the face-to-face-contact angle comes in.)

After the event, make sure all the people you interacted with are in your Contacts and you've left notes to yourself in Google Contacts to ensure that you remember how you contacted them.

✔ **Organize regular Google+ Hangouts to encourage employees to get to know each other and solve problems together.** As with online Hangouts with your regular Google+ friends, you can organize Hangouts, at first allowing only those in your domain to join (you can take over the world a little later on). Hanging out is a handy way to get to know your fellow employees, share information about what you're working on, and even collaborate and work together on projects, especially if you work remotely . Track these interactions and use this as an opportunity to build relationships among your coworkers.

Turning internal conversations into external sales

Ultimately, your conversations — and all you do inside your company — should be focused on the customers who buy and use your products. Google+ for Google Apps provides an effective tool for this purpose, as good as (or better than) many competing software products on the market. Here's why: You can target contacts both inside and outside your company network. The idea is to turn your internal conversations into external relationships and interactions with customers. Try these approaches:

✔ As you're discussing your company's products in your internal company domain, consider bringing in a customer or two (or many) to that conversation to get their input and feedback. Assuming there's nothing too private (or commercially sensitive) being discussed, you can solicit feedback from customers on the topics you're discussing.

- ✔ Consider using Hangouts to bring customers into the loop. A Hangout that involves up to ten people could become a remote focus group: Invite a couple of people from within your domain and a few people from outside it. Result: People inside your company have a chance to talk, face to face, with people who are interested in your brand.

- ✔ If you notice a customer with a problem on Google+, consider resharing that person's post in your internal domain. (Depending on the situation, you might consider asking the customer first.) You can even opt to include the customer in the conversation and then the entire company can work to help this one customer.

Chapter 12

Building Website Authority

I say it throughout this book, and here it comes again: Google+ is about people — which makes it a powerful tool for improving your authority and authenticity on the web. Using Google+ provides this boon for your company, for the people who build your brand, and for your brand as a market presence. This means better search rankings, more trust from your users, and a much larger audience.

In this chapter, I show you how you can build your brand's online authority using Google+ — and why that's important. My hope is that you'll be able to grow both your personal and business brand as a result, and in the end you'll have a lock on why Google+ is such a powerful platform.

Bringing Identity to Your Website Through Google+

Building *authority* on the web is, at heart, creating a reliable, trusted, widely recognized identity for yourself and your brand. For people to trust you, they have to know what your brand is, that it's real, and that it's produced and supported by the efforts of real people. Several elements of Google+, especially when used in tandem with other social networks, are critical to establishing this identity:

> ✓ **A web profile available at a trusted location:** Most social networks offer such a feature. Google+, in particular, provides a Google+ Page where you can specify such basic (but essential) brand information as its name, a company location if you have one, contact information, and a website where people can find more information. You can also include identifying photos and images to help people recognize your brand.

Because a Google+ Page exists on Google the moment you create it, people can easily find your brand's identity — and (just as easily) link to it, interact with it, and follow it from around the web. Your profile can be seen across all Google properties and can easily be added to third-party websites. The +1 buttons and Circle buttons are easily noticeable and recognizable to anyone who uses Google products.

✔ **A voice:** On Google+, you get your online voice from your Google+ Page's news feed. When people circle you, they give you an audience. At that point, you have multiple opportunities to encourage others to circle you — and to hear from you. Because you can speak directly to your customers and potential customers, you become much more identifiable — and real — to them. Having a real voice means having people to hear and recognize your voice.

✔ **A home base that you own:** This is critical in establishing your identity on the web. Don't just trust Google+ or Facebook or any other social network to identify you automatically to your customers. Many of your customers will recognize your brand and your home page more than anything else, so make sure you don't neglect those identifiers.

Throughout Part III of this book, I call this development of an online customer base "creating your fish-farm" — in effect, bringing all your fish to your farm so that you can cultivate and nourish them. Then you can reel them in for the sale much more easily. The fish on your own farm also identify with you much more easily.

✔ **A way to identify the people who make your brand:** Here's where Google+ really proves itself as an asset to your brand's identity. Sure, you can link an employee's Facebook or other profile to your website, but such isolated links can't match the boost to your brand's value and authenticity that you get by associating a Google+ profile with your content. By linking people to your content and your brand through your website — and by allowing them to interact with employees through your brand's Google+ Page — you're firming up the identity of your brand and spreading awareness of the company and its people. The result is more authority for your brand among your fans and customers.

✔ **A way to link all your brand's online assets and to demonstrate that they're all linked:** Google+ shines here. Google provides a way for you to link your website to your Google+ Page and then point your Google+ Page to your website. The two-way link leaves no doubt in the user's mind that both the page and the site are indeed your brand's identities on the web. Also, as mentioned earlier, you can link yourself, your employees, and anyone else responsible for making your brand to your website by establishing the same link to and from Google+ to your website. This connection makes your people more accessible to the customers — and the website much more closely associated with real people. Result: more authenticity for your brand. And the stronger your brand's established identity, the better your search ranking within Google search results on Google.com.

Using your Google+ Page to identify your website

Establishing your website's identity on Google+ (and on all of Google) starts when you add a website to your Google+ Page that links your customers to the website that serves as your brand's home base on the web.

To add your website to your Google+ Page, just do the following:

1. **Go to your Google+ Page, and click the Profile section.**

   To go to your Google+ Page, just click your name in the upper-right of Google+ and select your Google+ Page. Note the list of icons (as I write this, at the left of the screen); click the Profile icon to open your page's Profile section.

2. **Click the Edit Profile button at the upper-right.**

   Edit mode opens for your Google+ profile.

3. **Click Website.**

   The Website line on your profile changes to a field that you can edit, providing buttons to either Save or Cancel the changes you make to your profile (see Figure 12-1).

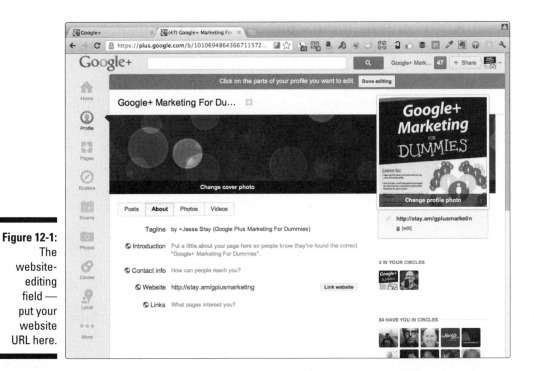

Figure 12-1: The website-editing field — put your website URL here.

4. **Type in the URL to your website.**

   Enter the main URL for the website associated with your Google+ Page.

   This URL should lead to a strong landing page, ideally with a Google+ Page Badge on it. I show you how to do that next.

5. **Click Save.**

   Your website appears on your Google+ Page, displayed prominently.

Using your website to identify your Google+ Page

To complete the process of adding authority to your website through Google+, you link your newly Badged website back to your Google+ Page. You have two basic ways to do this task, but a word to the wise: The more you do, the more of a boost you get in Google search results and in visibility across other Google properties. In the end, either approach provides a little *Verified* check mark next to your name on your Google+ Page — which tells your users that your Google+ Page is owned by the website that it displays.

So to start simple, here's the easiest way to link your website to your Google+ Page. All it does is put a link on your site that says Find Us on Google+ or a meta `<link>` tag that Google can read but doesn't show anything to your users (which I recommend against). That said, here's how to integrate your website into your Google+ Page:

1. **Click your name in the Google bar at the top of Google+, select your Google+ Page, and click the About tab to get to your page's profile.**

   The Profile section of your Google+ Page opens.

2. **Click Edit Profile.**

   The editing view opens.

3. **Click the Link Website button (see Figure 12-2 and Figure 12-3).**

   A pop-up window shows you the code you need to copy into your website (the same code shown in the next step) so that the site displays a link to your Google+ Page.

   If you don't want your users to see the text link to your Google+ Page on your website, refer to the next step. Otherwise you're done.

4. **Copy the following line of code, and paste it somewhere on your website:**

```
<a href="YOUR_URL_HERE" rel="publisher">Find us on Google+</a>
```

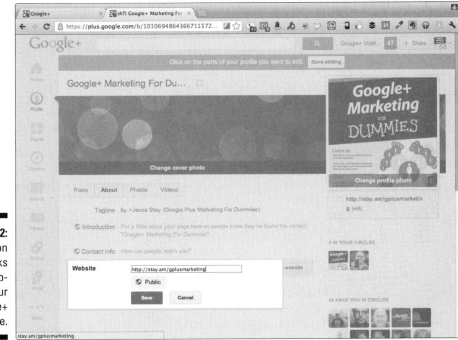

Figure 12-2:
The button
that links
your web-
site to your
Google+
Page.

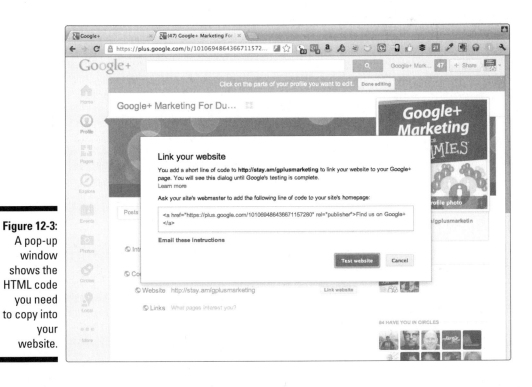

Figure 12-3:
A pop-up
window
shows the
HTML code
you need
to copy into
your
website.

Be sure you replace `YOUR_URL_HERE` with the URL of your Google+ Page. If you're keeping the text of this link onscreen for your users to see on your website (recommended), you can also replace the `Find us on Google+` text with a more enticing message specific to your brand.

From here, you can just skip the upcoming Step 5 — which I suggest you do, because you get better results by keeping the link text visible onscreen. But okay, in the interest of full disclosure, here's Step 5. . . .

5. **If you don't want the text of the link visible to your users, follow these steps:**

   a. *Make sure you can still identify your website with Google.*

      You do so by replacing `<a` with `<link` and `</a>` with `</link>` so the line of HTML reads like this:

      ```
      <link href="YOUR_URL_HERE" rel="publisher">Find us on Google+</link>
      ```

      Note that you still have to replace `YOUR_URL_HERE` with the URL of your Google+ Page so your users are taken to the right location. Skip adding an enticing message if they won't be seeing the text anyway.

   b. *Put the line somewhere in the `<head>` section of your HTML.*

      Now the link exists. Your users will never see this, but Google+ will, and it should start recognizing the link.

If you followed the most basic procedure outlined here (Steps 1 through 4), you'll need to have an ad account with a good amount of ad spend in order to get a Verified check-mark icon next to your Google+ Page's name that people will see when they visit your Google+ Page. The icon tells visitors immediately that this Google+ Page really does belong to you. Having this link should improve your ranking in `www.google.com` search results, however.

If you want to build even more trust among customers, a better identity and (in the long term) even more authority for your brand so that Google sees your website as the real deal, you'll also want to integrate a Google+ Page *Badge* for your website. The Badge is a prominent widget that makes your Google+ Page easier for visitors to find, circle, or +1 — without ever having to leave your website.

In the ideal scenario, a Google+ user should never have to leave your website to interact with Google+. Such an arrangement works out better for Google, because people will see Google+ throughout the web. It also works out better for you — your *bounce rate* (the rate of people leaving your site, and how quickly) will be a lot lower because visitors no longer need to visit Google+ specifically if they're going to interact with your site. The Google+ Page Badge is convenient for both the site owner and the customer.

Setting up your Google+ Page Badge is also fairly simple and straightforward. Here's how you set it up:

1. **Go to** `https://developers.google.com/+/plugins/badge`.

    Here you're presented with a form to fill out that also enables you to get HTML code to paste into your website (see Figure 12-4). Every step of the way, you're presented with a preview on the right, showing you what your configured form options will produce on your.

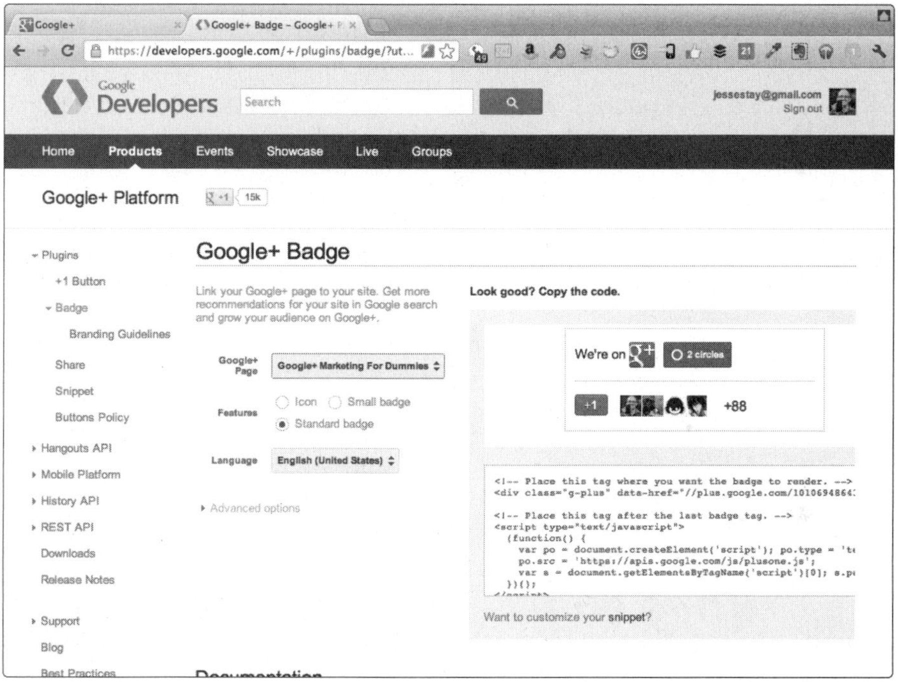

Figure 12-4: The form you fill out to get your Google+ Page Badge code looks like this.

2. **Select your Google+ Page from the drop-down list.**

    Select the Google+ Page to which you want to link this Badge on your website. You may only have one option here if you have only one Google+ Page — and that's okay. (If you're like me, you have multiple Google+ Pages to choose among.)

3. **Select the type of Badge you want.**

    You can choose Icon, Small Badge, and the default Standard Badge. Click through each choice to see how it looks in the preview; you may like one better than the others. I like my Google+ Badge to have the greatest visibility and the most screen real estate possible, so I stick with the default Standard Badge.

4. **Choose your language.**

   In general, you can leave this choice at the default — but if your website is in a specific language, specify the language here so your Google+ Badge also appears in that language.

5. **Look over any advanced options.**

   Adjust the width, the color theme, or any other advanced options, if necessary. If everything here makes sense to you as is, that's okay — you can usually leave the defaults in place. Defer to a developer if you need any help configuring this section.

6. **Copy and paste.**

   When you've filled out the form, just copy and paste the HTML code, and place it where you want your Page Badge to go. Your Page Badge code should appear onscreen under the preview at the right of your form, as shown in Figure 12-4.

Building Authority Along with Identity

When you've established your presence on Google+, start finding ways to bring Google+ over to your "fish-farm" via features like the Google+ Badges mentioned in the previous section. Identifying not only your brand, but also the *people* behind your brand, enhances the natural authority of the brand and establishes that you are an authoritative source, made up of real people, behind the content you produce or the products you sell.

Using brand identity on your website

Building authority on the web begins with how you use your brand's identity on your website. Here are some suggested approaches:

✔ **Making the most of the Google+ Page Badge:** I cover the details of the Badge in the previous section, but here's the method behind the madness: Your first step in identifying yourself on your website is to link your website to your Google+ Page. There's no better way to do so than through a simple Badge you place on your website to show your visitors more about what or who your brand is. The more people +1 and circle your brand because of your Badge, the greater the online authority you build. The idea is to get to the point at which Google can trust the source of information your website provides.

✔ **Linking authors of content to their actual Google+ profiles:** A more people-focused approach always makes Google+ a much more successful tool for you and your business. That's why I strongly suggest bringing people into the design of your website as a more active presence. With Google+, the best way to do so is to make the authors of your content more visible and accessible in the design. Show off your employees and the people behind your visitors' online experience of your brand. Then you can use (for example) Author tags to link those authors with their actual profiles on Google+. Google sees this mutually reinforced content as much more authoritative because it puts a real identity behind the content; as a result, your content ranks higher in Google.com search results.

✓ **Integrating a Log In with Google+ button into your website to identify your customers and visitors:** The Log In with Google+ button (just in its infancy as I write this) allows your visitors to log in using their Google accounts. Then you can create experiences using the data that users have given you permission to access. At the same time, you can publish experiences throughout your website to Google+, and users can choose which of those experiences they want to share with their friends through a yet-to-be-launched service named Google+ History, which will likely surface soon with more details.

Identifying associated Google+ profiles and pages through your website

Google has provided a way to use your Google+ profile to identify content you've written on websites you contribute to. In terms of your business, this also enables you to include your employees and those behind the content and products you provide on your website. Proper integration of such provides three benefits:

✓ **It personalizes your website a lot more, increasing the trust you build between your brand and your users.** Seeing the smiling faces of the people behind your content and products makes your website much more real and much more identifiable by displaying the pictures and names of the people who are writing your content with the content that is published. This means you build greater trust in your visitors, and they become more likely to convert in the manner you want them to.

✓ **It gives your search listings on Google.com much more real estate onscreen.** Identifying your content with real people gives each of those content pages a much larger listing in Google.com search results. Each listing includes a picture of the person who wrote the content, a link back to his or her Google+ profile, and (on occasion) an opportunity to circle that individual. If the content's creator shares content for your company, your brand gets even greater visibility.

✔ **It does give you some search advantage, especially in personalized search results.** Some of my own preliminary (if unscientific) testing has shown that listings with a linked Google+ profile to the content do rank a little better than content that is not associated with a Google+ profile. Perhaps this advantage comes about because the Google folks know that the content is associated directly with a real person on their network. If you're looking for a guaranteed way to rank your website higher, consider linking your landing pages to the actual authors of your content who have Google+ Pages. You'll thank me later.

Google, unfortunately, only allows you to get the additional author data to show up in Google.com search results if you link the author's name or image to a Google+ profile page. Google won't attach that data if you link it to a Twitter or Facebook profile, for instance. Although this policy does put Google in a walled garden of sorts, I'd say stick to the practical benefits for now and make those links.

There are essentially two ways you can link your Google+ profile to your website content. I show you how in a later section, "Using author tags to bring out your employees." In brief, here they are:

✔ **Linking the byline of your content directly to the author's Google+ profile:** This simple link format (which I'll show you in the next section) is easy to set up.

✔ **Linking the byline of your content directly to the author's profile page on your website and then linking that profile back to his or her Google+ profile:** If you prefer that your authors have their own profiles on your website, you can still link each author's profile, using an HTML format called *microdata,* back to the author's Google+ profile.

When you've implemented either method, give it a couple of weeks, and you'll start to see your content show up with an author image and name in Google.com search results.

Bringing Attention to Your Search Results

Knowing what you can do is a first step. Here are some effective (general) next steps to take:

1. Figure out and implement your best strategy for calling attention to your search results. You can start by integrating profile tags and Badges throughout your website.

2. Make sure you're checking Google Webmaster Tools regularly and testing the data that Google is extracting from your website. The idea is to be sure Google knows as much about your brand and those who are behind your content as possible.

3. Test your efforts by doing a Google search for your content. How better to see how your results appear inside Google?

I've already mentioned a few techniques for improving your brand's authority on Google by using Google+ and how that process enhances your identity on the web. Here's where I show you how to make each of those processes work to best advantage.

Using author tags to bring out your employees

Making your website much more personal can be one of the greatest (and easiest) ways to start improving your search results on Google. When Google knows your content is authentic (that is, created by real people — which is apparent when your content includes bylines, author names, and profile images), it doesn't have work as hard to sift your content from (say) SEO spam and content that isn't as relevant to the people who are searching on Google.com for what you have to offer.

Google uses *microdata* (defined in the sidebar "Understanding microdata") to (a) identify the authors of content and (b) identify the authors' social network profiles, including those on Google+, in an easy-to-find way. The idea is to help you prove your authors' identity this way by

✔ Linking to each author's Google+ and other social networking profiles

✔ Linking back to your website from the authors' social networking profiles

To make this technique work, you have to know (a) the proper HTML syntax for linking to the author's social networking profile from your website and (b) how to establish a working link from that social networking profile back to your website in a way that Google can understand.

In theory, this linking can be accomplished with any social network out there. (Google used to do just that, supporting multiple social networks for identifying profile data on the web through an old Application Programming Interface called "The Social Graph API.") Presently, Google only supports linking this profile data through Google+ profiles. Therefore, at minimum, you'll want to provide a proper link back to your Google+ profile for every named individual or profile picture on the site.

Using rel="author" to identify authorship links

The way to link back to a Google+ profile is to use a special attribute on your HTML links (the <a> tag) that tells Google that the currently linked text is identifying who the author of the post is and takes the user back to that author's Google+ profile.

To link the user back to the author's Google profile, just do the following:

1. **Create a link to the author's profile anywhere on the page.**

   Your link will look something like this:

   ```
   <a href="http://profiles.google.com/jessestay">Jesse Stay</a>
   ```

   On my blog (`http://staynalive.com`), I link the name in the byline for each article. So where it says *by Jesse Stay* or *by Another Author,* I link the *Jesse Stay* or *Another Author* to each of our individual Google+ profiles. Figure 12-5 shows the code on my blog. When I link the byline, the code behind the text looks something like this:

   ```
   <a href=http://profiles.google.com/jessestay>by Jesse Stay</a>
   ```

Figure 12-5:
The code behind the text on my blog.

I can actually do this bit of magic for multiple authors and multiple people on the same site. Google then reads the data about each author and attaches it to the individual post in the search results (see Figure 12-6).

2. **Append the text** `rel="author"` **to the link, either before or after the** `href` **attribute.**

When you create the link as you would any other HTML link, all you need do now is tell Google that the link is identifying a place that users can click to find the author's profile on the web. To do so, just add the text `rel="author"` to the link. The final link HTML will look something like this:

```
<a href="http://profiles.google.com/jessestay" rel="author">by Jesse Stay</a>
```

You can go over to my blog at `http://staynalive.com` and look at the source for the page to see how I link the bylines of each article.

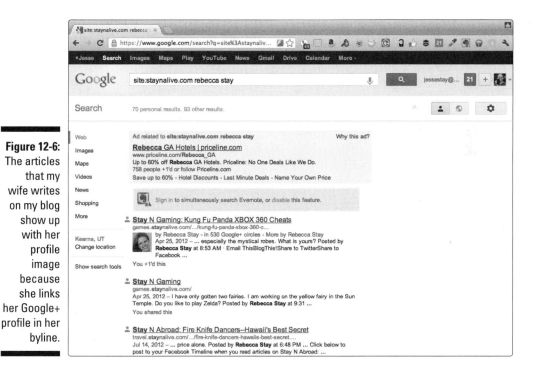

Figure 12-6:
The articles that my wife writes on my blog show up with her profile image because she links her Google+ profile in her byline.

Using rel="me" to identify profile links

In the event that your website has individual profile pages for each author, you can continue to link author names back to the profile pages on your website. You can also tell Google, on each of the profile pages on your website, that the profile page itself is associated with a Google+ profile.

Instead of using an `<a>` link tag like you do if you're just going to link directly to the author's Google+ profile, on the profile pages on your own site you'll put the invisible tag `<link>` in the `<head>` section of your HTML. It's structured just like the `<a>` tag, only users don't see it unless they look at the source of the profile pages on your website. The end `<link>` tag looks something like this:

```
<html>
<head>
<!--Other stuff can go here. The user doesn't see this-->
<link href="http://profiles.google.com/jessestay" rel="author" />
</head>
<body>...</body>
</html>
```

With the `<link>` tag on each author's profile page on your website, Google now knows the associated Google+ profile for that author — and can properly link that person's profile information with his or her content in Google search results.

Linking back to your website from each author's Google+ profile

You have one more step to take before Google can properly see the link between your authors' content and their Google+ profiles: linking those Google+ profiles back to your website. You can do so in one of two ways:

✔ Add each author's profile from your website to other profiles on their individual Google+ profile.

✔ Add your website under Contributor To for each author's Google+ profile.

To change this data, do the following:

1. **Go to the author's Google+ profile.**

   To do so, go to Google+ under the user's account, and click the Profile link.

2. **Click Edit Profile.**

   This should be a big button at the upper right.

3. **Click Other Profiles or Contributor To (or both).**

   The section becomes a set of fields that you can edit or add to.

4. **Add the author's website profile or your website name in the space provided.**

   Just type in the URL to the author's profile (or type in your own website URL if there is none) and click Save to finish linking the author's Google+ profile to your website.

It can take a few weeks for Google to start recognizing the link between the author's Google+ profile and your website — and to start detecting the data. Have some patience. If you want to verify that your HTML is formatted correctly, the later section "Testing your microdata with the Rich Snippet Tool" gives you the lowdown.

Using page Badges to grow your audience

After you've created page Badges as described earlier in this chapter, you can start taking advantage of the value that page Badges bring to your brand's search results.

The fact is, by identifying your website with a Google+ Page, you're giving your website greater visibility and attracting more attention to your brand, which grows an audience organically in Google search results. Make sure you consider adding a Google+ Page Badge if you're looking for simple ways to improve your visibility in Google.com search results. From this page Badge, users can circle your page or +1 your page right from Google.com search results and other parts of Google (say, from a Gmail message). At the same time, users are getting encouragement by association when their friends show an interest in your website or brand. When those folks circle your Google+ Page, you have an audience you can start advertising to for free.

Using Webmaster Tools for optimization

You can actually use Google's tools for webmasters, Webmaster Tools, to see how the posts you make on your website — as well as those you create on Google+ — are doing in search results. You can get a handle on how your content is gaining authority on Google search and elsewhere by checking these two locations:

✔ **+1 Reports:** This feature provides a way for you to find out — on your website — what pages are getting new +1s and how your site is ranking as a result of those +1s. The reports that Webmaster Tools provides show you how many people are clicking through on search results as a result of the +1s you've garnered in your posts and how successful your +1 campaigns are. It also shows you how many +1s from your site and others, per article, have accrued over an interval you can specify. This information is vital when you're trying to determine how successful your +1 campaigns are in relation to Google.com search.

✔ **Author Stats:** Currently, this feature is accessible under Labs. You can use a special tool called Author Stats to gauge how your own personal posts are doing in Google search. This tool is for *you,* the author — and shows only the content you've personally posted on Google+ or websites linked to Google+. From this tool, you can view

- How many times your content has been shown in Google.com search results

- How many people have clicked through to the original post as a result of those impressions in Google search (see Figure 12-7)

- Average position in search results for each post you make

Using this tool, you (as an author) can personally track your content, no matter where it is on the Internet — and test how different types of content can produce different rankings in search results.

Figure 12-7: Author Stats in Google Webmaster Tools provides a useful interface for authors of content to track how their content does in Google.com search results.

Testing your microdata with the Rich Snippets Testing Tool

Also in Webmaster Tools, Google provides a tool you can use to test how your content is structured on your website, so that you can understand how it will be shared on Google+, as well as what Google is indexing as it reads your content for Google.com search results. Here's how you get to the Rich Snippets Testing Tool:

1. **Go to Webmaster Tools.**

   I usually find this just by searching for *Webmaster Tools* in Google. The URL http://www.google.com/webmasters/tools will take you right there.

2. **Click Other Resources.**

   Doing so opens several resources that webmasters can use to augment the way Google indexes data from their content.

3. **Click Rich Snippets Testing Tool.**

   The Rich Snippets Testing Tool appears.

4. **Using the Rich Snippets Testing Tool, specify the data you want to see.**

   You can either enter the URL of your content, or you can copy and paste your HTML directly into the boxes provided.

   Google shows you the data that it has parsed and how the data will appear in search results (see Figure 12-8). If your site has no markup, it tells you that it doesn't detect markup — in which case, you may want to go to this site to see how to add markup and Rich Snippets data to your website:

   ```
   www.google.com/support/webmasters/bin/answer.
        py?answer=1408986
   ```

Pay particular attention to the author links that this tool detects. Try putting in a couple of different URLs from your website to see whether Rich Snippets detects different authors for each URL:

✔ Verify that the publisher has been linked through your Google+ Page Badge or the appropriate markup and that Google has verified that the publisher is linked.

✔ Check out what title, description, and image Google is detecting for each URL (you want these identifiers to appear onscreen appropriately on Google+).

Figure 12-8:
The Rich
Snippets
Testing Tool
from Google
Webmaster
Tools.

When all looks fine, and you're happy with the preview of how the data looks in your Google search results, you should be all set. Google, as it indexes this data, should start reading your microdata appropriately and rendering your content in a way that gives your website authority and makes your postings stand out in Google.com search results.

Google understands Facebook's open-standard Open Graph Protocol (learn more at `http://opengraphprotocol.org`) when using microdata to structure content. The Rich Snippet Tool may not identify all this data, but it's worth testing out with Google+ if you've already integrated this type of syntax into your HTML for integration with Facebook.

SEO is another whole complex topic in itself, but clearly, Google+ and social networks can benefit any marketer's campaign by driving traffic and sales to a web property. Search is a big part of that approach; Google+ can give your search strategy a major boost. Your SEO specialist or consultant can use the benefits of Google+ as a starting point for further structuring your content for better search gains. As you start reaping the rewards of improving your presence on Google+ search, consult an SEO expert to get the whole picture on how to take optimization to the next level.

Understanding microdata

Microdata is a set of standard supplementary attributes that you can add to the HTML tags on your website to identify the content within. They make up a set of standard attributes that Google and many other websites all understand.

For example, the `"rel"` attribute helps identify how items of content are linked together and the types of relationships they have. Other microsyntax formats identify profile information, titles, descriptions, and the main images that show up when your content is shared.

It's always a good idea to make sure your developers are properly adding microdata to your website so that it's shared most effectively, and is easily identifiable by sites such as Google. To find out more about the microdata that Google supports, visit this web page:

`http://support.google.com/`
`webmasters/bin/answer.`
`py?hl=en&answer=176035`

Increasing page ranking through social SEO

People are the new major criterion for effective SEO. Not to discount other factors (say, superior content) that can improve your search presence, the online landscape has changed: With the advent of social media, search engines are starting to look at a person's friends — and identity on the web — as significant factors that help marketers to identify the content that a particular person wants to see when conducting a search on the web. That's the point at which Google+ can take your SEO strategy to the next level. Here are my best suggestions for using social factors from Google+ to improve your presence in search on Google.com:

- ✔ **Improve the number of +1s on each page of your website.** These days, social endorsement by an individual — and by his or her friends — plays a significant part in the ranking of content on Google.com. This happens both through Google personal results through Google Search Plus Your Web, as well as through the natural results. Google now includes the +1 as a ranking factor in search results; look for the importance of that factor to increase over time.

- ✔ **Grow your page audience and link that to your website.** Linking your Google+ Page to your website — and using that connection to grow that audience — gives additional authority to your website by establishing that your website has a strong audience of followers — exactly what advertisers want. Not only does this improve ranking in search results, but it brings out more opportunities for Google to feature your page and website more prominently in search results.

✔ **Link authors of content to their Google+ profiles through your website, and focus your content around people.** Preliminary studies show that content linked to real authors does rank higher in Google.com search results. But even if it didn't, when you link your authors to their Google+ profiles through your website, you're increasing their visibility in Google.com search results. As a result, searchers' eyes are drawn to your results over those of your competitors, regardless of ranking. You'll see more click-throughs this way.

✔ **Post lots of content on your Google+ Page and your employees' Google+ profiles that you also link back to your website.** Content truly is king; Google+ gives you opportunities to post lots of it. Post frequently to your Google+ Page and link frequently back to your website. Get your employees, customers, and fans to do the same. The more this happens, the more your content will appear in Google.com search results — and the more click-throughs and visibility your brand will have.

Part IV
Taking Google+ Further

In this part . . .

When you've taken in all the essentials of Google+, what next? The answer is to never stop looking for more! Google+ will always be an ever-evolving social network, and every change brings new things to learn and do with it. Make sure you stay on top of it to keep your edge against the competition!

To get you started, this part of the book gives you a more advanced look at maximizing the value of Google+ — angles that your competition probably isn't paying as much attention to yet — which could give you just the boost you need to outpace your competitors.

Chapter 13

Measuring Google+ Activity

. . . .

In This Chapter

▶ Getting a perspective on your data with Google Analytics

▶ Measuring your ads

. . . .

*A*ny good marketer knows that measurement is core of an effective strategy — and that's especially true on Google+. Knowing not only the number of comments and +1s on your posts, but also how those posts actually perform in click-throughs to your site and conversions in sales will make you stand out from your competition.

You can't really say for sure that you're fully successful until you've measured and proven the success that you're trying to achieve. In the end, as marketers, we're all marketplace scientists: We have to come to a conclusion in our experiments, using reliable measurements. In this chapter, I show you some techniques you can use to measure the success of your Google+ strategy and prove to the top brass (even if the bigwig exec in your business is you) that your campaigns are working. As you read here, I also recommend you visit Chapter 12 for a refresher on the use of Webmaster Tools to measure the integration of Google+ on your website.

Using Google Analytics to Measure Google+ Activity

Google provides a powerful free tool that all webmasters can use to track the success of their web activity: Google Analytics. It's so powerful that I heard Omniture's founder and former CEO, Josh James, suggest in a talk that the threat of Google Analytics was part of the reason he sold Omniture to Adobe.

Other analytics solutions

There are many other analytics solutions you can use besides Google Analytics to track Google+ growth. Most of these products cost a lot of money, but they may be worth your investment if you have needs greater than the simplified free offerings. Make sure you do some research on social-analytics products and assess whether they offer enough bang for the buck.

Despite what Josh James said, and although Omniture's Social Analytics is one of my favorite products for tracking Google+ conversations, it's built (and intended) for the large-scale enterprise. It can be pricey, especially compared to Google Analytics. Other products you may want to consider include, among others, Oracle's BuddyMedia, as well as SalesForce Radian6. Each of these enterprise products has its own unique offerings, so research is the key.

If you're a big business, you're probably using an analytical tool like Omniture, but you might also have integrated Google Analytics to get additional data. If you're a smaller business than (say) the average huge multinational corporation, you're likely using Google Analytics to track your small-business website for free. If you're not in either scenario yet, my guess is that you probably will be after you read this chapter.

To get started with Google Analytics, just go to `http://analytics.google.com` and click Create an Account (or just follow the instructions).

Google Analytics also allows you to track your social activity from Google+, as well as other social networks. With Google Analytics you can

- ✔ Track which social networks are providing the most traffic.
- ✔ Find out what pages on your website are gaining the most social web traffic.
- ✔ Track which posts on your social channels convert the most visitors to customers on your website.
- ✔ Zero in on the pages on your website that get the most +1s, likes, or tweets.
- ✔ Study the flow of how visitors use your website from social channels.

Figuring out traffic from social signals

Google Analytics allows you to learn which social channels are providing the greatest traffic. From Google Analytics, you can determine whether Facebook, Twitter, Google+, YouTube, or other social networks are providing traffic to your website and which pages on your website are getting the most traffic from those channels. Figure 13-1 shows the screen you get when you choose Social⇨Sources.

Figure 13-1:
The Sources section under Social in Google Analytics shows data about what social networks are providing traffic.

To study this traffic, follow these steps:

1. **Go** to www.google.com/analytics.

   This is where you go to get all your analytic data from Google.

2. **Select your site from the list.**

   If you haven't set up your site for Google Analytics, you'll want to do that first. Although the details of setting up your site on Google Analytics are beyond the scope of this book, you can always click Help if you have questions. Google Analytics has a terrific Help section.

3. **Click Traffic Sources.**

   All information about where your traffic comes from is stored in this section of Google Analytics.

4. **Click Social under Traffic Sources.**

   Doing so expands the options available for monitoring the traffic that comes to your website from social channels. If you want a bird's-eye view, you can look at the Overview section under Social.

5. Click Sources under Social.

This is where you need to be. In this submenu, you can see a list of all the social networks that are providing traffic for your website. You can even break down that data by activity stream and see who on Google+ is linking to your website (the later section "Listening to your audience" provides the how-to). Browse around the Sources section — check out the various ways you can get the lowdown.

If you explore this section a little, immediately you'll notice a graph of all the visits driven by social networks for your website. Below that you see a corresponding graph that shows total visits to your website. Compare the two graphs, and you can spot any correlation to the spikes you see in your total traffic. From there you can get a bird's-eye view of social channels as drivers of your traffic. You can also adjust the time period as needed.

You can do even more tweaking under Social➪Sources. Try these approaches:

- ✔ **Evaluate how much of a role social channels play in driving traffic to your website.** Just comparing the two graphs can give you a good idea of whether social channels are primary influencers of traffic for your website — and what items on your website get the most social traffic. Zeroing in on those attractive items can help you decide how to share your website on your social network channels.

- ✔ **Break down the traffic to your website by social network.** Below the graphs you'll see a list of the social networks driving traffic to your website. From this you can see which social networks are the most influential in driving traffic for you.

   This list can give you some strong hints about which social networks you should be more involved in. Also pay attention to the growth of traffic from each network. See one growing faster than another? (I see that happening quite significantly with Google+.) If so, maybe it's time to give that network some more attention.

- ✔ **See which pages on your website are getting the most traffic from particular social networks.** Click any of the social network names in the list below the charts, and you get a view that shows all pages on your website that are being linked to from social networks. Here you can tell which pages are attracting the most traffic from each social network. This can help you identify the types of content your social networking audience likes most.

- ✔ **Evaluate how many new visitors social networks are driving to your website.** If you click Advanced Segments at the top of your Social Sources page in Google Analytics under Social, you have the option to narrow down the audience you're looking at (see Figure 13-2). If you want to see how many of those visiting from each social networking channel are new visitors, check the box next to New Visitors (and then be sure to click Apply). Doing so shows you stats that reflect how many new visitors are being driven to your website by each social network. You can also click through and figure out which articles attracted the most new users.

Play around with the Advanced Segments box. There are some interesting demographics you can tie into these stats, and I'm sure they'll only get better as Google integrates more social factors into its analytics.

✔ **Track conversations about your website on Google+.** This is a powerful feature. Next to the Social Referral tab there is an Activity Stream tab. Click that, and you'll see an *activity stream* made up of social mentions of your website. Here you can see everyone talking about your website on Google+ and even a few other supported social networks (such as Delicious). For further details, check out the "Listening to your audience" section, later in this chapter.

✔ **Identify when people are interacting with your website on other social networks.** Also under the Activity Stream tab, you can click the Events link below the activity stream. This will show you a list of *events* — instances of people interacting with your website (see Figure 13-3). If (for instance) someone links to your website and provides a trackback, that event appears onscreen for your perusal. Or, because Delicious has partnered with Google Analytics, every time someone bookmarks your website on Delicious, you'll see that bookmark in this section. You can even see who bookmarked you (handy info).

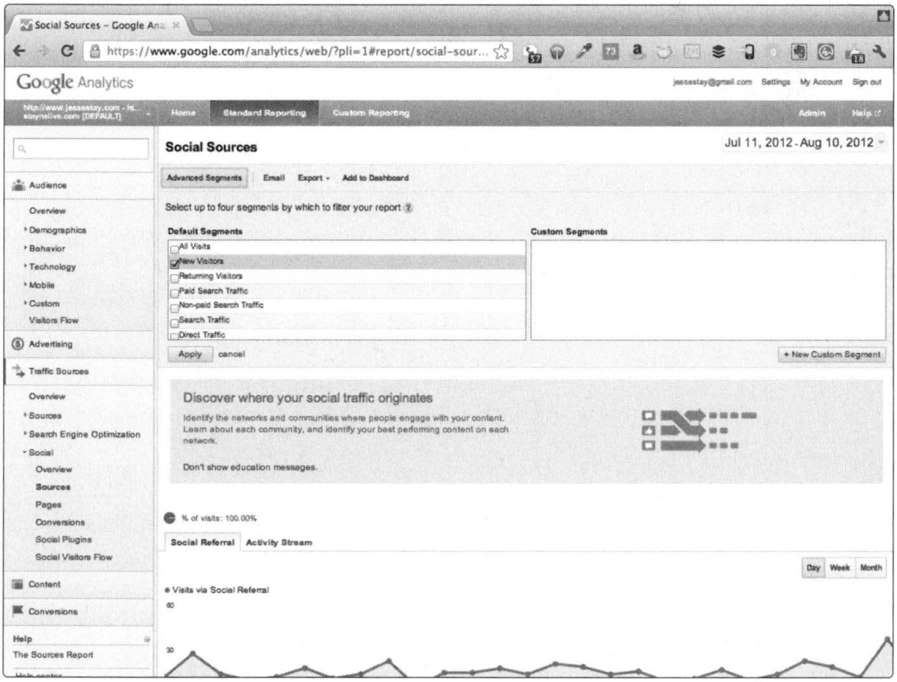

Figure 13-2:
You can narrow down your analytics to just new visitors by going to the Advanced Segments box.

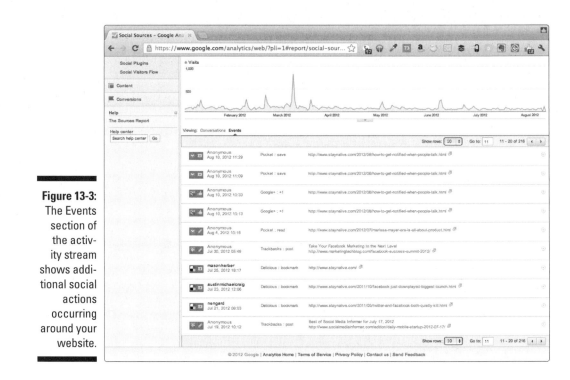

Figure 13-3:
The Events
section of
the activ-
ity stream
shows addi-
tional social
actions
occurring
around your
website.

Tracking +1s

Google Analytics will allow you to track the +1s you have on your website as well. Google stores this under a section called Social Plugins (see Figure 13-4).

The idea here is to offer a place where you can take a closer look at the results you're getting from *social plugins* (such as Like buttons, +1 buttons, and other such plugins that indicate visitors' approval) on your site. Presently the Social Plugins feature only supports the +1 button.

To get to this section and start tracking your +1 buttons on your site, follow these steps:

1. **Open your site in Google Analytics (**`http://google.com/analytics`**).**

   Your Google Analytics site appears. If there's a specific time period I want to track, I like to specify it here on the landing page, but you can set or change it on any page in Google Analytics.

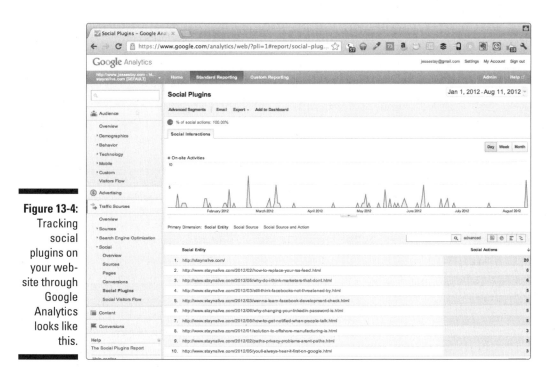

Figure 13-4:
Tracking
social
plugins on
your web-
site through
Google
Analytics
looks like
this.

2. **Click Traffic Sources⇨Social⇨Social Plugins.**

   The Social Plugins page shows you a graph of all the times someone
   clicked a +1 button on your website over the time period you specified.
   Below that graph, you can see which pages on your website have
   attracted the most +1s.

Presently, checking out the effect of social plugins on website traffic really is
that simple. So far, this section of Google Analytics only supports +1s — but
I expect that Google will soon support the tracking of Like buttons and such
on your website, all from one interface.

I've found the Social Plugins section to be a bit buggy. It doesn't always seem
to report all the clicks of +1 buttons.

Studying conversions

Everything you do on Google+ and other social networks should be centered
on converting visitors to customers — using methods like the following (for
openers):

✔ Turn a post on Google+ or Facebook or Twitter into sales by purchasing your products or clicking ads.

✔ Get people to click an ad.

✔ Entice visitors to visit a particular page on your website.

✔ Invite your visitors (with a call to action) to click a link.

You can track all these events on Google Analytics — and you can link them to social network activity.

First, you'll want to go to the Conversions section of Google Analytics. To get there:

1. **Go to your Google Analytics web page by going to** `http://analytics.google.com` **(be sure to log in)**⇨*Your site name.*

   Google Analytics opens.

2. **Click Traffic Sources**⇨**Social**⇨**Conversions.**

   You're presented with a page that shows you how well different social channels are converting visitors to customers on your website. Before this page can work effectively, you have to define exactly what you think constitutes a conversion — and attach a value to that goal. The next step shows how you set up a goal in Google Analytics.

3. **Click the Admin tab in the orange bar at the top right of the Google Analytics page.**

   The Admin tab offers you all kinds of advanced stuff you can do with your website.

4. **Click the Goals tab.**

   Options appear for adding and modifying conversion goals for your website.

5. **Click +Goal to add a new conversion goal for your site (you can also group these under goal sets).**

   A form appears, allowing you to customize your goal to your liking.

6. **Fill out the form, specifying the steps that lead to the goals you want to achieve.**

   Clicking URL Destination, for instance, will open a form that allows you to specify a URL that you want all your visitors to visit (or at least that you want to track). When visitors visit the URL, any conversion is tracked. You can also do this with visit durations (marking a conversion when people have been on the site for over a certain time), as well as the number of pages per visit.

7. **Fill out the form, name your goal, and click Save.**

   After you click Save, Google Analytics starts tracking the conversion goals you've set up.

   The useful and free AdSense Tracker can be used with a URL Destination goal to track when visitors click AdSense ads if you're displaying Google AdSense ads on your website. Get instructions at

   ```
   www.seobook.com/archives/001370.shtml
   ```

When you have some goals set up, you can start tracking conversions from social channels — and the report you get back is quite simple. It shows you how many conversions you've had over your specified time frame, which social networks have led to those conversions, and (if you specified a monetary value as a criterion for conversion) how much money you made from the conversions that came to you via social networking channels. Pretty powerful stuff, isn't it?

Getting notified

With every report on Google Analytics, you can have Google e-mail you a copy of that report on a regular basis (as shown in Figure 13-5).

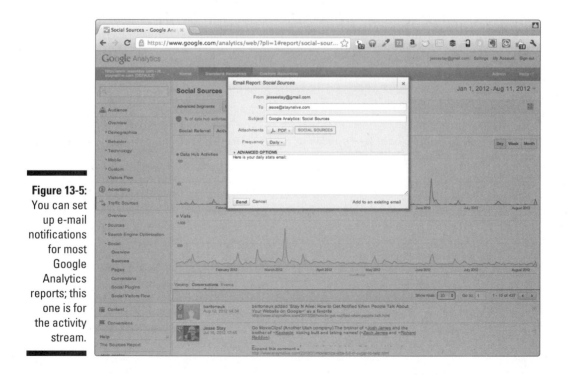

Figure 13-5:
You can set up e-mail notifications for most Google Analytics reports; this one is for the activity stream.

On almost any report you're on, just do the following to set up a notification e-mail for that report:

1. **If the notification option is available, you see an Email link above the report; click that link.**

   In the dialog box that opens, you specify how you want to receive your notifications.

2. **Choose who will receive your notification e-mail.**

   In the To field, enter a single e-mail address or a comma-separated list of e-mail addresses that you want to receive your report.

3. **Specify the format of the report that will be attached to the e-mail.**

   Your report gets attached to an e-mail sent to the recipients you specified in Step 2. Presently you can send the report in CSV, TSV, TSV for Excel, and PDF formats.

4. **Choose how often to send the e-mail notification.**

   You can choose When, Daily, Weekly, Monthly, or Quarterly. You can also identify days within that repeated time period.

5. **Set the duration, by clicking Advanced Options and selecting from the drop-down list.**

   When you click Advanced Options, you can specify how long you want to receive the notifications on a regular basis. Presently you can't receive the notifications for longer than 12 months before having to reset them.

6. **Type in the text you want to appear in the body of your e-mail.**

   This can't be blank. I usually put something brief and friendly here ("Here's your report," for example), but you can also use this space to describe the report to those who will receive it.

7. **Decide whether you want to add this report to an already existing e-mail notification report.**

   You can also opt to just add this report to an existing e-mail so people aren't receiving more than one e-mail for their website, filling up their inboxes. To do so, click the Add to an Existing E-mail link in the lower right.

8. **Click Send.**

   Your e-mail notification should now be set up, and your first report will be sent out.

Listening to your audience

One of the coolest features of the Google+ integration with Google Analytics is that you can track the number of clicks and referrals from Google+ to your website, and also identify who is linking to your website on Google+ and where their posts are. Here's how you do it:

1. **Choose Social⇨Sources (as described earlier in the chapter).**

   This takes you to the analytics for social traffic.

2. **Click the Activity Stream tab below the charts.**

   You see a list of posts and of people who have posted or commented on Google+ and also linked to your website.

3. **Check the list of posts from Google+ to find posts that mention your website (see Figure 13-6).**

   By default, you see ten posts at a time. Click the right and left arrows to move through the list and look for any good posts you might have missed.

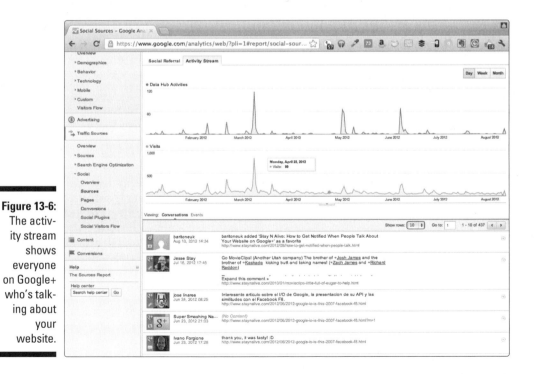

Figure 13-6: The activity stream shows everyone on Google+ who's talking about your website.

4. **Click the little down arrow/triangle at the upper right of each post.**

    A drop-down list appears, offering these options you can click:

    - Page Analytics provides analytics for that specific page on your website.

    - View Ripple shows the ripple of influence for that specific share on Google+ (see "Understanding Ripples," later in this chapter).

    - View Page takes you straight to the page on your website.

    - View Activity takes you to the actual Google+ post.

Spend some time absorbing what's being said about your website. The activity stream is where the conversation is happening; it's an extension of the comments already on your website. It's your audience and your community.

I like to go through each post linking to my website (by clicking View Activity) and click the +1 button on the post. This shows my acknowledgement of their share of my content. Occasionally, I might also participate in the conversation, which will then send future comments to my Google+ notifications so I can follow the ensuing conversation. Sometimes a simple thank-you will suffice to turn on notifications for that particular post.

You can get notifications of every new mention of your website on Google+ by creating an e-mail notification for this report. Just go to your Activity Stream tab and click Email. Then follow the instructions in the earlier section "Getting notified."

Learning the Effect of Your Posts

So far Google+ doesn't give you much specific data about how your audience reacts to your posts on your Google+ page. That shouldn't stop you from looking into the basic features that Google+ provides for tracking and learning from every post you make on your Google+ page.

Understanding ripples

Google has given one piece of analytical information for each URL that a user chooses to share on the service. The available public data includes posts from normal user accounts (your own and those of other people) that Google+ Pages can use to determine *ripples* — how the URLs you share spread around Google+.

Here's how to access the Ripples feature on Google+:

1. **On any post with a URL in it on Google+, click the little upside-down triangle (or down-arrow) in the upper right of the post.**

   A drop-down list appears, showing what you can do with that post.

   This works for any post with a link in it, whether it's on your profile and pages or posted by other people and pages in your news feed.

2. **Click View Ripples.**

   A new page opens, showing you all the ripples belonging to the shared URL across all of Google+.

The Ripples page is a graphical representation of all the times you or others share any URL on Google+ (see Figure 13-7). Each share is represented by a circle; the size of the circle depends on the influence of the person or page doing the sharing. You also see circles within circles and arrows pointing between the circles; each of those is a person who shared as a result of another person's share, resulting in *chains of influence.*

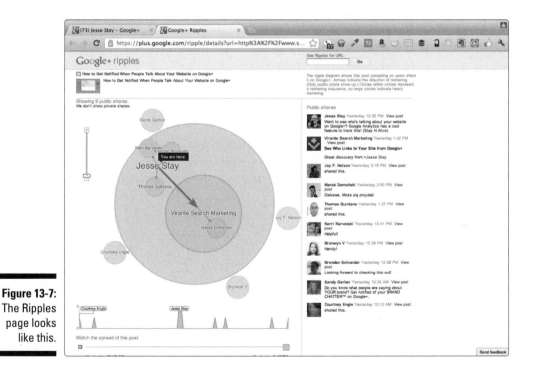

Figure 13-7: The Ripples page looks like this.

Here is what you'll see beyond just the circles of different sizes on the Ripples page:

- ✔ **The ripples themselves:** The main section of the Ripples page is the visualization of the ripples themselves. You can zoom in and out of these representations to see the names and dive into the specifics of who shared and how they're connected.

- ✔ **A list of all the public shares, who shared them, and what they said:** On the right of the ripples is a list of all the people who shared the given URL and what they said. You can scroll through this list to get an idea of people's impressions of your post as they share it.

- ✔ **A link to the original URL:** At the top is the link to the original URL. If you want to visit this URL, you can use this link as a shortcut.

- ✔ **A timeline of how the URL was shared:** Below the ripples, you can see a timeline graph of how the URL was shared. Clicking the Play button (the triangle button) plays the timeline for you and shows you, in real time, the momentum of how the URL spread — and who shared it at what times. The ripples update in real time as they are shared by each individual.

- ✔ **The top influencers:** Below the timeline you'll see some miscellaneous stats. One of these is a short list of the top influencers to share the URL and how many shares resulted from their own shares of the URL.

- ✔ **Statistics about how the URL was shared:** In this part, you can see the average chain length (how many shares on average resulted from an individual), the longest chain (who caused the most shares and how many resulted from that one individual), and the number of shares per hour.

- ✔ **Languages the post was shared in:** Want to see how well a URL is doing internationally? Use this to see what languages the given URL is being shared in and how fast it's growing in each language.

Although ripples are fun to look at, they can also be a useful tool for determining how you can grow your audience around a given share. Here are a few nuggets of information you can find in your ripples:

- ✔ **The real reach of your shares:** Normally the number of shares on a post is not an accurate enough measurement of how well your post did. Knowing how many of those who shared your post also had their posts shared — and how many times the URL you shared actually got shared after you posted it — gives you much more accurate data on your influence for every post. (It may not even be through the Share button; it may be posted as a link explicitly by someone who noticed your website and then copied and pasted it into an update.) Use this to measure how you're doing and track it frequently (see the "Measuring manually" section later).

✔ **How fast a URL (or your shares) spreads and why:** Using the timeline feature, you can see how quickly the post spread after you shared the URL. Was it because another person had already shared it? Was it because a particular influencer took hold of it? Did it start growing right around a particular ad campaign or product launch?

✔ **Who your top influencers are in a very real metric that follows the entire chain down:** Because you can track the total number of shares caused all the way down the chain from a particular influencer, you can measure true influence of an individual. Who influences the influencers? Who was the real reason for all your traffic? You can look at this through Ripples. Seek to reach out to these influencers after you learn this data.

✔ **The ability to be a part of the conversation as a URL that you own or have shared spreads:** Because you can see all the people talking about a given URL, you can go through their conversations and comment on them. Participate in the conversations so you know what people are saying about your content. Make every share you make on Google+ a personal one.

Measuring manually

Although Google+ doesn't provide built-in tools for measuring each post (at least not yet, though I anticipate this will come soon), you can still monitor your success for each post manually. That's how we did it in the olden days.

Here are a few ways you can monitor your posts that you should consider as you post on your Google+ page or profile:

✔ **Use a spreadsheet.** The age-old spreadsheet that my accountant dad uses is still the best tool for monitoring and keeping up with your own growth on Google+. Enter each metric you track into a spreadsheet, sort it by date, and keep a record of every post. Then you can sort, filter, and chart whatever data you like, and create reports that help you focus on what you need to learn about your data.

✔ **Track dates and times.** Knowing the best dates and times that provide the most comments, likes, or shares is important. They'll be different for every Google+ page you own, so track those dates and times for each page and get to know when your posts are most successful. Post at those times whenever you can.

✔ **Pull in Ripple data.** In particular, track the influencers. Track the average length of each chain. Track the number of shares per hour and what languages the post was shared in. This is all valuable data — which, visible as a whole on your spreadsheet, can give some interesting insights and ways to see further success.

✔ **Measure number of comments, +1s, and shares.** This is a given, but for every post, you'll want to keep a keen eye on the number of comments, +1s, and shares, and every time you get a new one you should mark it in your spreadsheet so you have a total tally. The shares with the most comments, +1s, and shares are the ones you want to study the most to see how to replicate that success.

✔ **Attempt to measure the sentiment(s) in the response.** Because you're measuring manually, you can also take a close look at whether a post was generally positively or negatively perceived by the people commenting on it or sharing it. If you're looking for more positive response, from this data you can then evaluate the posts that generate the most positive sentiment. Or maybe you'll notice that posts that generate negative sentiment bring more attention to your brand. For example, a more controversial post, such as one about climate change, can cause lots of comments, +1s, and shares, and also incite argument and banter within the comments. Follow the numbers, and they usually won't fail you.

✔ **Keep track of general subject matter for each post.** Write down some tags that summarize what is in each post. This will help you get a good idea of what types of posts and what types of subject matter see the most success. Put the topic in the spreadsheet I mention in the first bullet in this list.

If you see a repetition of particular tags with lots of comments, shares, or +1s, you'll know that those types of posts generally do better.

Track page growth. Besides the posts themselves, track how many new people follow your page or profile after each post. An increase in new visitors can be a reflection of a post's success; you should be tracking it. If you're seeing a greater page growth after certain types of posts, you'll want to focus on that type of content — provided, of course, that the content advances your goal and you're interested in growing your audience.

Chapter 14

Building Apps on Google+

In This Chapter

▶ Incorporating social design into your marketing strategy

▶ Checking out the available apps with Google+ and a developer

---

*T*o truly have an edge on your competition, you need to understand what tools are available to you so you can properly execute a strategy for getting the most exposure for your brand or product. Even if you're not a developer (or maybe you have some experience), you need to understand what you can do to best integrate Google+ into the experiences your company builds online. Whether you have a website or a mobile app, you'll want to understand the available Google+ features you can use to build the *best* experience, baked right into the online experiences you own.

This chapter doesn't require that you be a developer to understand the principles of building apps on Google+. If you look closely at these principles, however, they can help you figure out what types of online experiences will give your business the best bang for the buck; then you can hire a developer to build what works for you.

Thinking Socially — Integrating Social Design into Your Website or App

Long gone are the days of lonely experiences where visitors to your website (or users of your mobile app) came and went, without any possibility of interaction with their friends. Now, with Social APIs (Application Programming Interfaces), you can build experiences that bring in each visitor's friends. The user experience no longer has to be lonely — and as a result, your visitors share more, stay around longer, and participate more as they visit your website or mobile app.

This concept of bringing visitors' friends along with them is called *social design*. It's the essence of the "from fishers to fish-farmers" concept I mention in Part III. In every aspect of your company, you should be thinking of how users can bring their friends with them throughout the experience.

Designing around social interaction

To make social design a seamless part of your app or website, you have to "think socially" — that is, always imagine what the user or visitor might be able to do if his or her friends were part of the same online experience at the same time. Some questions you should ask yourself as you design your app or site are

- ✔ **Where are the closest friends of the individual visiting my site located?** Those close friends may not always be on Google+. Sometimes they might be found in your own user database and the relationships you've already established there. Maybe you already know who a particular visitor's friends are. Maybe you already know who the visitor's family is. If so, you'll want to find ways to utilize your own database to identify those friends and family of the user and start building online experiences that connect you and your brand with them.

- ✔ **How can I do better at bringing those friends along for the ride with each visitor who visits my site or app?** When visitors come to your site, they should immediately be able to see their close friends and family there in some way. Maybe you show them articles their friends are reading on your site. Perhaps you show them other products their friends are purchasing. Or maybe you just show them the most recent friends of theirs to visit your website.

  The goal is to make your site a social, welcoming experience for each visitor.

- ✔ **What products does my company provide that I could be featuring with each visitor's friends?** Do you sell products? You could be featuring the products most popular amongst a user's friends. Is content your bread and butter? You could be sharing the most popular articles from the user's friends. When you share your money-making material in this manner, it becomes much more interesting to the users. They become more likely to read your articles or purchase your products.

  When users are surrounded with things their friends and family are participating in, they're much more likely to share those things with their other friends because they know what's being offered is already trusted by people they trust.

✔ **How can you reduce barriers to allowing visitors to share with their friends?** Every step a user takes on your site should have opportunities to share intriguing finds via links to places _outside_ your website or app where users are most likely to participate. Consider Google+ as one of those places:

- Consider putting +1 buttons, Google+ Badges, and Facebook's Like buttons at convenient locations around your app or site.

- Consider integrating with Facebook Timeline and Google History.

- Make sure you have author tags and are linking your website to your Google+ Page and Facebook Page (and vice versa).

- Prompt the users to share when they find content or activities that they might want to share; if you do so, they're more likely to share what they find.

- Give users a feed that shows what their friends and family are doing on your website, and allow your users to share items to that feed as well (which brings all that sharing back to your "fish-farm").

Bringing the conversation to your site

Spontaneous conversations about your brand boost its authority more than anything — and you have much greater control when those conversations are happening on your own site, rather than on someone else's, such as Google+ or Facebook. (Yes, I did just suggest that something is more important than Google+.) The minute people are coming to your site to converse with their friends over their favorite social network, you know you've been successful. There is a good chance your most passionate audience will start up some of those conversations. When they're talking about your brand on your site, you now produce the news about your brand. They get the story from the horse's mouth — you're in control of your own message at this point.

The only way to get people conversing on your own site is by utilizing profiles you've created and building ways for them to communicate, or by using profiles they've created on social networks like Google+ and pulling those profiles into your own user experience for communication via the APIs that those social networks provide.

In the next section, I talk about the APIs that Google+ provides. If you want a closer look at the APIs that Facebook provides, I've written a book that can help: _Facebook Application Development For Dummies_ (John Wiley & Sons, Inc.).

There are a couple of ways people can communicate with each other on your site, and you can start using your site as a communication tool to build community and make your audience more passionate about your brand. Here are a couple of ideas:

- **Create your own news feed.** I know people don't enjoy the thought of "creating another Facebook." That's not really what you're doing here. Instead, you're providing a place where people can get a link to the latest activity on your site from their friends. This link is a feed that focuses solely on your site — every product purchased, every article read, every Like or comment registered — you can share it all here, inviting the individual's friends to comment and share to their friends as well.

   The idea is to create a social network around your products and content — and then allow your users to share to the other social networks they participate in.

- **Add comments to content and product listings.** Facebook makes it easy with plugins they can provide for your content. With Google+ you have to do it on your own. You may also consider a third-party platform like Disqus.com. Or, for the greatest benefit, you may consider creating your own commenting system for every product or piece of content on your site. At that point, if your site supports profiles, you have two options:

   - Use the profiles of users on your own site.

   - Integrate, via APIs, the profiles of those users from Google and Facebook.

   To get information on Google+ APIs, go to `http://developers. google.com+`.

   Integrating comments on individual pieces of content or products allows your users and customers to get to know each other and builds community around your brand. It also gives you feedback and helps you play a part in the conversation. If you allow comments to share out to other websites and social networks, it can bring new people back to the conversations on your own site or app, bringing potential new customers to your website or app.

- **Create a forum.** The old-style forum isn't dead yet. You may benefit by creating a forum that links from your website or app where users can discuss content or products from your website. This medium provides a place for your users to communicate, build community, and get to know each other while giving them some level of control over the conversation. At the same time, because you own the forum and the community it's based on, you still can lead and guide what happens there. It's probably better that conversation happens on your own turf instead of someone else's.

Case study: Huffington Post Social

HuffingtonPost.com is an excellent example of social-design integration that I like to show off whenever I speak or consult with others. As I write this, you can find it at `http://huffingtonpost.com/social`.

When you visit the site, you are presented with the opportunity to log in through Facebook.

When you log in, you are presented with a news feed of the activity of all your Facebook friends who are also using Huffington Post Social, as shown here. The news feed shows articles they

are reading, have liked, and have commented on. This view is much more interesting to a marketer than the traditional, edited flow of content you find on the main site.

As a result of this integration, Huffington Post reported significant upgrades in the number of comments on their articles. They also showed huge increases in the number of referrals from Facebook from this integration. Huffington Post was "thinking socially" in this design, and their thought process paid off.

There are plenty of open-source, as well as COTS (Commercial Off-The-Shelf), solutions for forum software out there.

My favorite forum software is phpBB (`www.phpbb.com`). It's free of charge and has plenty of features.

✔ **Start a blog.** The blog gives you a place to start conversations. You post the article to start the conversation. Your users and customers can then comment. The advantage is you're writing the news in this case and controlling the conversation. I recommend this for at least any new feature you launch or news you might want the world to hear about.

Using well-established blogging tools like WordPress or Tumblr, you can host on your own blog. I use Blogger.com, which is very flexible and free, and I don't even have to host.

Using Google+ Features to Build Your Site or App

Now that you're thinking socially and creating social design in your websites and apps, it's time to start thinking Google+ again. In this section I'll talk about what you can do with Google+, an API, and a developer, and how you can start creating social designs using Google+ as your infrastructure for that design.

Updates to Google APIs

Google+ APIs are a moving target. They're brand-new. They're constantly changing — and so are the rules. So keep in mind that everything I tell you about APIs in this chapter is subject to change; it's the nature of the beast. For the latest word from the source, always consult Google's own docs at `developers.google.com/+/api`.

Presently, Google+'s API does have a few limitations:

✔ **Publishing to Google+ through an API is limited to select developers.** Google+ is gradually opening up its publishing capabilities to select developers — the idea is to give you a way to publish to a

news feed on behalf of a user through your website or app. At the moment, this feature is available to only a small group of apps that have a legitimate need to publish to Google+. Unfortunately, you have to know the right people at Google to even consider this option.

✔ **Google+ limits the number of requests per minute (or per hour), so you can't create high-traffic integrations without Google's express permission.** In order to put a throttle on growth so Google can handle the initial phases of its API rollout, Google is throttling bandwidth to a limited number of requests in a short time period. You'll have to live by these rules to use the platform. However, you can request that Google increase your available request quota if you find your app is using the limit, and you have a legitimate app that isn't spamming or doing anything sketchy on the Google+ platform. Google is gradually increasing these limits as it grows and solidifies its platform.

✔ **Google+ is testing a beta of a feature they call Google History, where users can vet what apps publish to their news feed.** Google History is a tool that lets users choose which items published by apps go to their news feed. It's intended as a way to prevent the spam that some users have received on Facebook and other social networks. To the side of the Google+ interface, a History link offers users the chance to select and approve specific posts from apps, as shown here. The area is completely private until users approve each item and specify that it go to the circles they want to publish to. Although Google History is still in the works, look for it to launch soon.

One highly useful magic trick you can do with the Google+ API is retrieve content. For example, you can go through a user's news feed and retrieve individual posts or comments on those posts. You can retrieve the photos that the user posts, the events he or she participates in, and the Hangouts he or she joins or starts.

Being able to get this content means you can build some unique experiences on your website or app. Here are a few ideas:

✔ You notice a user is participating in a Hangout. You can post a link that the user is participating in the Hangout and allow that user's friends visiting your website to join them, right from your website.

✔ You have an Events page for events related to your brand. From that page, you can show the other events a user's friends are attending.

✔ You allow the user to create a profile on your website or app. You let that user pull from his or her list of Google+ photos to create a profile photo for your website or app.

Retrieving people and connections

Social design requires pulling in the friends and connections of a user. Although sometimes you find the user has relationships you can use right in your own website or app, connections from Facebook and other social networks are worth pulling in; you should also consider the possibility that a person's closest connections might also be in Google+.

Consider this: Many of the original contacts belonging to each user on Google+ have been retrieved from their Gmail address books. That means many of the connections that a user has on Google+, whether active or not, are people with whom that user has actually communicated through e-mail. In many cases, that's a powerful link to a user's friends and family — even more powerful than Facebook. Definitely consider Google+ as a source for connections when you're trying to transfer those relationships from Google+ over to your own website.

I have several favorite techniques I use when I integrate social design from any social network into my website or apps (or those of my clients):

✔ **Feature the user's friends and their activity.** Get the list of a user's friends from Google+ (those in the user's circles). Do a search through your database to see whether any of those friends have purchased products or looked at content on your website. This will give you the list of friends who have interacted with your website or app. Feature those friends — or the products they purchased or articles they read — somewhere on your website.

✔ **Automate the friending process.** Want to build a social graph on your own website? There's no sense asking a user to identify his or her friends manually anymore. Now, with a simple API call to Google+, you can access the social accounts of all the people in a user's Google+ circles, and go on to create experiences that automatically pull in the friends of that user as friends on your website or app. You can do so with multiple social networks, if you like.

The cool thing about this approach is that you can have your website automatically add people as friends on your website every time a new friend from Google+ for a particular user joins your website. So if I want to follow certain people on your website, it automatically determines when my friends from Google+ join the site — and either prompts me to add them or automatically adds them as friends, without any intervention from me. A great example of this is Pinterest (see Figure 14-1).

Figure 14-1:
Pinterest automatically lists friends from Facebook who have followed you on Pinterest, whom you can follow back.

✔ **Simplify registration and purchase pipelines.** This is one of the coolest ways to use social APIs such as the one you can use for Google+. Simple is good: The more steps you have in your registration or purchase process, the more likely users are to abandon the purchase or registration — which kills conversions. If you have any doubt about this scenario, just test it using Google Analytics or another analytics tool. As more steps are added, more people leave without buying. It's that simple.

You can significantly simplify your registration and purchase processes by giving users a one-click way to provide name, address, phone, e-mail, and other data — removing the need to type in that information as they try to register or pay for your service. Using the data they've already entered on Google+ and other social networks will make registration fast and convenient; users don't have to type their data twice.

Every time you create a feature that requests user data or data about the user's friends, consider using the Google+ and other social network APIs to automate that process for the user. In many cases, the process of logging in can be as simple as one click. (Figure 14-2 shows how `cinch.fm`, a previous client of mine, does registration.)

Figure 14-2:
Cinch.fm allows users to log in with their Facebook and Twitter profiles to register. The moment a user is logged in, an account is created automatically.

Publishing and sharing to Google+

When a user is in an environment surrounded by friends and family, the natural inclination is to share. You make that process simple for your users by using tools that Google+ provides:

✓ **Use the +1 and Share buttons.** Google+ provides both a +1 and a Share button. I generally suggest the +1 button because it kills two birds with one stone: Immediately after users click the +1 button for products and articles they like on your website or app, they're prompted with the opportunity to share that link with their friends on Google+.

With these buttons that Google provides, you can use Google's own interface and methods for sharing straight to Google+ — with very little integration on your part. Just copy and paste, and you're done.

✔ **Give users an opportunity to automate sharing through Google+ History.** This feature is just on the verge of being launched; it may change, but another approach you should consider is to find actions that can be automatically shared to a user's Google+ History tab on Google+. If a user is reading an article, prompt him or her to send it automatically to Google+ History; after that, continue doing so automatically for the user. If the user is purchasing things, give him or her the opportunity to share the purchase information to Google History after every future purchase.

Every post to Google+ History remains private until the user opts to share it to his or her circles. Thus the user incurs no risk of intrusion by the app developer and can afford to share a little more detail when the time is right. There is (for example) no risk that the gift you bought for your significant other will be shared out for the world to see before you say it's okay. No surprises will be spoiled with Google+ History.

✔ **Consider publishing for users.** With approval, Google+ is giving select developers access to publish on behalf of users to the users' news feeds on Google+. Right now this feature is limited to enterprise-level and business social media clients such as HootSuite, Hearsay Social, and Omniture's Context Optional. Google+ may limit this capability to such businesslike uses, but consider whether you have a legitimate use case that you think Google+ should approve. If you get that approval, being able to publish on behalf of your users is a powerful way to enable sharing from a website or app. It's a limited capability just now, but that may change.

Building branded layers on top of Google+ Hangouts

Google+ Hangouts provides a special API as well, and you can build yet another layer of online experiences with a developer and a Google+ Hangout:

✔ **Build an app experience that multiple people can participate in live and use at the same time.** The classic example of this would be a board game. You could create a board game for your brand and have every member of the Hangout play in that board game, communicating and enjoying the time together in the experience you built live, on video, with friends.

You should think of experiences you can build that allow multiple people to participate together and allow each of them to have a part. You can access the names and profile IDs of all participants in a Google+ Hangout. Find ways to incorporate those participants into the Google+ Hangout experiences you create.

You can then create Hangout experiences for your users and customers that they can launch — and play along with their friends. Those friends can then share with their friends. Soon, you're creating face-to-face experiences among those who are passionate about your brand, and giving new customers the opportunity to be introduced to those people (and their enthusiasm) at the same time.

✓ **Create layers on top of the videos of each participant in a Hangout.** Google+ has created its own experience around this, providing reindeer antlers, bunny ears, and clown faces that you can put over your face during the video. (Not all apps have to be this silly. Honest.)

Maybe you create a dashboard that goes around the user's picture in the Hangout, showing stats about what that user is doing in the Hangout. Maybe you give your users the opportunity to brand themselves in the Hangouts they participate in. Maybe you give them a little virtual badge they can "wear" to each Hangout they join. All these tweaks are possible with Hangout overlays.

✓ **Control elements of the Hangout.** You have access to every element of the Hangout through the Google+ Hangouts API. You can use that API to create your own dashboards, and even control (for example) whose image appears as the main image in the middle of the screen and create your own stats around each Hangout.

Although you can't create your own Hangout experiences on your own website (not yet, anyway), you can launch them *from* your website, and maybe from there you can start to provide information that supports your brand — say, which customers of yours are currently participating in Hangouts or the average length of time they participate. This feature offers multiple opportunities to entice your customers to get in and meet other customers in Hangout experiences that you create.

Part V
The Part of Tens

"I know it's a short profile, but I thought 'King of the Jungle' sort of said it all."

In this part . . .

If you've read any *For Dummies* book, you know the drill! In this Part of the book, I give you several chapters of top-10 lists that offer easy-to-read summaries — as well as advanced tips — about what the book covers. Read these chapters to gain some extra ideas about taking your brand to the next level!

Chapter 15

Ten Ways to Add Value to Your Website Using Google+

• •

*I*f you've wanted a one-stop place to go and find what you need to improve your website and integrate it better with Google+, this chapter is it. Thinking socially (as outlined in Chapter 14) and using Google+ to build a full social design for your website will help your site retain users, grow your brand's presence in online searches, bring more sales, and convert more visitors into customers. Follow the tips in this chapter, and you're sure to see success!

Integrating +1 Buttons

The easiest and first thing you should do to your website when you create your Google+ presence is add +1 buttons to every piece of content or product you feature. On every landing page where you want better search engine rankings, you should have a +1 button.

The +1 button gives you several benefits:

✔ **It shows visitors that there are more people than just them visiting and endorsing the product or content where the +1 button is placed.** That +1 number can make anyone feel a little peer pressure to click the button and join the crowd. Seeing a number greater than 0 shows your visitors that you have an audience and that people are interested in your products and/or content. The effect still happens if the number of +1s is 0: That 0 tempts a visitor to be the first one to click that +1 and grow the number of endorsements for the page.

✔ **It allows visitors to both endorse (through the +1) and share content from your website with only a couple of clicks.** Every time someone clicks the +1 button, it also prompts the visitor to share that page to friends on Google+. The combination of button and prompt makes it easy for people to share content on your website — and to make it count.

✔ **It displays other content on your website that others have endorsed, showing off your most popular content amongst a user's friends on Google+ (which makes your design much more social).** When visitors mouse over the unclicked +1 button, they see a list of other pages on your website that have been endorsed by others. This handy tidbit of info encourages more traffic to your website and keeps visitors around longer.

✔ **It improves your search ranking on Google.com.** Every endorsement your site or app gets via a +1 button improves your ranking on Google.com search results. Even better, when a friend has endorsed an article, that friend's +1'd articles on your website will rank higher for everyone who has friended the person. So even if it doesn't bump you up much in the default Google.com search results, it will still give you a bump among an individual's friends on Google.com. No matter what, your ranking is going to go up.

Adding Share Buttons

Did you know that in addition to +1 buttons, you can add a share button? Google+ provides a share button for websites that want a little extra prompt to get users sharing content (see Figure 15-1). Personally, I like the +1 button in place of the Share button because it gives the user the opportunity to share as well, but in the event that the +1 button isn't enough, you'll want to consider a Share button.

The Share button puts the word *share* a little more prominently on your content or products that you want shared on Google+. This way, if users don't know much about the +1 button but still want to share what they've found, they can still have that option — in an easy-to-find way.

Make sure you A/B test having the Share button in place or not having it — does the button really improve shares, or is there no difference? No matter what, you'll still want to have the +1 button in place because the +1s improve search. However, having the Share button might be a good way to improve the number of shares for a given page on your website.

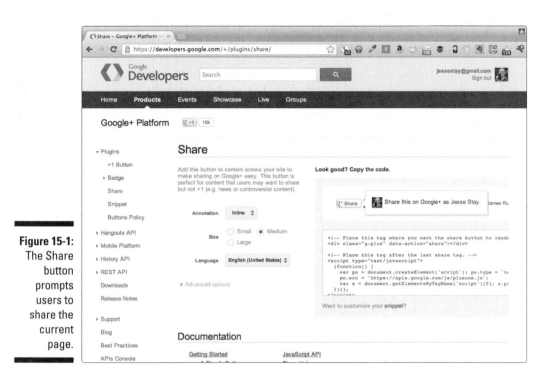

Figure 15-1:
The Share button prompts users to share the current page.

Implementing a Google+ Page Badge

If you have a Google+ Page, the next step you'll want to take is to implement a Page Badge on your website. The Google+ Page Badge is a little widget that you can put on your website to point visitors back to your Google+ Page (see Figure 15-2). It allows visitors to +1 and circle your Google+ Page without ever having to leave your website.

The Google+ Page Badge has some handy benefits:

✔ **It verifies your Google+ Page as being owned by you.** Not only does your Google+ Page Badge show your visitors that you own the Google+ Page, but it also tells Google+ that you acknowledge this Google+ Page as yours. Then Google+ can put a Verified check mark next to your Google+ Page's name, signaling visitors that it's the real deal. This assurance of authenticity means more people circling your page, more people +1'ing your page, and (as a result) more people visiting your website.

✔ **It allows visitors to follow your Google+ Page from your website.** Because they can circle your Google+ Page right in the widget, visitors can stay on your website when they follow your Google+ Page — which means a much longer time on-site for each visitor.

✔ **It improves your website's search ranking.** Google views every +1 that your Google+ Page gets as an endorsement for your brand. If you've linked your website to your Google+ Page, that gives your website authority — and when people search in Google.com, Google will rank your content higher than content from websites that don't have this authority. The more authority you can give your website (among other factors, of course), the better your rank.

✔ **It gives you a shot at getting a Direct Connect Listing in Google. com search.** The Direct Connect feature puts your Google+ Page in the suggestions that show onscreen as a visitor types in search words on Google.com. If you preface your search with a plus sign (+) and it includes your Google+ Page's name, Google may allow your Google+ Page to show up in this advantageous position, taking users right to your Google+ Page from the suggestion.

This feature only works for some Google+ Pages at the moment; keep in mind that you must link your website to your Google+ Page before the feature can work.

Figure 15-2: The Google+ Page Badge, when implemented, can improve your website's visibility.

Adding Author Tags

Author tags are one of my favorite secrets for improving a website's visibility in Google+ — and, more specifically, in Google.com search results. Here's what a simple `rel="author"` link can do for your website:

- ✔ **Improve your search listing's screen real estate with an added profile image of the author of your content.** Each search listing with a profile image in it is nearly twice the size of traditional listings in Google.com search results. This brings the user's eyes to your listing over any others on the page. Even if you don't have the first listing, you've managed to distract the user from other listings with pretty pictures and a bigger image.

- ✔ **Give the content and pages on your website more authority with Google.** Google gives content with authority a higher rank. Generally, when Google knows content has a real person behind it (there are many automated "SEO experts" out there trying to game Google with automated content generation), it ranks that content higher than if Google can't tell.

- ✔ **Author tags give your website personality.** When you see content linked to individual Google+ profiles, it shows your visitors and users that your content is written by real people. This is a general social-design principle. When you design around people, people want to interact with your content more. Make your content owned by real people, and visitors will be more likely to read it, purchase it, or do whatever you want them to do with it.

 Consider making your content even more personal by making it more obvious that people are behind the content on your site. Try to include profile pictures and names of individuals, and link those names back to their Google+ profiles. Doing so not only makes people more eager to interact with your site, but also helps your ranking in Google because Google sees that your content is genuine.

Linking Your Website to Your Google+ Page

If you can't get a Google+ Badge on your website or it takes up too much screen real estate, you'll still want to link your website to your Google+ Page. You start by adding your website to your Google+ Page's Website Info section in your Google+ Page's profile. Then, by adding a small bit of HTML that Google gives you, you can have Google index your site and immediately signal your visitors that it's associated with a Google+ Page. Doing so provides a couple of immediate benefits:

✔ It verifies your Google+ Page, adding a little Verified check mark next to your Google+ Page's name.

✔ It gives you a potentially stronger ranking in Google.com search results.

Optimizing for Search

The ultimate benefit you get from Google+ is a much greater search presence on Google.com. That's no surprise — search is Google's bread and butter, after all, and it's what they started with. Therefore you can expect that Google would naturally want Google+ to improve its search experience.

Here's a roundup of tips for optimizing your chances to shine in Google search results, complete with chapter references where you can find more information:

✔ Implement Google+ Page Badges (see Chapter 12).

✔ Add `rel="author"` `Author` tags to pages you want to index well (see Chapter 12).

✔ Link your website to your Google+ Page (see Chapter 12).

✔ Add +1 Badges (see Chapter 12).

✔ Post often on your Google+ Page, giving Google more content to index, linking back to your website so more people can +1 and endorse pages on your site (see Chapter 7).

Of course, just creating a Google+ Page can be the first big step in optimizing search. If you have a Google+ Profile and have also created a Google+ Page, you're already one step ahead of those who haven't done so! Pat yourself on the back.

Building Around People

Social design with Google+ calls for a slightly different approach from social design on social networks like Facebook or even Twitter. With Facebook and other social networks, you design around relationships (which is still possible in Google+ — though the relationships may not be as close as those other networks, at least not yet). With Google+, social design focuses more on the profile — and on the people behind your content — which can make it easier to bring in other visitors who like those people. Before you know it, you've got some relationships growing around your brand.

Designing around people and profiles personalizes your content — which makes the visitors to your website feel that they're in friendly territory, on a site run by real people. If they feel that way long enough and often enough, they'll feel they're part of a community rather than lone visitors wandering around. Implement `Author` tags to ensure that users are seeing the Google+ profiles of authors behind your content. Feature profile pictures and names. Make sure users can see the owners of each piece of content very clearly.

This approach means changing the main focus of your site from content or product per se to the people who create the content or product — and if you can make that change, you'll be on the right path toward implementing an optimal Google+ website strategy. People will stick around longer because they see people they recognize and trust. They'll go to your site instead of your competitors' sites for the same reasons. They'll find your website more easily because you'll appear with a higher rank in search results. It's a new way of thinking, but you ought to see results as you take this approach.

Designing Around Social Connections

As I mention in the previous section ("Building around People"), Facebook is more about relationships and connections than is Google+. The connections you find on Facebook tend to be much tighter — close family and (often) friends already known in real life offline. Google+ is a different kind of social network for that reason — often, the connections made there are with people the users have newly met.

However, there may be some advantages to pulling in just that type of connection: Some Google+ users feel more tightly connected to the people they know on Google+ than they do to their Facebook friends, even if their Google+ gangs aren't made up of family and face-to-face friends! For this reason, you ought to consider integrating some design principles that make specific use of the user's connections on Google+.

Here are some considerations to think about as you're designing your website or (for that matter) your mobile app:

- ✔ What types of content or products do you own that the user would find more interesting if his or her friends were viewing the same content or purchasing the same products?

- ✔ How can you build community through adding comments that link back to users' Google+ profiles?

- ✔ Can you implement an activity stream that connects the various types of activity that a user's Google+ friends have participated in on your website?

✔ How can users share content back to Google+? Are you automatically sharing activities back to each user's Google+ History private feed? Can you pull from those resources to improve the online experience that your website offers?

Always think about ways social design could improve your visitors' experience. Be sure to A/B test — and then track results — as you develop an effective social design for your website or app. You might be surprised by what you find out.

Launching Hangouts

You can add links to launch specific Hangouts from your website. Maybe you have a Hangout running, and you want to bring your visitors' attention to it. Or perhaps you have an application you've created that your website's visitors can use to interact together in a Hangout.

Google has given apps access to Hangouts to create more versatile experiences for their users in Hangouts. You can create a special link from a Hangout to your website, one that launches the Google+ Hangout with your app installed. This means you can now launch a Hangout that features a focus on your brand as its main experience.

With a brand-specific Hangout up and running, you've created a place where visitors can chat live, in real time, with your brand at the center of their shared experience. These relationships are as close to face to face as you can get online, which improves the community you're growing through your website. See `https://developers.google.com/+/hangouts` to learn more about what you can do on your website with Google+ Hangouts.

Tracking Growth with Google Analytics

Measure! Measure! Measure! I can't stress it enough. Whatever you do, don't just take my word for it! I really mean that. Your analytics and measuring will always give you much more (and more relevant) data than I could ever provide, and what I say won't always apply in every single situation — because the situation is always changing.

Google Analytics provides some very valuable data that can sharpen your understanding of what people are saying about your website on Google+. In addition, this feature can show you how Google+ is converting users to customers by nudging them toward purchases, ad clicks, or other items you're trying to track. Be sure to keep on top of results, either through Google Analytics or another tool such as Omniture, so you have solid data to guide you when you adapt your social strategy.

As you see changes happening, adapt your website and Google+ Page strategy to improve your brand's response to those changes. You can, for example, utilize Ripples to get a handle on how viral your content is, and adapt as necessary. Google Analytics can work powerfully as both a set of gauges and as a steering gear on your marketing voyage.

Chapter 16

Ten Good Google+ Business Practices

. . . .

*I*f you've dug into any of this book, you're already on your way to implementing good business practices on Google+. I figured you might also want a look at how some folks have used Google+ to boost their success while maintaining a vital online community around their brands. Coming right up: This chapter shows you ten solid examples of doing Google+ right — businesses, brands, and the people who run those small businesses (and put a human face on those brands). A couple of these examples also appear elsewhere in the book, but my hope is that by reading this chapter you can see them in a new context — with their fellow Google+ star performers — and I'll point out some highly useful features of those cases.

Separating Fans into Audiences (+Intel)

Intel engages its fans superbly by separating fans into different audiences and then catering its messages to those audiences. The brand does so by making the individual images across the top of its profile a way for users to "vote" on topics that they might be interested in.

Each image at the top is an animated GIF — currently, the topics are Technology Enthusiasts, Trends, IT Experts, Newsroom, and Software Developers. Each animated GIF flips around to show a circle that prompts the user, "+1 to join" (see Figure 16-1).

Figure 16-1:
Intel uses
images to
get people
to decide
which
interests to
follow.

When fans of the Intel Google+ Page circle the page and click the image, they have the option to +1 the image. When a user chooses and +1's an image, Intel adds him or her to the circle requested. From that point on, the user will get targeted messages about the topics that he or she is interested in. The idea is to ensure that the company's messages are always connecting with the chosen interests of each member of the audience. Intel's approach also does a couple of other things equally well:

✔ **Intel uses images to attract user attention.** Intel's Google+ Page at `https://plus.google.com/111660275132722215045/posts` shows an image attached to almost every post. Images drive more attention to posts, and bring more comments, shares, and +1s in almost all cases. (As always, be sure to test this principle to see how well it fits your own case.)

✔ **Intel utilizes popular hashtags to connect with trends.** Recently trending hashtags that Intel is using to advantage include #ThrowbackThursday, which prompts users (every Thursday) to share something from their own past experiences. #London2012 encourages them to talk about their involvement in the Olympics. By keeping a savvy eye on trends, Intel is participating as a member of the larger Google+ community — and so sees more active conversations, eyes seeing the company message, and shares.

✔ **Intel focuses on people and highlights people who use its products.**
Almost every post on Intel's Google+ Page is about people in some way.
I see posts about science-fair winners, posts about the people who make
Intel computer chips, and pictures of actual chipmakers. The whole page
feels very personal to me and makes me want to comment on the posts
and converse with the Intel people.

You can add +Intel to your circles at `https://plus.google.com/111660275132722215045`.

Allowing People to Taste Your Brand (+Cadbury UK)

Cadbury UK — you know, the delicious, fun, oh-so-fattening-for-me chocolate-
maker known here in the United States for crème eggs — is also one of the
most popular Google+ Pages at the moment (see Figure 16-2). With over two
million people following Cadbury (and that number's growing), the company
must be doing something right.

Figure 16-2: Cadbury UK is one of the most popular Pages on Google+.

The secret is that Cadbury UK uses Google+ features that are among the best strengths of Google+. Unwrap these tasty morsels:

- **The brand embraces animated GIFs.** As I go through Cadbury's stream, I see a few posts that use animated GIFs to get the brand's point across. This is a Google+ feature that's uniquely effective in comparison to other social networks. You should consider utilizing — but not overutilizing — animated GIFs if they can help bring attention to your posts and your images are relevant to what you're talking about.

- **Each post has pictures.** I think you'll see some common themes amongst the examples I share in this chapter. It's clear that images in posts show results and bring attention to each post.

- **Cadbury people ask questions and start conversations.** Remember — every post you make is a conversation. Your post should have a question or some sort of phrase in it intended to start a conversation in the comments. The more people who comment, the more people will discover your content. The more people who discover, the more +1s and shares you get. The more +1s and shares you get, the better your posts will show up in Google search results.

- **Cadbury posts are often about their fans.** Did I mention Google+ is about people? The more you post about the people passionate about your brand, the better you'll perform. Cadbury UK does this well, highlighting fans who are eating its chocolate. I don't know about you, but when I see someone eating chocolate and enjoying it, I want to eat some too!

- **The brand embraces Hangouts.** For the launch of one of its products, Cadbury UK did a Google+ Hangout to have select customers try out the new product in a "chocolate tasting," an event that the company organized. Each participant in the Hangout was sent the new chocolate; then, one by one, the lucky fans tasted the product, sharing their experiences with viewers.

Be sure to add +Cadbury UK to your circles at `https://plus.google.com/117517201037060589294`.

Hanging Out with Your Fans (+Kaskade)

Kaskade, the popular DJ, used an approach I haven't seen others utilize enough: He asked his fans to create their own Hangouts in a given time frame and posted the links to those Hangouts in the comments of his post; then, during that time frame, Kaskade visited each and every fan's Hangout and bestowed a bit of personal attention.

I don't know about you, but if one of my favorite artists joined me and my friends in a face-to-face video chat, that would be pretty darn cool! You should consider trying something similar, especially if you have celebrities involved with your brand in some way. Some intimate, one-on-one access to the celebrities or executives involved with your brand can get your customers and fans jazzed up.

Follow +Kaskade at `https://plus.google.com/110804007745043534935`.

Getting to Know Your Customers (+Michael Dell and +Dell)

Getting to know your customers is an approach that Dell does well. Not only does Dell Computer have a superbly run Google+ Page, but they also have a social-network-savvy CEO who likes to use Google+ himself on occasion. Many companies could learn from the way Michael Dell has used Google+. He does a couple of things especially well:

- ✔ **He uses Google+ Hangouts to learn from his customers face to face.**
  In the early days of Google+, Michael Dell used to start Hangouts with the first ten people who could join (those slots usually filled up pretty quickly), and he'd chat with them about Dell — and about what the customers would like to see from Dell on Google+. These conversations helped Michael Dell establish his company's presence on Google+. Not many companies can say that their social media presence was a result of the CEO's direct involvement. In this case, it worked big-time.

- ✔ **He actively posts on Google+, soliciting advice from customers.**
  Michael Dell's profile features active, regular posts from him that show he's interested in the service — and makes an active effort for his customers and fans on Google+. As a result, they comment and discuss topics related to Dell and the various topics that Michael shares. Michael Dell gets to control the conversations about his company in this way.

If you think Michael Dell is impressive, go over and check out his company's Google+ Page as well. The company is implementing many of the same strategies you see in this chapter — to advantage.

You can circle +Michael Dell at `https://plus.google.com/100523784851251213675`. Add +Dell to your circles at `https://plus.google.com/117161668189080869053`.

Performing for Fans (Black Eyed Peas and +Will.i.am)

One of my favorite uses of Google+ was a concert put on by the popular band Black Eyed Peas through the artist Will.i.am's Google+ account. They allowed the first ten lucky fans who could get in to participate in a concert they were performing in New York City and broadcast the Hangout out to their audience there. At the same time, those in the Hangout and watching live On Air were able to watch the concert from a very unique perspective.

The entire concert was one of the most personalized experiences I've participated in. Here are the reasons they were successful:

- ✔ **They catered their message to their Google+ audience.** The Black Eyed Peas figured out a way to personalize the experience and connect with fans so that fans would come back.

- ✔ **They used Hangouts to point back to their Google+ brand.** Those watching the Hangout discovered Will.i.am's Google+ account — another avenue of involvement — and his audience grew as a result. In addition, those in the band's real-life audience saw that Will.i.am was on Google+ as they watched in person.

- ✔ **They utilized Hangouts On Air to amass a significant audience.** I learned of the Hangout because my friends were watching it. In fact, hundreds of thousands of people were watching it. Each one of those people probably saw it because of their friends and followed Will.i.am as a result.

Follow +Will.ia.am at `https://plus.google.com/109351399938437494273`.

Discovering Planets (+Venus Transit)

I wanted to share this one because it isn't necessarily a specific brand, but a great business case. In some ways, I wish a brand like +NASA were hosting the idea. In 2012, Venus crossed the path of the sun in what was called the Venus Transit. Astronomers and enthusiasts everywhere got together to watch the transit occur.

An amateur astronomer and enthusiast named Fraser Cain organized a Hangout around the Venus Transit and broadcast it live On Air. As a result, thousands of people could watch Venus's transit across the sun safely, *online* (no elaborate eye-protection measures needed) — and experience it *together*. Other members of the Hangout were setting up their own custom rigs to watch the transit, and each member was showing a new, creative way of sharing the Venus Transit.

As a result, even though it was cloudy here in my home state of Utah, I still got to see the Venus Transit. In fact, I was on the road at the time and watched it on my phone, in the middle of nowhere! This was a great application of Google+ Hangouts that I think shows what a Hangout can do to bring the world together, especially around an event, product, or topic. Your brand can be at the center of these events!

+Fraser Cain's profile can be found at `https://plus.google.com/110701307803962595019`.

Learning Together (+Scott Jarvie)

With the passionate audience of photographers on Google+, I thought it would be appropriate to present this example of a small photography business run by my friend Scott Jarvie, a wedding and profile photographer with a great Google+ presence. Scott loves to share what he does, and he was perhaps one of the first on Google+ to really start sharing his photography skills with his audience.

Scott likes to meet his audience face to face, and he has built up an incredible community of photographers, amateur photographers, and those who just like good photography all by meeting many of them through Google+ Hangouts. I was able to HIRL (Hangout In Real Life) with Scott here locally when he brought out a bunch of photographers to Utah. Many of those folks came out because they met him in Google+ Hangouts and in face-to-face interactions through Google+ Hangouts. I was impressed with how he had already built relationships with many of these photographers!

In his Hangouts, Scott often shows off one of his favorite things and strengths: Lightroom editing. Lightroom is a photo-editing program that pros use to create their final images; Scott takes those who show up in the Hangout through what he does to process photos of weddings and other events he photographs. To him, Google+ truly is about sharing!

If you're running a small business, Scott is a great example of how to use Google+ to "open the covers" on your business and share a little of what you do, what you're good at, and how you do it. Share as much as you can, and people will naturally come to you to learn. Build community with that audience.

Learn from +Scott Jarvie at `https://plus.google.com/100962871525684315897`.

Engaging Community (+Chris Pirillo)

There's no one better at building community than my friend Chris Pirillo. Chris has a popular YouTube Channel at `youtube.com/lockergnome` where he talks tech and all things geek. Through his videos and live broadcasts, Chris has managed to build an incredible community of geeks who are passionate about geeky things like software, hardware, *Star Wars,* and LEGOs.

Chris has extended his community over to Google+ in an incredible way. He truly engages his audience in every single post he makes and tries to make each person feel welcome. When you comment on a Chris Pirillo post, you can expect him to interact with you and participate in the conversation.

On Chris Pirillo's Google+ profile (see Figure 16-3), he is just as much a part of the community as his fans are. As a result, he's gained a ton of control over his audience and what they'll stand up for. If you're looking to build community, look at the example of Chris Pirillo and how he's built such a passionate community. He's one of the best.

Join +Chris Pirillo's community at `https://plus.google.com/107234826207633309420`.

Figure 16-3:
Chris Pirillo
engaging
his fans.

Getting to Know Fans (+Jeri Ryan)

Star Trek fans may know her as Seven of Nine in *Star Trek: Voyager.* She is currently starring in the TV show *Body of Proof.* The lovely Jeri Ryan is one of the most active celebrities I know on Google+. She truly interacts with her fans (see Figure 16-4).

In fact, Ms. Ryan was one of the first celebrities on Google+. What immediately got my attention about her online presence was its two-way social connection: Not only was she willing to chat, as well as even share and highlight posts by people she followed on Google+, but she also posted on Google+ herself and followed posts of her fans. Now, there's a canny use of star power!

I remember giving her some advice on Google+ in response to her comments and being surprised when she responded to my comment. Not to say I was starstruck, but I never wanted to delete that comment thread. She makes every one of her fans feel that special, and Google+ gives her an efficient, natural way to do so. As a result, she's built a great audience of fans — including some who hadn't followed her career before. Now, as one of her fans, I'm aware of what she's up to and am interested in supporting her work. Other celebrities should take note of what Jeri Ryan is doing on Google+. Don't be surprised if they follow suit — soon.

Add +Jeri Ryan to your circles at `https://plus.google.com/101765416973555767821`.

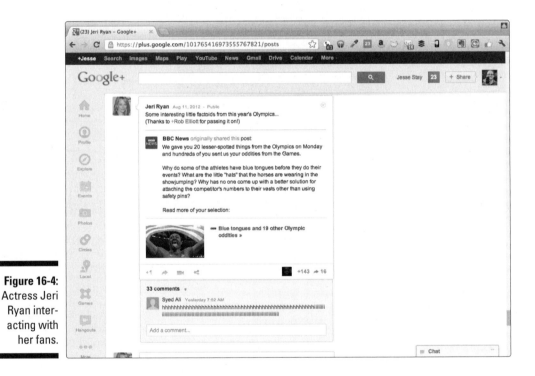

Figure 16-4:
Actress Jeri Ryan interacting with her fans.

Embracing Google+ (+H&M)

H&M was brought to my attention as a result for its huge audience on Google+. To be honest, I had never shopped at H&M before I found its Google+ profile. It was always a store I passed as I went through the mall.

What caught my attention was their Page growth — and then I started seeing some of my friends sharing their posts. I also started seeing them showing up in Google search results. All of a sudden, they had my attention!

H&M has some particular strengths that I think make the brand popular. Specifically, I think the brand uses Google+ for the unique advantages it provides, a secret that many of the Pages you see in this chapter share. Here are a few:

- ✔ **H&M uses lots of photos.** If you've perused the other cases in this chapter, you may notice a pattern here. It's no accident: As with many of the successful Pages on Google+, H&M posts a photo with just about every post it makes on its Google+ Page. This practice brings in more eyes and shows some behind-the-scenes content to make the visitors' experience more personal.

- ✔ **H&M links to other profiles on Google+.** One of the big brands they work with is David Beckham — the famous football/soccer player who has become both a successful human being and a high-profile brand. Whenever the website mentions his line of clothing, it always links to his Google+ profile, bringing visitors' attention over to him — which eventually leads traffic back to H&M through his involvement with the company.

- ✔ **H&M's photos are albums, not just individual photos.** H&M makes frequent and impressive use of photo albums instead of just isolated photos. If the company has an entire line of clothing to feature, it shares a photo of every item of clothing in that line — *and* shares all those items together as a photo album. Google+ photo albums are (if you'll pardon the expression) tailor-made for sharing collections of photos like this, and they're a natural advantage for H&M.

H&M can be found at `https://plus.google.com/115900903196483234016`

Chapter 17

Ten Rules for Small-Business Success with Google+

• •

*Y*ou may find bits and pieces of this advice scattered throughout the book, but if you run a small business, this is the chapter you want to read for a good summary of what to consider so you can keep your feet when you hit the ground running with Google+.

Business Starts with People!

You can't run a business without considering the people who make your business run. This goes for your customers as well as the employees and founders who keep your small business functioning! Google+ provides just the right tools to allow your business to focus on people — did I mention Google+ is about people?

There are several ways you can focus on people with Google+ — be sure to read Chapter 16 for some great examples:

✔ **Dropping in to Hangouts:** The best way you can focus on people is to talk to them face to face. Google+ provides Hangouts to allow you to meet customers via live video, ten people at a time. You should take advantage of this feature — join other people's Hangouts that focus on similar topics that you might be interested in. Or start your own Hangouts, meet your customers, record them, and share them for further opportunities to meet your audience.

✔ **Focusing on your employees:** Google+ gives you the opportunity to open the covers a little bit and share what goes on behind the scenes at your company. Spend some time sharing things you're doing from day to day. Help your customers understand what goes into the products they've come to know. Utilize Hangouts to share these things live with your customers.

✔ **Optimizing the social design of your website (see Chapter 14):** You should design your website around people. Use `rel="author"` tags to link the Google+ profiles of your employees to content on your website. This will also make your content more personable as people find it in search engines and make your site rank better. At the same time, make sure visitors are seeing a site full of content and products that have people behind them in some way. Feature the employees behind your products, and you will humanize your small business.

✔ **Coordinating your efforts through Google Apps:** Google+ is supported through Google Apps for your business. If you use Google Apps to provide e-mail, document sharing, group functionality, or any of the other services it provides, you should consider getting your employees using Google+ through Google Apps as well.

Through Google Apps, you can post messages to Google+ that just those in your Google Apps domain can see. This arrangement allows further communication between employees — and if you ever want to take the conversation outside your domain, you can just add the circles you want to see the conversation when you post your content. Use Google Apps and Google+ to help your employees get to know each other as well.

Google+ Pages — Your Secret Weapon in Search

One of the first things you should consider doing as a small business after joining Google+ is set up a Google+ Page for your company. A Google+ Page not only gives your company a presence on Google+, but it also helps you gain an advantage in Google.com search. Start with a couple of tips:

✔ **Post content frequently, and engage your fans to +1 and comment on your posts.** Frequent content means more content that will appear in Google search results. It also gives your audience something to remember you by and makes them much less likely to miss your posts.

Engaging content will get them to +1 and comment more. The more +1s your content has on Google+, the better your content will rank on Google.com search results. Try to come up with content that increases your +1s and comments and shares on your Google+ Page.

✔ **Link your website to your Google+ Page with a Badge.** If you go to `http://google.com/+/business`, you can find all kinds of resources for your business. One of the things you can get there is a Google+ Page Badge that will link your Google+ Page to your website. This Badge can go anywhere on your website, and allows visitors to +1 and circle your Google+ Page right from your website. This means a greater audience for your Google+ Page, and the link between your Google+ Badge and your website means you'll rank better in Google.com search results as well!

Give Your Website Authority

One of the greatest advantages to Google+ is the authority it can give your website in Google.com search results. Simply by having a Google+ profile or Page, your content can immediately have more authority — and, as a result, greater ranking in Google.com search results.

There are a few additional ways you can improve your website's authority however. Here are some good tips:

✔ **Use Google+ Badges.** I mention this in the previous section — integrating a Google+ Badge that links back to your Google+ Page is a simple, effective way to improve the authority of your website.

✔ **Implement Author tags.** In Chapter 12 of this book, I show you how to implement these. By simply adding `rel="author"` to a link of the author on each piece of content for your website, and linking that to his or her Google+ Profile, you'll immediately give authority to the content on your site. Because Google now knows there is a real person and real author behind that content, it can rank your content better in search results and give it enhanced authority against other websites that don't do this.

✔ **Add +1 buttons to your content or products.** Every +1 your content gets gives your content more authority in Google.com search results. You can implement +1 buttons on every article, and this allows visitors to "endorse" the content and products on your site. Use this effect to build authority and ranking for the content you publish.

People Are the New SEO

A year or two ago, Facebook launched a cool feature that allowed website owners to have their content appear in the search results of Facebook just by adding a simple Like button to their pages: When Facebook users liked (clicked the button next to) the content on a website, they added the content to their likes and interests. Then, when friends of theirs who hadn't liked the content yet searched for keywords related to the content (especially its website's title), the content would show up in their Facebook search results. I see this capability as a new era of "social SEO" where people's attention is what you optimize your site to attract.

Google has now jumped into the "social SEO" game with the launch of Google+, and you should be taking advantage of this situation. When you create a Google+ account, you'll immediately start seeing content that your friends have +1'd and shared on Google+, mixed in with the normal Google. com search results. The feature is called Google Search Plus Your World.

By integrating +1 buttons and building authority through the steps I mention in the previous tip, you can have your content ranked and seen among the friends of your customers. When a customer's friend sees that your customer +1'd a product on your website, that friend is much likelier to click that product than would be the case if it had just appeared as a random item in Google.com search results. As a smart marketer, embrace this feature, and optimize your website and content to get people +1'ing and sharing your content as much as possible.

Developers! Developers! Developers!

Everyone who owns a small business knows that the owner has to wear multiple hats. Fortunately, such versatility doesn't mean that you have to be a full-fledged developer to be successful with Google+. Of course, knowing a little code may help, but you can still achieve a lot on Google+ without having to hire (or be) a developer.

Some enhancements you may want to consider right away include integrating Google+ Badges in your site, +1s, or linking author tags to your content (for details, review Chapter 12). Or you may want to consider some content strategy to get your content ranking well in www.google.com search (see Chapter 7).

Of course, if you want to take your business just that extra step farther toward "social SEO," consider hiring a developer and finding ways to integrate Google+ into your website or app. If you can customize your web presence for each user while still providing a social experience for all those who visit your website, you practically guarantee that those folks will spend more time on your site — and that more people will refer their friends.

Once you have a developer, you'll want to consider trying a few things that your developer can put in place for you. Here are a couple of ideas:

✔ **Integrate Badges and +1s.** You can start doing this integration your own if you know how to copy and paste (see Chapter 12 to learn more). If you don't yet have the capability of integrating these vital sources of authority, your developer can do it for you. Resources for the purpose reside at http://google.com/+/business.

✔ **Focus on improving your SEO.** You may want to hire a consultant on (or buy a book about) SEO (Search Engine Optimization). Although the book you're now reading has some useful tips to get you started, there's a lot more to SEO. An SEO consultant, along with an SEO-savvy developer, can help you take a really customized approach to ensure that search engines like Google find and read what you want them to about your site — and rank it as high as possible in the search results. Use your developer to help implement your SEO consultant's recommendations.

✔ **Build social experiences.** I talk about this in Chapter 14 — a *social experience* is when users visit your website and see their close friends and family there with them. Find ways to embrace the Google+ APIs to learn who each visitor's friends are on Google+, and build experiences out of those connections.

✔ **Build social connections into website experiences.** You should find ways that your website's offerings are attached to each individual's connections on Google+. If someone buys a product, find a way to show the most popular products to each visitor's friends. If someone reads an article, show that person which articles his or her friends have read. These website experiences should be social; bringing in each person's friends on Google+ can be a naturally attractive way to create social experiences.

Bring Home the Bacon

One of the most popular *memes* (viral topics) on Google+ — and perhaps most social networks — is the topic of cats. Many people love 'em, and folks love to share postings about the things they love. (Here's a meow-out to cat-lovers!)

Cater your content to elicit responses from your audience. They'll likely enjoy posts about (say) cats, so if cats are your meme of choice, consider a picture of cats here or there. And while you're at it, here are some other ways to engage and elicit responses (+1s, comments, and shares) from your audience:

✔ **Find out what memes are currently popular on Google+.** Google+ shows a list of trending topics and hashtags in the upper right of each user's feed. Pay attention to those indicators. You may notice that every Sunday, people participate in #SacredSunday, or every Saturday, people participate in #Caturday. I also like to use #Photography to join other photographers with my photos. You may consider your own meme — perhaps #SacredSaturday if Saturday has sacred meaning to you and you want to associate with those of like faith or beliefs. Use this affinity to your advantage, and find posts, ideally related to your brand, that embrace such topics. Include the hashtags in your posts if you can (or post from the search results for that hashtag), and then others following those memes will be able to discover your posts and participate in your conversations. This brings you greater search traffic and encourages more people to follow your Page and profile.

✔ **Ask questions.** Questions are a handy way to get people following your content. If you ask questions that start conversations, you build community among your audience. At the same time, for every person who comments, others who follow your Page or profile will see those posts bumped up to the top of their feeds when they refresh the page.

Google+ bumps most recently commented posts to the top of users' news feeds. This gets more people involved in the conversation and drives more people to your Page or profile.

✔ **Know your audience.** Get to know your audience. What do they like? What do they not like? Create posts that reflect their interests.

✔ **Use calls to action!** People will not always know what to do when you post on Google+. If you want them to +1 your post, ask them to! If you want them to comment, ask them to, or present a question so they are prompted to respond. If you want them to share, just ask! If you don't ask, they won't do it.

✔ **Pictures, videos, and animated GIFs bring attention.** Google+ is a very graphical social network. Posts with images and even animated GIFs bring more attention to your posts. When you catch their attention, people comment. Consider an attention-catching image to go with your content, and more people will pay attention.

✔ **Measure! Measure! Measure!** All marketers should have this message tattooed on their brains. Measuring is in the blood of every good marketer! Make sure you're measuring each post you make and writing posts that are based on the results of those measurements. Track what days and times work best. What content does your audience like? If you measure, you'll know your market better — and you'll progress.

✔ **Circle people and *build relationships*.** I always laugh when I see critics of Google+ talk about how they don't get any interaction on Google+ — but when you look at their profiles, they're not following anyone! Success on Google+ means adding interesting people to your circles. In particular, add people to your circles who are interesting to you or reflect well on your brand, and then participate in their conversations. People will naturally start following you as they get to know you. You have to build relationships to get relationships!

"Hang out" with Customers

To be a successful Google+ user, embrace Google+ Hangouts; they're an especially useful feature of Google+. They represent one of the best ways online for brands and customers to get to know each other face to face. Here's a checklist for embracing Google+ Hangouts:

✔ **Show off your skills.** Hangouts are a highly visible way to show off what you are good at. Check out the example of my friend Scott Jarvie in Chapter 16. He uses Google+ Hangouts to show off his Lightroom photo-editing skills. If you figure out what you're good at and share it with the world, it puts a spotlight on what you value and on how you are valuable. People naturally follow people and brands that give them value. Consider Hangouts a way to pass around good karma on Google+.

✔ **Open the covers.** Google+ Hangouts can also showcase what's going on inside your company that the world needs to know about — and put a human face on your company at the same time. Chapter 16, for example, talks about how Michael Dell, CEO of Dell Computer, used Google+ Hangouts to talk to his customers face to face. Bring in your executives if they're ready to serve as online spokespersons for your company, or find creative, engaging ways to show what makes your company work.

✔ **Bring influential people together.** My favorite example of this principle is when the Dalai Lama and Desmond Tutu had a Hangout to discuss religion and philosophy: They broadcast their online interaction to the world. Hangouts are a great way to bring influential people together and get them talking while sharing that conversation with the world. If you can connect influential people, even as a small business, you should.

✔ **Join other Hangouts.** Chapter 16 mentions Kaskade, a popular DJ who invited his audience to start their own Hangouts — then he went in and joined their Hangouts. Use the Hangouts others are creating to join in, participate, and allow your fans (or even those who may not yet be fans) to get to know you better. Don't be shy — meet a few new people here and there, and they'll naturally come back to your Page and profile to follow.

✔ **Try 24/7 Hangouts.** I have a couple of friends who did a 24/7 Hangout where they left the cameras running for about a week, inviting new people to come join. Their Hangout always stood out on the side of Google+, making me want to join. In a sense, Google+ was giving them free 24/7 advertising because their Hangout was on all the time. They also had some interesting guests join; you never knew who or what you might find if you came and joined their Hangout. Intrigue stimulates curiosity, and that's useful for marketers.

Know Your Audience

You may find that your Google+ audience is slightly different from the audience you'll find on Facebook. That's okay — just make sure you're aware of that difference, understand who your audience is, and adapt your message to cater to that audience. The Google+ audience is a uniquely interesting community; keep a few general principles in mind when you connect with it:

✔ **Google+ tends to work well for professional industries, especially creative types like artists, photographers, or even programmers.** Maybe the graphical interface that Google+ provides is especially fascinating to creative folks and to those who try out new services just to see what happens; either way; they flock to Google+. Consider this creative atmosphere a potential advantage as you share on Google+. Share image-heavy posts where you can. Find things that that a creative audience will enjoy.

✔ **There's a good chance your mom is not on Google+ (but you may be surprised!).** Because it's such a new service, your family likely hasn't discovered Google+. That's okay — plenty of others have. Keep in mind that much of your audience is probably composed of people who have recently met each other and are not intimately connected (the way families usually are).

At the same time, many people come to Google+ because they want something new. Maybe your mom *is* on Google+ — if so, "Hi, Mom!" If she's aware of online trends, you'd better make sure that your brand is, too — and adapt your message to fit your audience.

✔ **There are plenty of opportunities to introduce your brand to new audiences.** Because so much of the Google+ audience is new, it pays to find ways to meet new audiences with your Google+ presence. Participate in other people's Hangouts. Comment on popular threads and memes. Get to know new people and their friends. It's about audiences.

✔ **As a result of catering to new audiences, your existing audience will start to naturally discover your presence on Google+ through Google. com search.** As you meet new audiences, folks who already follow you but aren't yet on Google+ will find your posts on Google+ through Google.com search. Try to optimize your Google+ presence to get the most from Google search.

Build Your Audience

When you know your audience, build it — focus on relationships and work on making your message attractive to the people you want to reach. Here are a few tips I've found successful in building audiences on Google+. As always, be sure to measure responses to find your own success stories!

✔ **Circle others.** The number-one way you'll see your audience increase on Google+ is by showing interest in them. Start by using your employee and individual profiles to add people to your circles. At the same time, consider adding the folks who follow your Google+ Page to the circles on your Google+ Page. As you do so, follow their updates, and pay attention to them. Participate in their conversations, and show that you care and have an interest in their conversations. As they get to know you, I guarantee they'll follow.

✔ **Relationships! Relationships! Relationships!** Building an audience is all about relationships. Go back and read the classic *How to Win Friends and Influence People,* by Dale Carnegie. Show genuine interest in people, and they will show interest in you — it's that simple!

✔ **Write interesting content.** If you have something interesting to say, people will follow. Make sure your content is interesting enough that your audience will want to read it. Spend time deciding what types of content will be most interesting to your audience, and integrate your findings into your posting strategy.

✔ **Engage!** (I had to get a *Star Trek* reference in here somewhere.) Engagement is extremely important for a successful content strategy on Google+. Find ways to engage your audience and get them commenting and +1'ing your content. Remember always that you're building community as much as you're building an audience. Find ways to get your audience helping each other. The more you engage your audience, the greater your audience will grow on Google+.

Sell! Sell! Sell!

Your Google+ presence is all moot if you're not converting followers into customers. For most people, this process means making money through your website or through some online presence that directs people's attention to where you want it. There are a couple of ways you can use Google+ to drive traffic to the conversion points on your website or app:

✔ **Use hashtags to drive people to content.** Pay attention to those trending tags on Google+! If the Super Bowl is generating the buzz, make sure you're doing a promotion on your website around the Super Bowl, and use the hashtags to drive people toward your promotion. Keep it classy, though — be sure that your messages don't come across as spam!

✔ **Consider contests.** Contests are a natural on Google+. A couple of photographer friends used the service to advantage that way: They submitted a new photo every week and asked their audience to post edits of that photo, identified with a particular hashtag. The contest Google+ Page would then share the favorite edits on the Page in a photo album; the edits with the most +1s would win the contest.

Utilize the strengths that Google+ provides — contests, photos, photo albums, Hangouts, and more — to challenge your audience to compete with each other. There's nothing like a healthy competition to build community and drive traffic toward an initiative that (in turn) drives sales toward your company.

✔ **Social ads.** Google+ provides a means for you to share the people who have +1'd your content alongside your ads on Google AdSense. This drives more people toward your content and products because people see that their friends have shown interest in what you're advertising. Chapter 10 goes into this feature in depth.

✔ **Social SEO.** Good SEO (Search Engine Optimization) can drive sales like nothing else. If your products or content rank high in search engines, they attract more traffic and sales than many other marketing efforts. For example, imagine if you sell skis (I live in Utah, which has some of the best skiing in the world!). When a potential customer wants some skis, she is likely to search for *skis*. When your product is number one in their search results, guess what? Your link gets that customer's sale! Google+ offers plenty of ways to influence your search engine ranking by just using the service. See Chapter 7 for more tips on building SEO with Google+.

Index

Math & Science

Algebra I For Dummies,
2nd Edition
978-0-470-55964-2

Biology For Dummies,
2nd Edition
978-0-470-59875-7

Chemistry For Dummies,
2nd Edition
978-1-1180-0730-3

Geometry For Dummies,
2nd Edition
978-0-470-08946-0

Pre-Algebra Essentials
For Dummies
978-0-470-61838-7

Microsoft Office

Excel 2010 For Dummies
978-0-470-48953-6

Office 2010 All-in-One
For Dummies
978-0-470-49748-7

Office 2011 for Mac
For Dummies
978-0-470-87869-9

Word 2010
For Dummies
978-0-470-48772-3

Music

Guitar For Dummies,
2nd Edition
978-0-7645-9904-0

Clarinet For Dummies
978-0-470-58477-4

iPod & iTunes
For Dummies,
9th Edition
978-1-118-13060-5

Pets

Cats For Dummies,
2nd Edition
978-0-7645-5275-5

Dogs All-in One
For Dummies
978-0470-52978-2

Saltwater Aquariums
For Dummies
978-0-470-06805-2

Religion & Inspiration

The Bible For Dummies
978-0-7645-5296-0

Catholicism For Dummies,
2nd Edition
978-1-118-07778-8

Spirituality For Dummies,
2nd Edition
978-0-470-19142-2

Self-Help & Relationships

Happiness For Dummies
978-0-470-28171-0

Overcoming Anxiety
For Dummies,
2nd Edition
978-0-470-57441-6

Seniors

Crosswords For Seniors
For Dummies
978-0-470-49157-7

iPad 2 For Seniors
For Dummies, 3rd Edition
978-1-118-17678-8

Laptops & Tablets
For Seniors For Dummies,
2nd Edition
978-1-118-09596-6

Smartphones & Tablets

BlackBerry For Dummies,
5th Edition
978-1-118-10035-6

Droid X2 For Dummies
978-1-118-14864-8

HTC ThunderBolt
For Dummies
978-1-118-07601-9

MOTOROLA XOOM
For Dummies
978-1-118-08835-7

Sports

Basketball For Dummies,
3rd Edition
978-1-118-07374-2

Football For Dummies,
2nd Edition
978-1-118-01261-1

Golf For Dummies,
4th Edition
978-0-470-88279-5

Test Prep

ACT For Dummies,
5th Edition
978-1-118-01259-8

ASVAB For Dummie
3rd Edition
978-0-470-63760-9

The GRE Test For
Dummies, 7th Editic
978-0-470-00919-2

Police Officer Exam
For Dummies
978-0-470-88724-0

Series 7 Exam
For Dummies
978-0-470-09932-2

Web Development

HTML, CSS, & XHTM
For Dummies, 7th E
978-0-470-91659-9

Drupal For Dummie
2nd Edition
978-1-118-08348-2

Windows 7

Windows 7
For Dummies
978-0-470-49743-2

Windows 7
For Dummies,
Book + DVD Bundle
978-0-470-52398-8

Windows 7 All-in-Or
For Dummies
978-0-470-48763-1